TRACING YOUR
Family Roots

THE COMPLETE GUIDE TO LOCATING YOUR ANCESTORS

LISE HULL

COLLINS & BROWN

First published in Great Britain in 2005
This paperback edition published in 2007 by
Collins & Brown
10 Southcombe Street
London
W14 0RA

An imprint of Anova Books Company Ltd

Designer: Lindsey Johns
Project editors: Nicola Hodgson and Anne McDowall
Proofreader: Libby Willis
Indexer: Margaret Binns

ISBN 978-1-84340-454-5

British Library Cataloguing-in-Publication Data:
A catalogue record for this book is available from the British Library.

10 9 8 7 6 5 4 3 2 1

Reproduction by Anorax Imaging Ltd, UK.
Printed and bound by SNP Leefung, China

This book can be ordered direct from the publisher.
Contact the marketing department, but try your bookshop first.

www.anovabooks.com

Contents

Starting work on your family tree may be daunting at first, but with perseverance the rewards can be great.

Waves of emigration, colonialization and forced movement of peoples throughout history have time and again created new nations filled with citizens of mixed ancestry. Yet, even though they take great pride in their present nationality, they often have questions about their immigration ancestors and what life was like for them before they journeyed across continents. The question 'Who am I?' brings up speculation about both one's purpose in life and one's personal heritage. Inspired by books like Alex Haley's *Roots*, which was published in 1976 and transformed into a popular television series, genealogy has become an incredibly popular pastime, as people navigate through this increasingly cosmopolitan and diversified world.

Starting your family tree

The quest to discover one's past – genealogy – usually begins with the creation of a family tree or pedigree chart. At first consideration, it seems simple enough to document names, birth and death dates and relationships on a flow chart or a drawing of a tree with projecting branches. But almost as soon as you attempt to complete the diagrams, the task shifts to something complex, confusing and often even overwhelming. Information 'remembered' by one family member may conflict with what another claims and you begin to wonder: did my father have six siblings or seven? Was that famous celebrity really my great-great-grandmother? When were my grandparents really born? And where are they buried?

Questions like these may well stop aspiring family historians in their tracks. What seemed simple creates an intimidating mental barrier to further research and the lines on the branches of the family tree remain blank. What you thought was going to be an enjoyable project has turned into a nightmare. Many of us give up too quickly and put off the heritage quest, deciding the answers are too difficult to find. But with a positive attitude and the right tools, anyone interested in tracing their roots can discover the ancestors and personal histories that influenced their development into the people they are today. Delving into one's genealogy may not produce a Pulitzer Prize-winning book, but, like Alex Haley, the most determined family historians can connect with kin living in the next county – or in the ancestral homeland.

In England another Alex – Alexandra Louise Nairne Myers – has discovered a lengthy heritage, which relatives have traced back to the Middle Ages when her ancestor, Sir John Baker (1488–1558), served as Chancellor of the Exchequer and Speaker of the House of Commons for the Tudor monarchy. Posthumously acquiring the nickname 'Bloody Baker' for his alleged persecution of Protestants during the reign of 'Bloody' Mary Tudor, Sir John is also notable for his ties to the historic manor in Kent centred by Sissinghurst Castle, a noted heritage site. Stately ancestors, such as the charismatic and highly popular Major William Bridges Webb, who twice declined the offer of the position of Lord Mayor of London, and Captain

Alexander Nairne, who served as a midshipman during the Battle of Copenhagen in the early 19th century, also grace Alex's family tree. Even though Alex's interest in family history has burgeoned relatively recently, she has memories of family stories and evocative family portraits that have always sparked curiosity about her past. Relatives with a keen interest in genealogy have helped point her in the right direction.

Inasmuch as our ancestors come from all walks of life, our pedigree charts normally include labourers, blue-collar workers and even the poverty-stricken, in addition to more prosperous citizens. Whether famous or humble, each of our ancestors has contributed in some way to our present. Each has a history to tell: some survived intrigue and notoriety, while others favoured the stability and commonality of daily life.

Tracing your family roots can be fraught with challenges, but perseverance will transform your life: Alex Haley discovered kinsmen in Africa; Alex Myers is still learning about her ancestors, pulling together the threads, building up a picture of her relatives and deciding for herself which family traditions are true and which remain family myth.

Your task as a family history researcher is to discover the reality behind the stories – to identify who was and who was not an ancestor and to explore the past using investigative skills perhaps equalled only by Agatha Christie's famed detective, Hercule Poirot. How do you differentiate fact from fiction when researching your past? That's the real challenge every genealogist has to face, and one that this book will help you resolve.

Begin the quest for self-discovery

Geared for both beginning genealogists and experienced family historians who have hit the proverbial research wall, this book will guide you from the basics of identifying the members of your family tree to the complexities of using historic records at home and abroad, and even to discovering blood-ties with hitherto unknown – and still living – relatives. Not only will you discover your ancestor's names and vital statistics and be able to complete your family tree, you will also acquire many other tools to give context and vitality to your heritage.

This book identifies some of the problems that are commonly encountered by family historians during each phase of the research process, and provides practical, understandable solutions that will allow you to move comfortably on to the next step of your quest. Topics include: how to create a family tree; resource materials and what information can be gleaned from them; using computer software and online resources; details on repositories and the specific kinds of records and archival information they hold; how to organize, document, confirm and share your findings; when and how to request professional assistance; points of contact for further information; and genetic genealogy – the latest innovation in family history research.

Tracing your roots may seem like a straightforward project, but don't be surprised when you have to branch out and follow several pathways to reach your goal.

'It is fascinating, once you get over the first few hurdles. It takes determination to find out real facts about your ancestry, and verifying the facts is all part of the challenge. I think most people vaguely think about tracing their family history, but it takes time to find out real information. If helps if you have something specific to do, i.e. set yourself a goal and stick to it. Then you may achieve something. Otherwise it's quite easy to go round in circles, or just give up. I couldn't help overhearing the odd conversation in the Family Records Centre (in London), when people pitch up and have a vague notion of wanting to trace their ancestors. You need hard facts, and then more!'

Common Myths about Family History Research

MYTH: *Tracing your roots is only about completing a family tree.*

REALITY: Filling in the family tree is just the beginning! And even that effort can be a daunting prospect. Don't be surprised to find yourself immersed in much more than names and dates. You will hit roadblocks, discover conflicting information and hear unexpected tales that will prompt further investigation.

MYTH: *Tracing your roots is easy – the Mormons have all the data in Salt Lake City.*

REALITY: While the Family History Library (FHL) contains the world's most comprehensive repository of genealogical information, the vast collections held by The Church of Jesus Christ of Latter-day Saints (also known as the Mormons) are comprised of donated materials and records accumulated over time. Their collections are dependent on the goodwill, research capabilities and storage practices of donors and they are ever-growing and ever-changing. Still, the Mormons do not and cannot accept every kind of material collected by well-meaning family historians – including family bibles, personal journals, written correspondence, school yearbooks, heirlooms, photo albums and scrapbooks – and cannot possibly hold every scrap of paper or every record pertaining to every family tree. However, as you will discover in this book, there are plenty of alternatives to the FHL. Different record repositories around the world hold thousands of records not stored in Salt Lake City and each offers a different pathway to your past.

Even though some of us have famous ancestors, such as Honest Abe Lincoln, always view reputed genealogical connections with skepticism, unless you have official records to prove your case.

MYTH: *If it's in print, it must be true.*

REALITY: Lured by the thought of self-discovery, many people purchase books that claim to trace the history of their family's surname. Then they discover they are generic at best or offer only vague or inconclusive evidence about a specific family's history. Read such books for enjoyment and let them stimulate your search for more concrete information, but never presume they are completely accurate – or even that they're related to your family's roots.

MYTH: *Official government documents are always correct and reliable.*

REALITY: Clerks and official transcribers are human and make mistakes. Typographical errors, especially in the age before computers, were – and are – common. Computerized spell-checkers also miss typos. And handwritten documents created before the invention of carbon paper and photocopying machines also contain errors. Always approach these items with a healthy degree of scepticism.

MYTH: *The Internet has all the facts about my surname.*

REALITY: As fantastic a resource as the Internet has become, not all the information touted as fact is accurate: mistakes occur. People may input incorrect dates, misspellings and misinterpretations of the historic record into online databases and articles. Changes in calendar systems and the inconsistencies of dating historic events can cause confusion. And assumptions about one's past are not necessarily true, even if many people cite the same information as factual. Remember, even historians debate the factuality of historic 'facts'. So, as with the information you may glean from the Family History Library, the Internet is only as accurate as the people who provide the data.

MYTH: *I can trace my roots to royalty or someone historically famous.*

REALITY: Wouldn't it be great to be related to Edward, the Black Prince, Abraham Lincoln or Winston Churchill? Even if you manage to dig up details that indicate you have blood ties to the British royal family, view them with suspicion. While you may love to have famous ancestors, family tales of glory and wealth and assumptions about royal links are rarely true. Neither are ties to castles based upon their name – Flint Castle, for example, is not the ancestral home of the Flint family.

MYTH: *I can trace my roots back to Adam and Eve.*

REALITY: Even though geneticist Bryan Sykes, researcher and founder of Oxford Ancestors, claims that Europeans can trace their heritage back to one of Eve's seven daughters and also to one of three African clans, don't expect to be able to trace your family roots that far back in time!

MYTH: *My surname has always been spelled the same way I spell it, so anyone with a differently spelled name cannot be related to me.*

REALITY: Wrong! Surnames change over time, either intentionally or owing to transcription errors. If you are searching for Hull ancestors, also check the following surnames: Hulle, Hoyl, Hoyle, Heyl, Heyle, Hohl, Holl, Hole, Hohle, Hell.

MYTH: *There are no skeletons in my family's closets.*

REALITY: Approach your family history with open-mindedness. You may learn that an ancestor was a petty thief, had a child out of wedlock or died from leprosy. If you uncover information that an ancestor led an unsavoury life, look for more details. Maybe the history has been exaggerated, and maybe not – but that's part of what makes you unique, so don't ignore it!

The idea of tracing your roots seems simple, involving identifying and recording the life histories of your ancestors and compiling the information. Almost like magic, you imagine, the family tree will sprout roots, but examining your genealogy is much more complex.

defining your goals

Beginning genealogists often expect the research process to be easy, but finding names of ancestors and filling in the family tree are just the tip of the iceberg.

If you're thinking about tracing your family roots, ask yourself what you hope to learn. Is your interest casual or intense? Is there an inheritance at stake? Do you want to know your medical history? Each of these issues can be addressed by delving into your family's history.

If you are clear about your goals, you will avoid wasting too much time following false leads or investing too much money. You can then organize and manage your efforts without becoming overwhelmed. Whether you decide to create a family tree, research your entire family history or locate blood relatives, genealogy can become a consuming passion. The process has its rewards and its disappointments and will help you discover how you became the person you are today.

Creating a family tree

Your goal may be to record the vital details (i.e., birth, marriage, death dates) of your ancestors as far back in time as possible. This is best accomplished by creating a family tree or completing a family group sheet. Also known as a pedigree chart, a family tree is a basic, useful tool for documenting your heritage. A family group sheet is similar, but also displays personal details for each individual within a nuclear family unit (parental couple and any children).

WHEN BEGINNING YOUR QUEST...

 DO

- define your goals.

- expect to stimulate your curiosity.

- be persistent when you hit the research wall.

- enjoy the discovery process, no matter where it takes you!

 DON'T

- assume that researching your family history is a simple process.

- expect to find all the information in one day.

- expect to find ancestors all the way back to Adam and Eve.

- expect your ancestors to include royalty.

Alex Myers has located a book with pedigree charts for her Baker ancestors. The hand-written additions are especially valuable: they help fill in gaps in the family history and provide clues for further research.

Full family histories

While identifying only names and dates may seem a sterile, monotonous process, compiling stories and intimate facts about ancestors – discovering the personalities behind the names – vividly brings them to life. Completing a family history can be a time-consuming – even a lifetime – project, requiring a considerable investment in time and effort and solid organizational skills, but it can be enormously fulfilling. Family histories are often the only comprehensive local history record for an area and as such are valuable research sources in their own right.

Locating family branches

Perhaps you need to find other branches of your family for health reasons – to establish your genetic makeup or for organ donation. Or you may simply want to connect with living kin, who have their own histories to relate. You may be able to locate them via the Internet, which features an abundance of genealogy-related websites, mailing lists and forums devoted to searching for relatives. Recent developments in genetic genealogy and DNA testing may also provide the links you seek. Hiring a professional research laboratory to do the tests can be costly, but the results can be truly exciting and may lead you to family members you never knew existed.

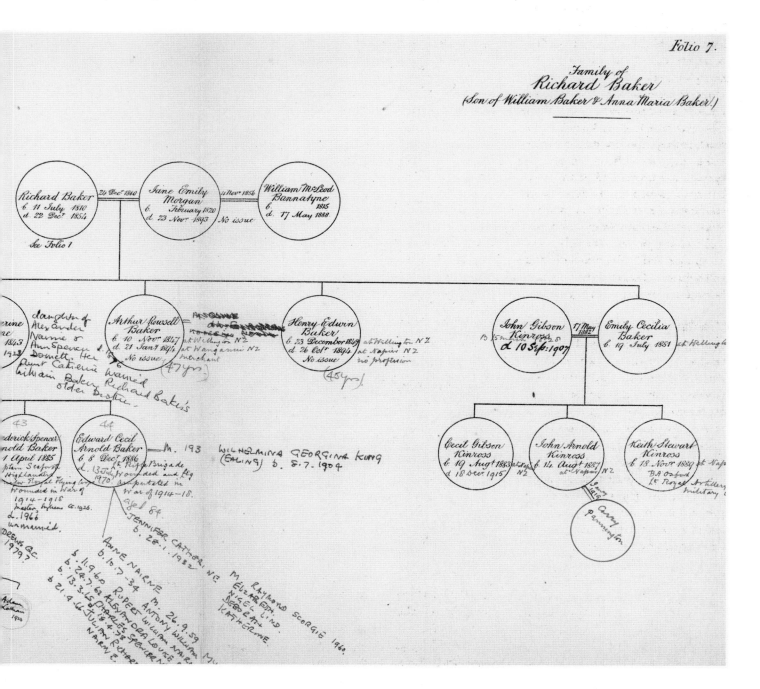

getting prepared

After identifying your goals, pause and take a breath before you rush to the library or archives office or start printing out pertinent genealogical data from the Internet.

Whether you pursue it as a hobby or a profession, genealogy is much more than jotting down a few names, adding them to a pedigree chart and filing the family tree somewhere your children might stumble upon it after your death.

Get organized!

If you have already begun researching your family history, you probably know how quickly the information piles up! If you are a complete beginner, help yourself avoid the nightmare of heaps of paper scattered on desks, shelves or tables. Losing the precious documents you've collected during your research creates unnecessary stress and wastes valuable time.

Whatever you do as you proceed along the pathway into your past, don't let the wealth of information get the better of you. Following a few basic steps can make all the difference between creating a teetering mound of incomprehensible pieces of paper and a well-organized, functional family archive. First, consider what you need to manage the project once it's underway. Begin the process by gathering essential supplies, using the checklist below.

Charts, logs and forms

If you are equipped with a computer, printer and Internet access, you can download or purchase charts, logs and other generic forms used by family historians. One click with your mouse will allow you to print as many sheets as you need – but begin with at least one copy of each form. Having the correct forms at your fingertips simplifies the process and allows you to move forward without losing track of what

you are doing as you make headway through the records.

Many websites, such as Thomson and Gale's Ancestry Plus (www.gale.ancestry.com/learn/start/surveying.htm) and ProGenealogists Family History Research Group (progenealogists.com/freeforms.htm), provide free, downloadable preprinted pedigree charts, family group sheets, family history questionnaires, correspondence and research logs. In addition, most genealogy software programs also include blank forms. See the Resources Directory at the end of this book for further details. If you don't have regular access to the Internet or a computer with a printer, contact a local genealogical society or a company selling items for use by family historians. Alternatively, if you want to save money, photocopy blank forms or design your own.

Where are you heading?

In many ways, tracing your roots is about having a system in place to record the information, store it properly and retrieve it with ease to update the details or share the data with family, friends and even local history societies. Making the time at the beginning of your project to plan out where you are heading will save you time as you get more involved and will keep you focused on achieving your goals. Whether you hope to fill in the blanks on your pedigree chart, write a family history or discover the health backgrounds of your ancestors, make sure you develop a game plan that is tailored to achieve your personal goals.

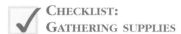 **CHECKLIST: GATHERING SUPPLIES**

- black ink pens and pencils
- blank paper or index cards for recording information
- file or archival folders
- filing cabinet or storage boxes
- loose-leaf binders and notebooks (avoid spiral designs)
- dividers or index tabs
- blank pedigree charts, family group sheets, correspondence and research logs (as applicable)
- coloured labels (optional)
- tape recorder and tapes (optional)
- camera and film (optional)

Where do I start?

problem

Tracing my roots looks so exciting. I want to get going now! But there is so much information and it all seems so confusing. How can I reach my goals?

solution

It's important to have a game plan that will help you identify – and ultimately achieve – your goals. Take the following steps to develop your personal plan of action.

- Identify what you wish to research (the task).

- Break down each task into manageable pieces (subtasks).

- Brainstorm potential sources of information.

- Make a list of sources you intend to examine.

- Make a tentative schedule for completing the task.

- Focus on one task at a time.

- Write your plan on paper or a computer file.

- Print and file a copy in your notebook.

- If you own a computer, save the plan to disk, CD or hard drive.

- Refer to your plan frequently.

- Revise it when necessary.

- Be flexible – but be organized.

- Be methodical.

- Track new leads with a new plan.

- Devise a new plan whenever you enter a new phase of your research.

where to begin

The key to researching your family history is to start at the beginning. Start close to home as you and your family are your own best resource.

Once you have defined your goals in researching your family history, established a game plan (a tentative one is better than no plan) and gathered enough pens, paper, blank forms and other supplies to record the information, you should feel ready to begin discovering your past. But where do you begin exactly – the library, the Internet, national archives?

Start with yourself

In fact, you can begin the hard work from the comfort of your own chair! You are your own best resource, so start with yourself and work backwards in time. First of all, write down what you know about your family. Ask yourself key questions and answer them to the best of your knowledge. Be specific, record everything, be precise and fastidious and don't abbreviate: you or whoever else may later read the data may misinterpret what you have written. Use a pencil and a blank sheet of paper, index card, pedigree chart or family group sheet to record your vital details. If you have transcription skills, consider tape-recording your memories.

Family documents and artefacts

Once you have written down as much as you can about yourself and your immediate family, gather the items that document your past (see the checklist). Consider each item a piece in a jigsaw puzzle that forms your family history. Treat them with care and store safely. The collection is your personal treasury, the artefacts of your past, and can provide research leads or corroborate other data you have acquired.

Question family members

Then, expand your research: talk to family members. Record their vital details and oral histories. Whether your goal is to fill in your family tree (pedigree chart) or to document as much of your family history as possible, preparing a list of questions ahead of the interview will save you time, help you remember to ask everything you want to know and keep your work on track. You may discover stories, myths and kin you never knew existed.

If you're aiming at a detailed family history, record special memories, favourite foods, friends' and pets' names, toys, school experiences, historical events that impacted on relatives' lives, the neighbourhood(s) where they grew up, jobs, memberships of societies and organizations, religious affiliations, as well as answers to the basic questions (see the Problem Solver on page 19). Even seemingly trivial information may lead you to a new discovery about yourself, so record minuscule details and curiosities. Above all, enjoy the process and jot down any questions that come to mind as you proceed – they will lead you into the next phase of your research.

✓ **CHECKLIST: FAMILY DOCUMENTS**

- birth certificates
- school records
- marriage licences
- divorce papers
- newspaper clippings and obituary notices
- wills, tax and property records
- family letters
- death certificates
- driver's licences
- military records and memorabilia
- religious records
- family bible
- diaries
- photographs
- heirlooms

tip **Subsequent marriages**
If there have been subsequent marriages, repeat the same questions listed in the Problem Solver on page 19, documenting the date and place of the wedding and the vital details for each subsequent spouse. If there are any children from subsequent marriages, establish their full names, dates and places of birth.

> 19. Nov. 1898

> THE ORCHARD,
> NORMANTON.

> Fred Bowes has been in my service as under groom for five years. He can feed groom and generally care for a horse very well.
>
> He can ride and drive, and has always done what he has been told.
>
> His general character has been satisfactory
>
> W. J. Mackenzie
> Surgeon
> J. P. West Riding Yorks.

Old photographs of your ancestors reveal more than just their physical appearance. This dapper image of Fred Bowes as an adult displays the clothing styles of the times, and the place and conditions where he worked.

Family keepsakes, such as this letter of reference from Fred Bowes's employer, not only bring you closer to your ancestors, but also give you insight into how and where they led their lives.

> Mrs Fred Bowes,
> Holstein Street,
> Preston.

Imagine finding an old postcard in your attic, like this one sent from France during World War I. What clues does it offer? Ask relatives what they know about your ancestor's participation in the war in France.

WHEN ASKING QUESTIONS OF RELATIVES...

 Do

- ask each relative the same basic questions in the same order.

- be specific, precise and fastidious in recording your answers.

- record the full name of the person interviewed and the date they provided the answers.

- encourage storytelling.

- jot down any questions that come to mind as you proceed.

 Don't

- ask 'closed' questions, i.e., the sort that elicit 'yes', 'no', silence, or a dead-end response.

- abbreviate: you may forget what you meant and others may depend on your research later.

- ignore trivia: it may lead you to a new discovery about yourself.

Completing the jigsaw puzzle of your past involves gathering as many documents on each relative as possible. Besides his vital statistics, Fred Bowes's birth certificate supplies personal information about his parents.

Talking to family members

Problem

What questions should I ask my relatives (and also myself) when I interview them for my family history research?

Solution

By asking your relatives the same questions that you ask yourself, you can identify blanks in your history, any inconsistencies in the data and tasks for further research. For consistency, repeat the same questions in the same order when interviewing each family member.

- **What is your full name? (And nickname, if you had/have one?)**

- **Where and when (exact date) were you born?**

- **What are your parents' full names? (And their nicknames?)**

- **Where and when (exact dates) were your parents born?**

- **Where and when (exact dates) were your parents married?**

- **When did your parents die and where are they buried? (if applicable)**

- **What are the full names of your siblings? (Include their nicknames.)**

- **What is each sibling's birth date and where were they born?**

- **If any siblings have died, when did they die and where are they buried?**

- **Where and when (exact dates) were you married?**

- **What are the full name, date and place of birth of your spouse?**

- **What are the full names, dates and places of birth of each of your children?**

- **If spouses or children have died, when did they die and where are they buried?**

- **If there have been divorces, when were they finalized?**

Whether you are tracing your roots for pure enjoyment or hope to publish a detailed family history, it's important to be consistent in everything you do.

Whenever you record information – whether you are taking dictation, jotting down notes from family members, transcribing taped memories or copying archival data – always use the same format to document names, dates and locations. Be complete: rather than abridging or abbreviating information, or planning to return at some later date for an in-depth examination, write everything down when you first come across it. Taking the extra time as you go along saves time later and you will avoid duplicating your efforts.

Problems with names

Surnames within the same family often evolve over time. Many people – not just actors, writers and newlyweds – change their surnames intentionally. They may abbreviate long names, anglicize or translate their names, or even make them more complex, for example, changing Wood to Woodford. In fact, before the mid-18th century, people commonly spelled names as they thought appropriate. Illiteracy was still common, so misspellings – even of one's own name – occurred frequently. Clerks and other officials also accidentally made transcription errors, misunderstanding the names told to them. Consequently, many old documents contain the same surname, but spelled more than one way. Although a single document may list John Smith, John Smithe and John Smyth, the names may all represent the same person. Therefore, copy clearly what you see or hear, word for word, exactly as it is presented to you. If you come across a surname that you think may be misspelled, don't alter or

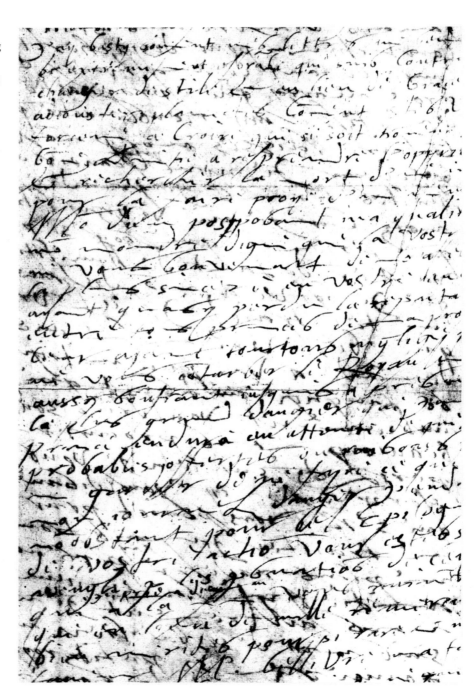

Old documents, like this letter from Queen Elizabeth I, dating from January 1587, can often be virtually impossible to read without the help of a paleographer.

How to record information

Problem

How should I record names, dates and locations?

Solution

Genealogists commonly use the following formats for recording vital details:

- Record the person's full name in its conventional order, using upper-case letters to distinguish the surname from given names:

  Example: Kathryn Anne JOHNSON (in the case of a married woman, record only her maiden name)

- Document 'nicknames' in quote marks:

  Example: Kathryn 'Katie' Anne JOHNSON

- Record also adopted or intentionally changed names:

  Example: Kathryn Anne JOHNSON (a.k.a. Kathryn Anne NORBERG)

- Be sure to include professional titles, as applicable:

  Example: Dr. Kathryn Anne JOHNSON

- Always record dates using the standard format: day, month, year. Spell out the month and use two numerals for the day and four for the year.

- *Example*: 09 October 1993

- Approximate dates should include abt (for 'about') or ca. or c. (for 'circa'):

  Example: abt October 1993, ca. October 1993 or c. October 1993

- Area designations will vary by country, so take care to list them accurately. Proceed from the smallest to the largest geographical area:

  Example: Old Tappan, Bergen County, New Jersey, United States

  Example: Haverfordwest, Pembrokeshire, Wales, United Kingdom

'revise' it because you think it should be spelled differently.

Handwritten signatures offer the best indicators of how people spelled their names, but they may be difficult to read. Ask for assistance with handwritten script. Record every spelling variation you find and then continue your research to determine the most commonly used variant during a specific time frame. Ultimately, different spellings may link you to relatives or lineages you did not realize existed.

Recording the data

Remember, you are recording not only your own family history, but also the history of other people – distant relatives or local historians – who may rely on your data to research their heritage. Use a pencil in case you make mistakes or want to update an entry at a later time. After you have recorded a person's vital details on index cards, notebook paper or computer disk, double-check the information to ensure its accuracy. Note any discrepancies or missing information. Transferring the information to a pedigree chart or family group sheet is an important part of the process, so do it slowly and meticulously. Conflicting or missing data are subjects for further research and should be noted as such on your research log or to-do list.

The pedigree chart

Begin by placing yourself on preprinted line number one, on the lefthand side of the pedigree chart (also known as an ancestor chart). Work backwards in time, adding your parents, grandparents, great-grandparents and so on. Most pedigree charts provide space for four or five generations, but they don't include space for your own marriages, children and siblings. You will have to fill out additional charts for those generations and for individuals more than five generations back in your family tree. The entry on line number one can be either male or

female, but for subsequent entries male relatives are always positioned on even numbered, upper lines, while female relatives are always placed on odd numbered, lower lines. Under each line, record the person's date and place of birth (b), date and place of marriage (m), date and place of death (d) and spouse's name (sp), as appropriate. Note blank spaces for further research.

The ahnentafel chart

When you add information to your pedigree chart, you can also complete an 'ahnentafel chart' (which means 'ancestor table' in German). This simple-to-use table identifies, in an organized way, the numbers you have assigned to each individual on your pedigree chart. The ahnentafel chart provides a cross-reference guide for you to locate quickly relatives listed on the pedigree chart. Ahnentafel charts exist in several formats: print out or design the one that suits your style. A simple, numbered list with each relative's name and their relationship to you may suffice.

The family group sheet

Each self-explanatory sheet focuses on a single family unit and includes blocks for recording vital details for parents (often labelled 'husband' and 'wife' on preprinted forms) and children in birth order. Each set of parents will have its own family group sheet. Complete separate sheets for you and your spouse (or spouses), your parents, their parents and any other couples in your family tree.

Follow the standard formats established in the Problem Solver on page 00 when entering data. Note anything and everything of interest: occupations, military service, school locations, grave sites, religious preferences, and so on. Leave blank spaces to indicate tasks for further research. Other researchers may want to use the sheets to continue your work or to complete their own records, so document every source you use for each piece of information (see below). Family group sheets generally include only a small block for citations, so if you need additional space, continue on the back of the sheet, attach another page or use a footnote/endnote system to identify which source supplied which data.

Citing sources

Although the effort seems tedious, fully and systematically documenting your resources is as essential to tracing your roots as is correctly transcribing vital details. When you need to refer to a source to verify data or check conflicting information, already having the citation will save you time and effort. You will lessen the likelihood of repeating research and avoid the confusion that is created by poorly cited records. And not only will other family historians be able to locate those resources for their own projects, they will also recognize that you have done your homework and feel confident that the information is accurate.

Use a separate research log, index card or notebook page for each family unit. Record your source (the author or the name of the person you spoke to)

tip **Citing yourself as a source**
Be cautious about citing yourself as the source. Unless you witnessed, participated in or have firsthand knowledge of the event, never cite yourself as the source. Some individual or some document had to have informed you of the details. You must cite that person or that record as your source.

along with the other information given in the checklist below. Once you establish a format, keep using it. After citing a few sources, the task will become routine and you will move along more quickly.

Primary and secondary sources

Original and unedited documents and contemporary accounts written by someone who actually experienced the event are called primary sources. Examples include manuscripts, wills, manorial records, letters, tithe maps, birth certificates, marriage records, obituaries, diaries, tape-recorded oral histories, government documents, paintings, photographs and artefacts. The people you interview or who tell you information about your family are primary sources, and should be cited as such. Wherever possible, try to use primary sources.

Secondary sources are documents about other documents – in other words, materials that interpret historical events or restate the information that is contained within primary sources. Secondary sources include encyclopaedias, textbooks and many magazine and journal articles. You should always cite the source that you actually used, not the sources mentioned in a book or that you learnt by word of mouth.

CHECKLIST: CITING SOURCES

Make sure you document the following, as applicable, for each source of information you acquire:

- the author of the source (or the person who gave you the information)
- the title
- the exact date (for archival information this often includes day, month and year)
- the publisher and location (as applicable)
- where you found the information (i.e., the library, records office, the Internet, etc.)
- call number or web page URL, page number, line number, etc.

Family Group Record

Husband _WILLIAM WOODS_
Born _JUNE 27 1875_ Place _ASHLAND, OHIO_
Married _JANUARY 6 1900_ Place _ASHLAND, OHIO_
Occupation _IRON MOULDER/PRIVATE CO 'C 8th OHIO VOL. INFANTRY - SPANISH-AMERICAN WAR_
Church Affil _____
✱ Died _FEBRUARY 23, 1933_ Place _CUYAHOGA HEIGHTS,_
Buried _CROWN HILL CEMETERY_ Place _TWINSBURG, OH OHIO_
Other wives _____
Father _HENRY ELMORE WOODS_
Mother (maiden name) _SARAH_
✱ _EFFECTS OF MALARIA FEVER CONTRACTED IN CUBA_

Wife _FLORA LENORA (NORA) STOVER_
Born _JANUARY 17, 1877_ Place _BELLE VERNON, OHIO_
Church Affil _____ Occupation _HOMEMAKER_ ✱✱
Died _OCTOBER 8, 1964_ Place _TEANECK, NJ_
Buried _CROWN HILL CEM._ Place _TWINSBURG, OHIO_
Other husbands _____
Father _ALONZO DELANCEY STOVER_
Mother (maiden name) _LYDIA RIEGEL_
✱✱ _AND PREP COOK_

Name and address of Person filling out this sheet
LISE E. HULL
_____
_____

Relationship of above to husband
GREAT GRAND-DAUGHTER

Relationship of above to Wife
GREAT GRAND-DAUGHTER

Names of Husband and Wife this chart are the same person as nos _____ & _____
on linage chart no _____

Sex M F	Children	Born Date And Place	Married to whom Date and Place	Died Date and Place
1	NITA RHEA	8-14-1900 CRESTLINE OHIO	HAROLD KENNETH EWALD JULY 31, 1921 CLEVELAND, OHIO	9-17-1977 TEANECK, NJ
2				
3				
4				
5				
6				
7				

The author's family group sheet for her great-grandparents documents each person's vital statistics. It also features a maiden name, nickname, cause of death, and employment details.

organizing your data

Almost immediately when you begin researching your past, you will accumulate an entire array of archival records.

Filing systems

Rather than stuffing all your documents into one folder, hauling loose papers with you to the library or record office and hoping you can find what you need when you need it, you should aim to establish a system that will logically organize your work for quick retrieval. Setting up a filing system even before you begin the research may seem premature, particularly if you think you only want to fill in a few blanks on your family tree. Rest assured: being organized has a practical purpose. Establishing a filing system at the beginning of the research process will help you avoid the rising mounds of seemingly random paperwork, help you prevent the misplacement of data and allow you to retrieve it with ease.

Not only will you want to file paperwork pertaining to specific relatives, you will also need a secure place to store the work as you make your way through the records. You will want to identify incomplete information and plan out additional research tasks. Do you prefer file folders, notebooks, boxes or briefcases of information? Folders are great for storing items, but the loose papers can scatter if you drop the file, or you may forget to replace an item that you removed from the folder. Where will you store the files: in a cardboard box, filing cabinet, fireproof file, safety deposit box? Purchasing acid-free folders and archive storage boxes will help preserve your information for future generations.

Choose a system that seems reasonable and usable to you. You may want to purchase a prepackaged system especially designed with genealogists in mind (see the Resource Directory and Further Reading for suggestions). Or you may want to devise a system to suit your particular needs and personality quirks. In time, you may decide to revise your system. Whatever you decide, it's always best to have a filing system in place before you begin investigating your past and cluttering up your house – not to mention your brain!

Organization is the key to tracing your roots. One of your first steps should be to develop a personal system for filing and storing the paperwork you gather.

How to file information

Problem

I have so many ancestors, with so many different surnames. Besides listing them on my pedigree chart and on family group sheets, how should I organize my notes and the documents I collect?

Solution

Take time to consider what you will need from your filing and storage system. A good system will help you recognize the work you have completed or determine what needs further attention. Ideally, you should create the following:

- A personal file for your pedigree chart and ahnentafel chart. Make working copies of each chart to carry with you when carrying out research.

- A family unit file for each couple for whom you have a family group sheet. Inside, file information all beginning with their marriage and working forward to their deaths. Each family unit file should also include a copy of the family group sheet. Update the table of contents every time you add new information and insert copies of all pertinent documents and notes, including marriage and children's birth certificates, death certificates, divorce papers, property records, wills, etc. Data related to your parents' childhoods go into the files for your grandparents. Identify each family unit file not just with surnames but also with each individual's position on your pedigree or ahnentafel chart. Example: Ralph James WILSON/ Matilda Eunice CARDIGAN 2/3.

- An originals file to keep original documents separate from your working files. They are one-of-a-kind items, which cannot be replaced, so store them in safe, fireproof containers. Make photocopies to keep in your working file.

- A working file, which, in addition to copies of your pedigree and ahnentafel charts, should include a research log, documenting the work you have done and the work you plan to do. Use one working file for each family group sheet or divide a single working file into sections. Use index tabs marked with the code you established for the couple, e.g., 2/3, 4/5, 6/7 and other number pairs, to distinguish the sections. You may prefer using coloured labels to identify different family units, surnames or generations.

- A communications file, which should include a correspondence log to identify communications you have sent out, that are pending and that you have received (and filed in the appropriate family unit file).

---

tip **Using computer filing systems**

Computer files can be excellent timesaving devices and allow you to store and manipulate data with relative ease. However, unless you carry a laptop to the library or records office, you will still accumulate notes, photocopies and actual records so it is still important to organize and store these properly, as suggested above.

identifying the gaps

As you begin recording details on your genealogy chart or family history sheet, you may notice dates and spellings that do not match.

Conflicting information

A family member may have reported your grandfather's birth date as 28 February 1931, while his birth certificate says 28 February 1932. Your relative may tell you an ancestor's name was Gerald James FULBRIGHT, but the death certificate may state it as Gerard James FULBRIGHT.

Such are the pitfalls of tracing one's family history. Not only can information gleaned from living relatives conflict with official records, but the records themselves may also differ. Gerald James FULBRIGHT's social security card may record his name as Gerald FULBRIGHT. At first glance, the discrepancy may seem like a minor detail, but just how certain can you be

that the two Geralds really are the same individual?

The simple answer is that you can't be certain! When you discover discrepancies in the information you have gathered on a person, additional research is warranted, indeed essential, but it does not guarantee you will ever determine the facts of an issue.

Use primary sources wherever possible – but remember, they can still contain mistakes. Secondary sources, including Internet files, are fallible; published genealogies may misrepresent the facts; clerks make mistakes; memories fade; transcription errors occur inadvertently. Some people may even have deliberately misspelled their names in order not to be traced

by relatives, the police, their employers, the Inland Revenue or the military. Others intentionally embellish their past or produce fraudulent genealogies without having corroborating evidence.

Some commonly encountered discrepancies and related issues – including problematic handwriting, date variations and problems with place names – are discussed more fully in Part Three (see pages 00–00).

Evaluating your data

Besides having a plan, being consistent and developing an organized system to approach your work and record your findings, you must train yourself to read between the lines and question every detail you learn about your

Be sure to crosscheck the details recorded on official documents. Does Fred Bowes's marriage certificate conflict with his birth certificate or any other papers?

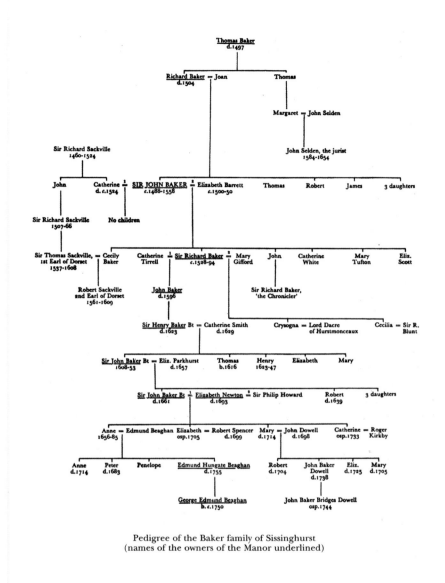

Pedigree of the Baker family of Sissinghurst
(names of the owners of the Manor underlined)

 Do

■ regularly and methodically review your pedigree chart, family group sheets, official documents and other notes in order to identify gaps and contradictory data.

■ highlight conflicting or missing information.

■ use a research log or discrepancy chart to note anomalies or missing information that you need to recheck or research further.

■ frequently reevaluate your findings.

■ identify what issues you wish to research.

■ update your to-do list, noting new tasks to pursue.

■ choose one topic or person to examine next.

✗ DON'T

■ overlook or change contradictory data just to make things consistent: altering information that someone recorded previously can destroy vital links to your ancestors.

■ take the content of previously published genealogies about your family or surname as gospel.

■ be insensitive should you need to ask your informants to verify what they remember about certain dates, events and people.

■ ignore unexpected connections between family members or new pathways into the past.

Don't expect to be able to put together a full family tree, like this one of the Baker family of Sissinghurst. It will take a lot of time and patience to find out this much information about your ancestors.

relatives. Become a modern-day Hercule Poirot: exercise your little grey cells! Never believe everything you read, nor everything you hear. Rather, consistently analyse, criticize, reconsider and crosscheck your information until you are reasonably certain that the data you have is authentic and accurate.

The key to producing an accurate family tree or history is to review and verify the information you collect and then crosscheck it against other sources. Every contradictory detail offers a clue to further research. You cannot predict where that piece of information will lead you, nor what new discoveries you may make.

Family historians often arrive at turning points in their genealogy studies. Gaps in the research can rapidly seem like impassable chasms. An abundance of archival repositories and Internet resources await your discovery. Your next step is to find out where these repositories are and how to use them.

As you fill in your pedigree chart or family group sheet, you will begin to notice blank spaces where names, dates, places or other information is missing.

Traditional family stories, related to you by grandparents or parents, may not match what you have recorded. You realize that the possibilities for further research seem limitless – and perhaps they are! However, you can control how much of your past you wish to examine and how you will proceed.

Your choices include mounting a major letter-writing effort to locate official documents, checking local bookstores and libraries, surfing the Internet for clues or actually visiting records repositories. Each of these pathways offers a valuable opportunity to fill in the information gaps or narrow the

chasms you encountered during your preliminary research.

Tracing your roots is an inexact process. It often involves trial and error followed by regrouping and renewing the quest for information. Once you have gleaned all the details you can from relatives, it's time to move outside your family circle.

Published family histories

Have you read through any previously published histories connected with your family? Libraries in the region where your ancestor lived or genealogical associations may hold copies.

You can review the Periodical Source Index (PERSI) to identify published articles about your family. Begun in the 1980s by the Allen County Public Library in Fort Wayne, Indiana, the database contains more than 1.7 million references to articles in journals, magazines, newsletters and other publications that focus on genealogy and historical topics of interest to family historians. Articles are indexed by subject matter and geographical locality. On the Internet, Ancestry.com provides searchable links

THE FAMILY OF NAIRNE.

ALTHOUGH it may reasonably be thought that the name "Nairne," or "Nairn," like so many others probably originated from the town or district of the same name, this is unlikely. Were it so, one would expect to find bearers of the name, and past records of it in the neighbourhood of the County of Nairn and the Moray Firth generally. But these are almost non-existent.

The name is not a very common one anywhere, but a fair sprinkling of Nairns and Nairnes in every class of society may be found in the County of Fife and in the eastern districts of Perthshire. Should a Nairn be met in London, Glasgow or the Colonies he will almost certainly claim that his folk came originally from Fife.

How a family living in this particular district came to adopt the name, which in the Gaelic means an alder tree, one can only surmise.

It has been suggested* that some early immigrant from the town of Narni in Umbria altered the "di Narni," by which he was known, to a name of Scotch form. It has come to my knowledge that some of the early Nairnes in the Tree of Nairne of Sandford actually spelled their name Narne. This is the only evidence I know in favour of the theory.

In the middle ages and down to the seventeenth century there appear to have been three important branches of the family, who were considerable land-holders. These were the Nairnes of Meiklour, the Nairnes of Dunsinane, and the Nairnes of Saint Ford (or Sandford). The head of the family associated with Meiklour was a partizan of the Stuarts and was created Baron Nairne in 1681.

The Nairnes of Dunsinane were baronets in the eighteenth century, and the fifth and last baronet, Sir William Nairne, was an ordinary lord of session, and as a Scottish judge took the title of Lord Dunsinane. The notorious Catherine Nairne, who in the eighteenth century was condemned to death with her lover for the murder of her husband, but who escaped from prison by a trick, belonged to the family at Dunsinane.

It is with the Nairnes of Sandford (or Saint Ford or Sanct Furd as it is earlier spelt) that our family claims connection.

Unfortunately this claim has never been proved, and is, I am afraid, never likely to be proved. James Nairne, W.S., in his manuscript has no doubt of the connection, but gives no evidence to prove it. Some account of the Nairnes of Sandford is given further on in my narrative.

Sibbald in his "History of Fife," published first in the eighteenth century, states "Saint Furd has been long the heritage of gentlemen of the name of Nairn. In 1446 Alexander "Nairn de Saintfurd is Comptroller, and in the same reign of King James II (of Scotland)— "Nairn is Lyon King of Arms." This last was Alexander Nairn, and I believe I am right

---

* A statement to this effect appeared in the "Peerage" of about 50 years ago.

7

Published family histories often contain details about your past that you will not be able to find anywhere else, such as the origins of the surname and notable historical connections.

tip **Using published family histories**

Remember that while they serve as short cuts to doing research, published family histories do not always contain accurate or current information.

Taking the next step

Problem

I have completed my pedigree chart and family group sheets and have noticed several gaps and discrepancies in the information. What's the next step?

Solution

Expand your research from what you can find at home and from questioning living relatives to the records stored by local repositories, then move on to larger political and geographical units, including archives held by state, provincial and national governmental agencies and organizations.

- Make a manageable, written plan before proceeding with your research.

- Select one individual or family unit to research at a time.

- Review your charts, sheets and research log and update them as you discover new details about your family history.

- Note any questions or information gaps.

- Identify which sources or record types you want to use.

- Identify the correct name of the town, county, province, state or territory where your ancestor actually lived.

- If you have Internet access, print and use a copy of the LDS (Latter-day Saints) research outline for the region where your ancestors lived. The outlines are located on the Family History Center's website at www.familysearch.org.

- Identify which repositories hold the records, e.g., the local records office, national archives, family history library, etc., in the geographical area associated with the ancestor you want to study.

- Determine if the record is available on the Internet or if you will have to contact or travel to the repository to use it.

- Prepare your working folders: gather the supplies and paperwork you need to carry with you to do the research.

- Before your visit, obtain a user's guide to the repository, if available, and know what records each type of repository holds before you contact staff for assistance.

- Familiarize yourself with different types of records, including their indexes.

- Contact the repository before your visit, via letter, email or telephone, according to their requirements.

- Read the rest of this book for further guidance!

---

to PERSI at www.ancestry.com/search/rectype/periodicals/persi/main.htm and also offers the database for purchase on CD-ROM.

Check your local library or family history centre for other genealogy periodical indexes, including the Genealogical Periodical Annual Index (GPAI) and the American Genealogical Biographical Index (AGBI).

Other primary records

Locating primary resources – those official and unofficial records directly related to specific family members – should be at the top of your priority list when you seek outside resources. If you live near or in the same area as the ancestor you are researching, you will be able to explore local cemeteries, newspaper archives and school and church records without having to venture too far beyond your front door. Governmental agencies, religious groups, military and civil authorities, and a myriad other sources hold records that will provide the keys to your past. Your task is to identify which repositories are most likely to contain those documents, and then get your hands on them.

local government repositories

The nations of the world subdivide and govern local areas in a variety of ways depending on their history and sociopolitical organization.

Not only do the names of these smallest governmental units vary from country to country, complicating the family history research process, but the records they produce and archive vary as well. Generally, local government repositories should be your first destination when you branch out from your home and family archives to seek more details and original records, including birth, marriage and death certificates, divorce records, probate and land records. The reason for checking such records first is that they normally contain full names, dates and places where significant life events occurred. With them, you may find data to fill in the gaps on your pedigree chart or family group sheet.

United States: county courthouses

Arguably the best-known and most commonly sought-out repository in the US is the county courthouse. As the governmental centre for each county within the 50 US states, the county courthouse stores vital records and is particularly valuable for documents originating before 1900. (After 1900 many states took over the registration process for vital details and other key life events.)

Before you visit a particular repository, check to see if it does have the type of record you need, as holdings vary from courthouse to courthouse. County names, seats and political boundaries change over time, so always contact the courthouse by letter or via the Internet to determine if you are looking in the correct county before you appear on the doorstep! A

good starting point for researchers with Internet access is the Family History Library website, www.familysearch.org. You may also want to contact your local Family History Centre, which stores vital records on microfilm.

Records typically held by a US county courthouse include:

- birth, death and marriage certificates
- divorce records
- probate records
- wills, deeds and land records
- voter lists
- tax lists
- court records
- naturalization papers (in some cases)

United Kingdom: country record offices

The UK's county archives services function as repositories not only for governmental records but also for family, estate, manorial, parish, school, business and maritime documents. Each office maintains a summary of its main collections, which family history researchers should consult before visiting the facility.

Many county record offices hold microfiche copies of the International Genealogical Index (IGI) – an invaluable resource for family historians – and many also provide short courses on using their archives to do genealogical research.

Records typically held by a UK county record office include:

- wills
- deeds
- hospital records
- school records
- shipping and valuation records
- census returns
- county council records
- poor relief records
- borough records
- water authority records
- parish records
- ecclesiastical and nonconformist registers
- private collections of families and estates, businesses and solicitors

France: archives départementales

In France, governmental units known as 'départements' serve as repositories for local records. Holdings include civil registration records (birth, marriage and death records), church records created before 1792 and census records. Usually located in the department's largest town, the archives are accessible to the public. Most departments provide inventories and guides to their collections, which researchers should examine before a visit to determine which records the particular office holds. Another resource for local records is the civil registration office (bureau de l'état civil). Located in town halls, these offices retain mainly original birth, marriage and death records created after 1792.

Germany

As Germany has no central repositories for civil records, your ancestor's records may be found in one of several places. The best place to start is the civil registration office, located in most towns, which generally holds birth, marriage and death documents. In some cases, vital records may be stored in larger towns close to your ancestor's home village. Descendants may obtain copies or information extracted from the records, but not the originals themselves. (You will need to be able to prove your relationship to the individual you are researching to obtain copies.)

Italy: comunes

In Italy, civil offices known as 'comunes' hold a variety of documents, including birth, death and marriage records created by the local government since 1865. Similar to town halls, the offices are accessible to the public. Copies of vital records may be obtained by writing directly to the comune or by visiting in person.

Mexico: municipio records offices

Comparable to county courthouses in the US, Mexico's local civil offices, or municipio records offices, maintain local archives, including vital records, divorce records, wills and probate records and land records. Roughly the equivalent of a US county, each municipio, or municipality, stores its own archives, the two most important of which are El Archivo del Municipio and El Archivo del Registro Civil.

County courthouses are among the best known and most widely used local repositories for tracing American roots. Many are historical structures in their own right.

Locating government records

Problem

How do I locate the local repository that keeps my ancestor's vital records?

Solution

There are several first courses of action you could take to locate such records, as follows:

- **To determine whether a specific US courthouse holds your ancestor's vital records, review the following sources, which should be available at most libraries:**

    - **Ancestry's *Red Book***
    - ***The Handy Book for Genealogists*, published by Everton's**
    - ***Kemp's International Vital Records Handbook***

- **Check the Resources Directory at the end of this book for contact information for other local repositories. Then write or telephone the office you believe may store the records you need.**

- **Internet users can contact records offices around the world. See the Resources Directory for website specifics.**

Whether a nation is subdivided into states, provinces or territories, it will have specific regional entities that create and store official records.

Many regional governments retain their most recent records until they are deemed no longer to be of immediate use. Records identified as having historical importance or significance as regulated by legislation may then be turned over to a regional storage facility. To manage, organize, preserve and safeguard the documents and to make them accessible to public scrutiny, most regional agencies have established records repositories, variously known as archives, record offices, state libraries and so on. In many cases, states maintain archives that hold records for a variety of governmental bodies, including county and national agencies as well as state or provincial ones.

United States

First, identify what type of repository exists for the state you believe holds the records for your ancestor. Many states maintain a Department of Vital Records, which stores recent records, while others deposit them at state archival repositories. Check the resource directory or ask staff at the local library or family history centre. If you are an Internet user, click on www.sos.state.ga.us/archives/rs/sarl.htm, the State Archives Referral List provided by the Georgia Secretary of State, for contact details for different states.

The following examples show the type of agencies that might be available in a given state:

The Connecticut State Library is the official repository for the archives of the state government. It operates a History and Genealogy Unit.

Georgia Archives is a division of the Office of the Secretary of State, and holds not only documents created by the state government but also certain county and federal records.

The Arkansas History Commission maintains the state's archives, as well as county records, including marriage, tax, probate and court records.

The National Archives and Records Administration (NARA) operates regional centres throughout the US as well as its main repository in Washington, DC. Facilities include an archival research room, microfilm research room and records centre research room. NARA also maintains presidential libraries in several states.

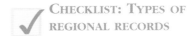

CHECKLIST: TYPES OF REGIONAL RECORDS

State, provincial and territorial repositories generally hold the following records, which are collectively characterized as 'regional' records. Before you visit, however, determine if the repository stores the records for your particular ancestor.

- vital records
- regional census records
- land records
- pension records
- voter lists
- vehicle registrations
- driver licences
- law enforcement records
- regional court and prison records
- regional cemetery records
- regional military records
- state-operated hospital and veterans' home records
- state university and school records
- indigenous records as they pertain to specific regions
- some family or business records

tip Planning a visit

Do not go to a state or provincial records office without prior planning, research and forethought. To get the most from these repositories, identify the types of records that they hold, whether they are accessible to the public and the best way to approach the facility for information: by appointment, telephone or mail, or via the Internet.

United Kingdom

The UK presently has no legislation that formalizes arrangements for the provision of archive services at regional levels. However, England has recently established nine Regional Archives Councils (RAC), which serve in an advisory capacity. The RACs also coordinate the services of each region's archival collections, including major archives services and archival collections in museums, libraries and other organizations, such as academic institutions. RACs have been formed for the Northwest and Northeast regions, Yorkshire, the West and East Midlands, the East of England, the Southwest and Southeast Regions and London. Scotland and Wales have the Scottish Council on Archives and Archives Council Wales respectively.

Canadian provincial/territorial archives

Each province and territory in Canada maintains a publicly accessible archives, which holds vital and church records, provincial census records, land records and other documents relevant to the particular region. The British Columbia Archives, for example, maintains vital records, land records, census records, church registers, pedigree charts and published family histories, as well as government documents, private manuscripts and papers, photographs, newspapers and publications that are related to British Columbia and the Pacific Northwest.

Australian state records

Individual states in Australia maintain archives or record offices, which hold records of state government departments, courts, local government authorities, ministerial offices and government-owned corporations. Repositories, such as the Queensland State Archives, also hold passenger lists, vital records, state electoral rolls, wills, records of death and fire inquests, naturalization records, land records, admission registers for state schools and many other resources.

Danish state archives

Even though Denmark maintains a state archives, each province also has a records repository. The Provincial Archives of Northern Jutland, for

Depending on the nation, regional repositories may be located in state facilities, such as the Massachusetts state house, which dates to the 1790s. Many nations store archives in state or regional libraries, which may have several branches.

example, is the oldest of the nation's four provincial repositories and holds material from state and local authorities and institutions, including the courts, law enforcement and bishop's records.

Poland's state archives

While the central government maintains three repositories of national significance in Warsaw, researchers will also find the 29 state archives and 53 regional branches, including those in Gdansk, Krakow, Lublin, Olszty, Poznan, Szczecin and Wroclaw, of particular value. These repositories store the records of local government and state authorities and institutions; educational and religious organizations; business, individual, family and estate papers and other documents of regional significance. Researchers from overseas are encouraged to use the facilities.

Confederate records

Problem

My great-great grandfather fought with a Confederate Army unit from Georgia during the Civil War. He even survived the Atlanta campaign, but was seriously wounded. What state records should I search to learn more about his post-war life?

Solution

A surprising wealth of information exists in archives often known as Confederate records.

Check the National Archives, which holds compiled service records for many Confederate soldiers.

The Georgia State Archives (www.sos.state.ga.us/archives/rs/cws.htm) holds microfilm copies of compiled service records of Confederate soldiers from the State of Georgia and similar records, which the public may review. They include information on battalions, regiments, legions and independent companies, and list soldiers by name.

Check Confederate pension records, which deal with state benefits granted to injured veterans, such as artificial limbs. Former soldiers also received pensions for blindness, loss of hearing, death due to wounds or disease contracted during the Civil War, poverty and infirmity. Widows were also eligible for pension benefits.

Check the rosters created by the Georgia Soldier Roster Commission, which document military service during the Civil War.

Review the records of the Confederate Soldiers' Home of Georgia, which include unit names, battles in which the individual fought, discharge date, next of kin, date of death (if it occurred in the home's hospital) and the place of burial.

Civil war archives often contain family photographs, such as this one of George and Elizabeth Custer and a relative in uniform, dating to 1874. Be sure to request copies for your personal files.

national government repositories

Many countries store all documents directly related to the daily operation of the national government and its branches, agencies or ministries in a central location.

Some countries provide online searchable catalogues of their holdings, easing the research process. Others require researchers to contact the archives or individual agencies directly or in person. All the repositories provide finding aids, guidance in the form of indexes, publications and other formats to assist the researcher.

United States

While the individual government agencies in the US often allow researchers access to official records, family historians will make more progress by starting with one of the major repositories listed below when researching records held at national repositories.

The Library of Congress is the research arm of the US Congress, and holds more than 40,000 genealogies, 100,000 local *histories* and a royalty, nobility and heraldry collection. Emphasis is on North America, the UK and Germany. Helpful bibliographies guides are listed at www.loc.gov/rr/genealogy/bib_ guid/bibguide.html.

Do

- research local public libraries before contacting the Library of Congress (LoC).

- identify the material you are seeking before contacting the LoC – 'advance reserves' are available.

- consider taking an LoC orientation class.

- allow enough time – the LoC operates a 'closed stack' system; it will take at least an hour to get the materials to you.

 Don't

- attempt to remove any LoC materials from the facility – photo duplication services are available.

- expect to find unpublished or primary sources for country, state or church records.

- forget to check the vertical files, for information on specific family names and general genealogical research.

Note: This advice will generally apply to using the facilities of other national libraries as well.

The US National Archives and Records Administration, in Washington, DC, holds millions of records that document the nation's history and family histories as well.

National Archives and Records Administration (NARA) is an independent federal agency, established in the late 19th century, which oversees the management of all federal records. While the main repository is located in Washington, DC, NARA also operates regional records and research centres. Records from the following federal agencies, which can be found at the NARA, are particularly useful to genealogists:

- American Battle Monuments Commission

- Bureau of the Census

- Bureau of Indian Affairs

- Bureau of Land Management

- Bureau of Prisons

- Bureau of Refugees, Freedmen and Abandoned Lands

- Immigration and Naturalization Service

- Internal Revenue Service

- Maritime Administration Military Services

- Post Office Department;

- Selective Service System

- Social Security Administration

- US Coast Guard

- US Court of Federal Claims

- US Courts of Appeals

- US Courts of Claims

- US Customs Service

- US District Courts

- US Soldiers' Home

- US Tax Court

- Veteran's Administration

- War Relocation Authority

United Kingdom

While the Houses of Parliament maintain archives for central government proceedings, most family historians will find greater success in learning about individual ancestors when searching the records stored with the General Register Office and National Archives. Researchers should be aware that many records are stored in central repositories located in Scotland, Wales and Northern Ireland.

The National Archives (NA-UK) in London is one of the world's largest archival repositories and consists of the records previously held by the Public Record Office (PRO) and the Historical Manuscripts Commission (HMC), which merged to form the single agency in 2003. As the main repository for the records of central government and courts of law for England and Wales and other portions of the United Kingdom, the NA-UK holds documents dating as early as the 11th century. It also advises governmental departments on records management. Besides ensuring proper care and management of the records themselves, the National Archives makes them widely accessible to the general public both on-site at the Family Records Centre in Islington (jointly managed by the General Register Office and the National Archives) and at the NA-UK repository at Kew.

Holdings include indexes of births, marriages and deaths in England and Wales; census returns; wills; naturalization certificates and criminal records; records of the Court of Common Pleas, Assizes and Central Criminal Court; medieval records; maps; records for members of the armed forces; Cabinet and Home Office Records and the records of all central government departments. The NA-UK also holds the National Register of Archives and the Manorial Documents Register. Researchers with Internet access should consult the NA-UK's searchable database of holdings at www.nationalarchives.co.uk.

National Archives of Scotland (NAS), which stores official records dating back as far as the 12th century, is the main repository for Scotland's public and legal records. NAS also holds many local and private archives. Records of genealogical interest include wills and testaments, deeds and estate records, taxation records, court records and church records.

Public Record Office of Northern Ireland (PRONI) holds records dating back to the 13th century from government departments, law courts, local agencies and other public bodies. PRONI also has documents from private individuals, churches, businesses and institutions.

General Register Office for England and Wales (GRO) is part of the Office for National Statistics and is headquartered in Southport, England. It oversees the activities of local registry offices in England and Wales, including civil marriages, births, deaths, adoptions and stillbirths. The GRO maintains an extensive archive of statutory records, which date to 1837 when civil registration began. Members of the public may order copies of certifications for a fee from the GRO website, www.gro.gov.uk, or by contacting the Family Records Centre in central London (see the Resource Directory for details), which acts as the GRO's public-access facility.

General Register Office for Scotland (GROS) is responsible for registering births, marriages, deaths, divorces and adoptions, and also conducts national censuses. Family historians may search GROS records and order copies of some certificates or records by letter, in person or by telephone. Researchers with access to the Internet may also use the fee-based services of the Scotland's People website, www.gro-scotland.gov.uk, which is the official government source for genealogical data for Scotland.

General Register Office for Northern Ireland maintains records of births, deaths, marriages and adoptions and will provide certified copies of birth, death and marriage certificates to applicants for a fee.

Australia

The National Archives of Australia has offices in Canberra and access points in every state capital, which are readily available to family history researchers. Primarily covering the activities of the Commonwealth government since Australia became a Federation in 1901, the archives contain a wide range of items that will be of interest to family history researchers, including passenger lists, naturalization certificates, war crimes and trial records, as well as records for statutory authorities, military units, law enforcement agencies, government ministers, customs and some maritime records and documents relating to Aboriginal and Torres Strait Islander peoples.

South Africa

National Archives and Records Service (NARS) of South Africa was created by official act in 1996 and preserves South Africa's national archival heritage for use by the government and the people. Repositories are located around the country, including in Pretoria and Cape Town. From rock paintings and oral histories to photographic and documentary materials, NARS offers an abundance of information to genealogists. Researchers over the age of 20 may examine national, provincial and local government records, court records, baptismal and marriage documents, death registers, probate and estate records and documents from the colonial and Apartheid eras.

Germany

The Federal Archives (Bundesarchiv) of Germany consists of three main branches, which maintain an extensive collection of records created by the central government since 1815 and the records of the kingdom of Prussia and the Electorate of Brandenburg from the 13th century to 1945.

The Bundesarchiv Berlin holds the records of the North German Confederation and the German Empire, except their military records. Emigration records can be found in the Ministry of the Interior (Reichsministerium des Innern) and the Foreign Office (Auswärtigesamt). The Berlin Archives also houses records for the SS (Schutzstaffel) and SA (Sturmabteilung), which were confiscated at the end of World War II but returned to Germany in 1994. The US National Archives maintain microfilm copies.

The Geheimes Staatarchiv Preussischer Kulturbestiz (the Secret State Archive of Prussian Cultural Heritage) stores the records of the kingdoms Westphalia and Prussia and the Electorate of Brandenburg. Document types include Prussian army military records, church records, royal family records, family archives, personal papers and local and provincial records.

The Bundesarchiv Abteilung Militararchiv, located in Freiburg, holds the personnel records of military members serving in the two world wars and hospital or medical records for individuals born before 1890 who were wounded or ill during their military career.

Other national repositories

Most large countries maintain national archives of some sort, though some delegate smaller political entities, such as states or principalities, to hold records on behalf of the central government.

People researching Asian and African heritage may have difficulty identifying or using national repositories: many nations offer only restricted access, while others have not created a central location to store and preserve archives.

The National Archives of Australia, in Canberra, stores documents tracing the 200 years of Australian history, including colonial, Aboriginal and immigrant records.

tip Accessing national archives

Make sure you can access archives before travelling to use them. Some restrict or prohibit public contact with their records, others require specific clearance. Some only keep documents and records for governmental agencies, and not hold information related to your ancestors.

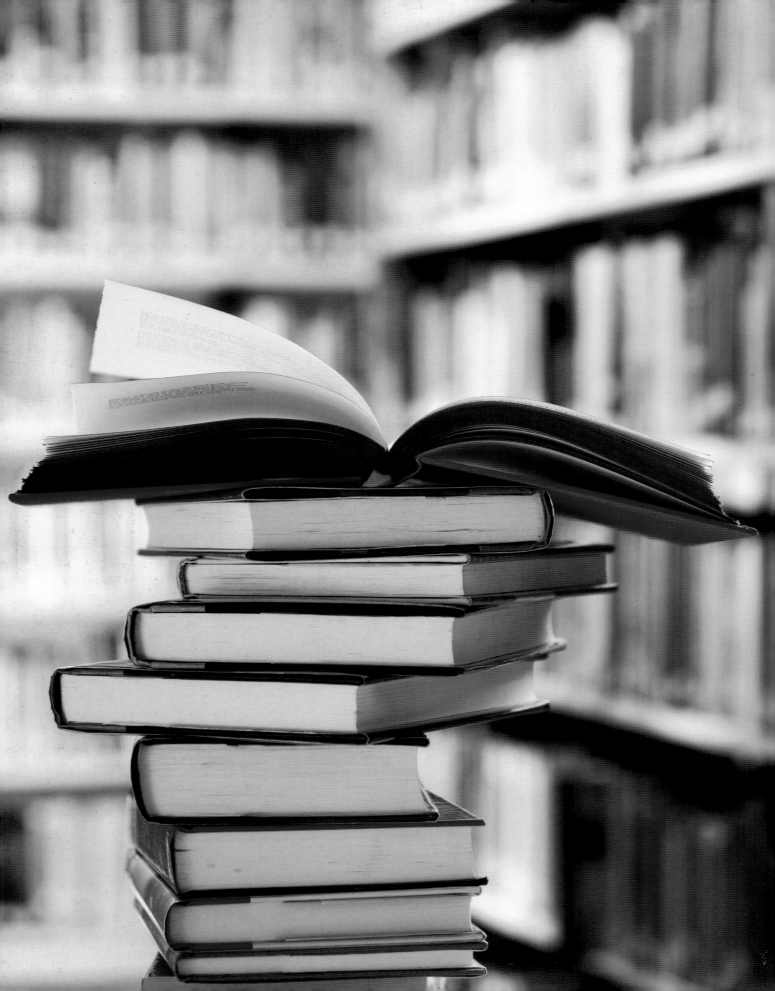

public libraries

For more than 3,000 years, people around the world have written books, created other documents and collected and stored them in repositories for learning and shared knowledge.

In about 300 BC, the Egyptians founded the Great Library of Alexandria to hold copies of all the world's books, which qualified members of the public could use. Sadly, the Alexandrian repository no longer survives, but before its demise it set the standard that modern libraries strive to achieve.

Today, libraries remain an essential part of the learning process and exist at national, state, university and local levels. Organizations and individuals maintain libraries for reference, leisure-time reading and study. Genealogical centres, often managed by genealogical societies, provide specialist services for researchers.

Public libraries

One of the best resources for family history researchers is the nearest public library. Public libraries not only hold books on how to study genealogy but often also maintain historical records, newspaper archives and a myriad other useful resources. Many have a family history or genealogy section, equipped with pamphlets on how to use the facility for genealogical research, research aids, family histories and other special collections.

Once you have identified some of the places where your ancestors lived, determine which libraries are located in that area. The following are examples of different kinds of regional and national libraries and their holdings:

Your local public library, genealogical centre or historical society library may hold published or unpublished documents related to your heritage.

The National Library of Wales (NLW), Llyfrgell Genedlaethol Cymru, which is located in Aberystwyth, arguably ranks second only to the British Library in the UK for the quality and size of its collections. Family history researchers should head to the Departments of Manuscripts and Printed Books, where scores of archival documents can be reviewed and photocopied.

As the national archive for the Church in Wales, the Department of Manuscripts holds registers of baptisms, marriages and burials; bishop's transcripts; marriage allegations and bonds. The NLW also has tithe maps and apportionments for all Welsh dioceses; probate records and wills from the 16th century to 1858; Nonconformist chapel records; Sunday school and society minute books, histories and legal documents; records for the Courts of Great and Quarter Sessions; Poor Law records; manorial records; estate and private collections and pedigree rolls and books.

The Department of Printed Books features copies of parish records and some Nonconformist registers; the International Genealogical Index for Wales, England, Scotland, Ireland, and the Channel Islands; local newspapers of Wales; indexes to civil registration, 1837–1997; copies of the Calendar of Grants of Probate up to 1943; copies of census returns for Wales.

The NLW also holds a variety of books that researchers may find helpful, including printed pedigrees and visitation books; trade directories and electoral registers; books of local interest relating to families, individuals and localities and articles from historical society journals.

The State Library of Queensland, which has its headquarters in South Brisbane, contains thousands of books and other resources in its branches around the Australian city. Family historians will find themselves almost overwhelmed with the selection of items, which range from general books on tracing one's roots to vital records, immigration and shipping records, parish records, convicts and miners records. A good place to begin your research is the John Oxley Library, located on the fourth floor of the Cannon Hill building, which contains finding aids, indexes and guides to the State Library collections and also holds a vast array of resources for researching indigenous family history, including the Norman Tindale Collection, which

tip   Get help from librarians

Reference librarians can assist with research, so don't be afraid to ask them for help. As well as being research experts, they will know about the library's holdings and facilities and may also have local knowledge that can provide you with useful leads.

requires special permission to access and maintains collections of manuscripts, photographs, oral histories, church and religious records, local directories, maps and much more. Portions of their collections are accessible online.

The Memphis and Shelby County Public Library and Information Center, which consists of several branches located throughout Tennessee's largest city, is a fine example of a local public library that provides extensive genealogical services. On the fourth floor of the Central Library, the History Department maintains the extensive Genealogy Collection, which not only focuses on Memphis and Shelby County records, but also features census records, family histories and other resources, such as marriage and probate records, copied on microfilm. They also hold a variety of indexes, including the Freedman's Bureau Marriage Index (1864–5), which African-ancestored researchers will find of particular interest. An index to all Memphis and Shelby County death records from 1848 to 1945 is accessible online.

The Newberry Library, a privately funded research library in Chicago, has a special emphasis on genealogy and is particularly noteworthy for its information on colonial America. The library holds 17,000 genealogies; local histories for the US, Canada and the British Isles; indexes for federal census records, vital records, probate, tax, court and cemetery records and other pertinent publications.

Genealogical libraries and specialist centres

Tenacious family historians may want to become members of a private genealogical library, such as the American Genealogical Lending Library (AGLL) in Bountiful, Utah, or the Genealogical Center Library (GCL) in Marietta, Georgia. If your local library does not participate in an interlibrary exchange with AGLL or GCL, become a member yourself. Paying membership allows you to rent books, which will be shipped to you for personal use but must be returned to the lending library.

Genealogical centres and heritage society offices provide research guidance and access to genealogical records. Large libraries often also house genealogical centres, while other genealogical facilities operate with their own personnel in their own buildings. Not only do they offer guidance on how to research specific topics and records, they often contain archives and records that family historians will find of particular value. Many, however, do not hold primary records, but maintain microfiche and microfilm copies for review. Many heritage societies maintain facilities for researchers, whether or not they belong to the organization; others require a fee to access specialized materials.

The Society of Genealogists operates one of the largest family history research libraries in the UK. Its extensive library, in London, contains family histories; indexes for vital, census and probate records; local histories; sections devoted to the peerage and heraldry; and religious, education and military records. It holds CD-ROM and microfiche copies of the International Genealogical Index (IGI) and also a wide range of textbooks and books dealing with specific counties, their genealogical records and other data.

The American-French Genealogical Society, based in Woonsocket, Rhode Island, US, lends microfiche records relating to Americans of French and French-Canadian descent. Access is by paid membership only.

The Daughters of the American Revolution (DAR), a volunteer service organization whose members all claim lineal descent from 'patriots' who served during the 18th-century American War of Independence, maintains an enormous research library in Washington, DC. Founded in 1896, the library is strictly a reference and research facility and is open to the public whether or not they belong to the DAR. Holdings include 15,000 volumes of Genealogical Records Committee Reports, unpublished compilations of records gathered by members since the early 20th century; a noteworthy manuscript collection, which is accessible online; an ephemera collection of pamphlets, booklets, newspaper items, etc. and historical records related to the Work Projects Administration.

Chicago's Newberry Library features a special emphasis on genealogy. Researchers find the library particularly useful for its wealth of information on colonial America and its substantial collections of genealogies and local histories.

the family history library

At some time during the course of your research, if you are able to get there, you may want to use the Family History Library in Salt Lake City, Utah, US.

The Family History Library

Established in 1894 by the Genealogical Society of Utah, the Family History Library (FHL), located at 35 North West Temple Street in Salt Lake City, is the largest facility of its kind in the world. Organized by leaders of the Church of Jesus Christ of the Latter-day Saints (LDS), otherwise known as the Mormons – who have achieved a well-earned reputation for collecting and maintaining genealogical records – the society's library gradually expanded its collections. Moving with the times technologically, it began to copy records on microfilm and then, in the 1960s, to transfer data on to computers. The library now holds millions of records copied on to CD-ROM, microfiche and microfilm and reproduced in books, periodicals and computerized records and has an international focus. Researchers can locate records for the US, UK, Canada and much of Europe, Asia, Africa and Latin America.

All members of the public are welcome to use the FHL and its associated Family History Centres (FHC) at no charge – though certain services, for example photocopying, do have fees. While funded and managed by the Mormons, the FHL and its subsidiary facilities provide services for people of all religions, ethnicities and races. They neither discriminate nor attempt to convert visitors to their religion. Staff are there to share their expertise and interest in family history research and to answer questions as thoroughly as possible.

The FHL acquires its holdings by donation and by purchasing records outright. It holds vital records from governmental and church sources; census records; court and probate records; manorial, homestead and other property records; cemetery records; emigration and immigration records; passenger lists; naturalization and citizenship records; some military records; published family histories; family tree databases and many other types of resources.

The public can access several databases of genealogical information via the FamilySearch (TM) system by visiting the FHL or one of the family history centres in person or by using the Internet to explore the library's website (www.familysearch.org). Databases include the FHL Catalog, the Ancestral File, the International Genealogical Index (IGI), the Pedigree Resource File, the US Social Security Death Index, Scottish Church Records and the Personal Ancestral File. Registration is free.

CHECKLIST: VISITING THE FAMILY HISTORY LIBRARY

- Educate yourself about the kinds of records and databases held by the FHL and FHCs.
- Determine what information you wish to research before visiting.
- Use the resources at your nearest FHC before heading to Salt Lake City to avoid duplication of effort and unnecessary expenses.
- Verify opening hours for the FHC.
- Request a brief orientation tour when you use the facility for the first time.
- Consider taking a specialized class on research methods, when available.
- Use information pamphlets to learn about the facility and also how to use the materials.
- Use the relevant research outline for guidance.
- Be patient and courteous.
- Don't demand undivided attention from staff – they often have many visitors to assist.

tip Using the FHL

The Family History Library is especially useful for tracing ancestors who lived before 1920. When using LDS resources, begin your research by locating the Family History Centre nearest your home.

Sometime during the course of your research, you will want to use the repositories at the Family History Library in Salt Lake City, Utah (shown here), or visit one of the affiliated family history centres in your area.

Family History Centres

The Mormons have also established more than 3,700 branch libraries, known as Family History Centres, in more than 88 countries around the world, including the UK, Australia, Canada, Mexico, Brazil, Venezuela, Spain, Hungary, France, Germany, Nigeria, Ghana, South Africa, Japan, Taiwan and Thailand. Internet researchers can identify the exact locations for worldwide centres at www.familysearch.org/Eng/Library/FHC/frameset_fhc.asp.

Like the Family History Library itself, most FHCs have microfilm and microfiche records, books, maps, published genealogies and local histories and provide access to computerized databases, including FamilySearch (TM). Staff can request records not held at the FHC from the FHL for a small fee. Each FHC varies in size, number of staff members (all volunteers), operating hours and holdings. Most provide access to the FHL Catalog and the IGI databases, the Parish and Vital Records List, US Census indexes and PERSI (Periodical Source Index), all of which are available on microfiche. FHCs also collect resources of local and regional interest not necessarily held by the FHL itself. They also sell genealogy supplies, including blank pedigree charts, family group sheets, logs, computer disks and some manuals.

The FamilySearch (TM) website

Arguably the best Internet resource for family history researchers, the FamilySearch Internet Genealogy Service website (www.familysearch.org) is owned and operated by the Corporation of the President of The Church of Jesus Christ of Latter-day Saints. This phenomenal resource provides not only access to scores of genealogical records and computerized indexes, but also a wealth of helpful information for professional researchers as well as beginners. Launched in 1999, the system features more than 957 million names in its searchable databases, encourages users to share their own findings and also provides a place for long-term storage of records and information accumulated by researchers.

Besides the records, the most useful area on the FamilySearch (TM) website is 'research helps'. Clicking on the section titled 'document types' takes users to indexes filled with downloadable forms, letter-writing guides, step-by-step guides, general guides to doing research and the all-important research outlines. Examine and print out the research outline relevant to your area of interest, whether it's the 50 US states, individual nations or specific ethnic, racial and religious groups. The selection is not all-inclusive, but covers a wide variety of topics. Each outline offers specific guidance on how to do research in particular states or countries, repository location, types of records produced by the country or state, accessibility at the FHL and at other repositories and much more besides.

Museums educate and entertain, reinforce awareness of national, regional and individual identities and encourage cross-cultural understanding.

In fact, the treasures museums exhibit to the public represent only a fraction of their total holdings. Space limitations make it virtually impossible to display entire collections, except perhaps for special occasions or as part of a travelling exhibition. Besides regular and temporary exhibits, museums have storerooms for their permanent collections, portions of which may have been donated by the very ancestors you are researching. Museums also hold archival information, historic documents and other items that may interest genealogists. Many provide special research and library facilities, some store vital records and operate genealogy departments, while others devote themselves entirely to collecting memorabilia and information on specific families, clans and lineages.

Using museums for research

A visit to a museum, particularly one you suspect has direct relevance to your family's history, can provide answers to lingering questions, fill in historical gaps and reveal new avenues towards your goals. Head to the museum with an open mind, a sense of curiosity, a research plan and a list of questions you hope to answer. Whether you learn about the social or cultural norms of the times in which your relative lived, discover long-lost heirlooms or explore archival sources, museums can provide valuable insights into your past.

Located in major cities, small communities and out-of-the-way rural locations around the world are art and science museums, industrial and maritime collections and natural and

tip **Ask the guides**
Don't forget to question museum guides and volunteers, those human repositories of information who may well know titbits about your ancestors that are not readily available in the archives.

local history museums. They may be operated on a national, regional or local level, serve specialist interests or offer a broad introduction to a community. Many are managed by historical societies or private trusts. Most struggle with funding and strive to stay open, even under the most dire of financial circumstances. The following is a selection of specialist museums, by type, that family historians will find of particular use, not only for learning about an ancestor's daily lifestyle but also for locating artefacts and memorabilia directly associated with them.

Museum collections often include old photographs, which may actually portray one of your ancestors performing the skills or creating the crafts, such as woven baskets, that have been passed down to you.

If your ancestors worked in the mines, a visit to a specialist industrial museum may connect you with collections of artefacts and gear that may have been used by them as they laboured in the earth's bowels.

Maritime museums

If your ancestor served in the merchant marine or navy aboard passenger ships or naval vessels, worked for a shipping company, died in a shipwreck or even operated a lighthouse, you may find valuable information in the records stored at a maritime museum.

The National Maritime Museum, located in Greenwich, England, holds more than two million items related to seafaring, navigation, astronomy and measuring time. In addition to photographs, manuscripts, artwork and equipment related to the maritime industry, the museum features the extensive Caird Library and collections of different maritime records, including master's certificates and crew lists, which family historians will find of particular interest. Family history researchers may access the collections in person or online.

Industrial museums

Did your ancestor mine coal or slate, gold or iron ore; work in a textile factory or woollen mill; make pottery or glassware? Industrial museums honour the age of mechanization, technological change and innovation. The men and women of the Industrial Revolution left evidence of their labours not only in the industrial sites themselves but also in artefacts, photographs and documents.

The World Museum of Mining,

in Butte, Montana, US, covers 13.4 hectares (33 acres) of land and the site of Orphan Girl Mine. which operated from 1875 to 1956. Besides original equipment and an underground mining exhibit, the museum features an extensive photographic collection and a wide range of holdings that family historians will find useful, including maps, diaries, log books, journals, company day books, payroll records and engineering diagrams. The museum offers research assistance by appointment, via email or by written correspondence.

Military museums

Countless men and women have served in their nation's military branches during war and peacetime. Most uniformed services maintain museum collections, which contain historical and personal memorabilia, documents, military vehicles and gear. Besides obtaining an ancestor's military records, family historians should contact the appropriate military museum to learn more about their relative or about the era during which they served. Regimental museums are especially valuable sources for genealogists.

The Imperial War Museum in

London, England, is one of the world's finest military museums. It houses an enormous collection of items and archives pertaining to all British military branches, men's and women's units, prisoners of war and Commonwealth countries. Family history researchers are able to use the collections in person and can also access information online at www.iwm.org.uk.

Specialist ethnic and racial heritage museums display artefacts and photographs related to a particular group's history. Visit them to learn more about your past and to discover the lifestyles of your ancestors.

Ethnic and racial heritage museums

Museums pertaining to or operated by specific ethnic and racial groups have appeared throughout the world as people increasingly celebrate their heritage, honour their differences and participate in the global community. Also known as heritage centres, these facilities safeguard precious cultural, artistic, technological and historical items, including tribal documents, artefacts, maps and histories.

The Pequot Museum and Research

Center in Mashantucket, Connecticut, US, specializes in archives and collections devoted to the lifestyles, events and natural environment that influenced the development of the Mashantucket Pequot Tribal Nation. The museum also features items of interest related to other Native American tribes and encourages the public to use its research and library facilities. Researchers will value the oral histories; photographs; family papers; minutes of tribal meetings; land, court and probate records and letters.

Museums operated by religious groups

Your ancestors may have belonged to a religious group that splintered off from mainstream society to form its own order or community, or they may have fled their homeland owing to religious persecution or to seek paradise in the New World. Museums dedicated to the history and heritage of particular religious groups can reveal intriguing facts about your past. Many have a special interest in the genealogies of their members and hold extensive and fascinating collections useful to family history researchers.

The Mennonite Heritage Center in

Harleysville, Pennsylvania, US, not only houses exhibits on the lifestyle and religious heritage of the Mennonites, whose founder, Menno Simons, gave his name to the new group in 1525, but

also features an outstanding library and archives. Staff readily provide assistance to researchers, and genealogical resources include family histories, cemetery records, newspaper obituaries, local church records, wills, tax and land records, immigration records and family bible records. Of particular note are the extensive databases that are devoted to early Mennonite families and local Brethren family names.

Historical society and community museums

Historical societies abound, and so do museums devoted to local or regional history, many of which are operated by society members. Each society's goal is to foster an interest in the history of the subject area it represents, whether that's a town, lifestyle, organization or local industry. Members generally collect, preserve and share memorabilia and knowledge. Over time, collections become large enough to warrant the establishment of a museum so that the public at large can have access. Most historical societies hold regular meetings, including lectures on an aspect of local history or heritage issues. Community museums likewise act as repositories of information and objects, which are catalogued, stored and displayed as time, space and finances permit.

The Scott County Historical Society,

located in Shakopee, Minnesota, US, not only locates, collects and preserves historical items related to the Minnesota River Valley, but also operates the Stans Museum. Honouring local entrepreneur, adventurer and governmental official Maurice Stans, the museum's research centre and archives contain a wealth of data, vital records, probate and naturalization records, photographic material, books, newspapers and artefacts, which family history researchers will find fascinating and informative. Staff also provide online assistance.

places of worship

Such religious records, whether individual documents or notations in a register, may be stored in the church or synagogue itself, the denomination's archives, historical libraries, research centres or in other repositories. Locating religious records can be time consuming – and often leads to dead-ends – but perseverance and creative searching can yield useful results.

One of your most challenging tasks may be to identify for certain to which denomination an ancestor belonged. The effort becomes increasingly difficult when people move from one region or country to another and join a different place of worship, as so often occurred with emigration or the settlement of new lands. Today, the plethora of Protestant denominations may make it difficult for new residents in a town to switch membership conveniently to a church of the same denomination. For example, the new town may offer Reformed, Episcopalian and Roman Catholic churches, but no Methodist chapel within easy reach.

If it appears that a community did not have a church associated with the denomination to which you believe your ancestors belonged, check the other churches in the area. Perhaps your relatives became members and left their vital details in the records of one of those churches. Or perhaps they chose to convert or forego attending church altogether.

Churches often store records that family historians will find of interest. They may also contain your ancestors' tombs and memorial plaques that honour them.

WHEN RESEARCHING YOUR ANCESTOR'S RELIGIOUS AFFILIATION...

Do

- check the family documents you gathered when you first began your research to verify religious affiliation.

- review published family histories, newspaper items (obituaries often note the deceased's religion) and any other records you have already gathered for that ancestor.

- check tombstone engravings for religious information.

- determine if the denomination you have identified actually existed at the time your ancestor lived – name changes and reorganization do occur over time.

- determine what kinds of religious records were created by that denomination at the time your ancestor was alive.

- locate the religious establishment for that denomination in the area where your ancestor lived.

- confirm that the establishment actually holds the records you seek, before visiting.

- contact the affiliated establishment in your local area to check its national directory, if available.

- ask questions of clergy, clerical staff and members.

- review published histories for the religious group and the particular establishment.

- document the information exactly as you find it.

- undertake further research to resolve conflicts.

✗ DON'T

- unquestioningly believe family traditions and oral histories about an ancestor's religion.

- take it for granted that your ancestor shared your family's current religious affiliation.

- assume that a particular establishment (church, synagogue, temple, etc.) existed during your ancestor's lifetime.

- be surprised if you find inconsistencies in the records.

Religious repositories

Scores of religious repositories exist around the world that store archival materials of interest to family history researchers. Some are located in individual places of worship, which are often tasked with making and safekeeping their records. Many religions have established central repositories for their records and some Christian denominations in the US and Canada also preserve their records in central archives, libraries or research centres and often hire archivists or church historians to maintain their collections. These individuals are valuable resources in their own right so make an appointment to talk with them whenever possible.

The following is a representative sampling of the repositories that hold religious archives.

The Catholic Archives of Texas, which is located in Austin, the state's capital city, acts as the main repository for information related to the history of the Catholic Church in the American Southwest. Tasked to gather and preserve records of individuals and organizations engaged in work reflecting the goals of the Catholic Church in Texas, the archives stores a varied range of materials. Holdings include the records of the Texas Catholic Conference and the Texas Knights of Columbus, the Texas Catholic Historical Society and Catholic organizations in the state; personal papers, correspondence, wills and administrative records produced by bishops and other clergy; diocesan and parish records; newspapers, books, photographs and artefacts related to the Catholic Church in Texas and sacramental records. Particularly notable are the manuscripts pertaining to Mexican religious orders and Texas missions. The facility also holds records of baptism, marriage, confirmation, first communion and death for churches established before Texas became a state in 1845.

The Friends Historical Library of Swarthmore College, Pennsylvania, US, is one of several repositories that family historians may use for researching Quaker ancestors. Established with the aim of collecting all works published by or about the Quakers, the library features books, manuscripts, archival records, photographs and other memorabilia. The collection of Quaker Meeting Records dates back to 1665. Researchers have controlled access to records of Quaker organizations, Quaker families and individuals, private correspondence, notebooks, genealogical charts, biographies, marriage certificates, deeds, business and financial papers, scrapbooks, charts and maps. Access is free and open to the public, provided visitors obtain a registration card. The library also provides a fee-based genealogical research service to individuals who cannot visit in person. Their website, www.swarthmore. edu/Library/friends, includes an inventory of family papers organised by surname. Begin your research with an online search for your surname.

The Methodist Archives and Research Centre, at John Rylands University Library in Manchester, England, features the world's largest collection of manuscripts related to the founders of Methodism as well as an extensive printed book collection, letters and diaries, records of theological colleges, magazines, newspapers, school records, trustees' papers, personal papers, appointment lists for itinerant preachers, indexes of obituaries and memorials and reference books. The centre provides special guidance, both online and at the centre itself, on how to research the history of a chapel, women in Methodism and family history. The website (rylibweb.man.ac.uk/data1/dg/text/method.html) has a lengthy listing of links to primary and secondary text sources dealing with all aspects of Methodism.

The Jacob Rader Marcus Center of the American Jewish Archives acts as a central repository for major records dealing with all aspects of Jewish life in the Americas. Located at the Hebrew Union College – Jewish Institute of Religion in Cincinnati, Ohio, the archives collects, preserves and provides access to manuscripts, records, photographs and genealogical materials. The staff encourage family historians to use the facility and will provide guidance on doing research.

Major collections include records of noteworthy American Jewish men, women and institutions of historical significance; the records of American Reform Judaism; the records of American Jewish communities and the records of the Hebrew Union College – Jewish Institute of Religion itself. The American Jewish Archives also makes copies of First American Jewish Families: 600 Genealogies, 1654–1988 available to the public, both in the centre itself and also on its website (www.americanjewisharchives.org/aja), which includes a searchable database.

The Presbyterian Church in Canada maintains its archives at the National Offices of the Church in Toronto. Documenting the history of the Presbyterian Church in Canada, holdings date to 1775. Items of genealogical interest include original and microfilm records for several hundred local churches in Canada, with vital detail registers, session minutes, congregational histories and communion registers; records of individual ministers and other personnel; records for the theological colleges; records of the Women's Missionary Society; private papers; photographs and biographical materials. The general public is welcome to view the records, by appointment only. Some church records created before 1925, when the Presbyterian Church became part of the United Church of Canada, are held at the archives for the United Church in Toronto.

Tracing its roots to 1839, New York's Central Synagogue is the city's oldest Jewish house of worship in continuous use since its foundation. Contact staff members to access documents that may deal with relatives who worshipped there.

Muslim Associations

Although not places of worship, the following might be of help if you are researching Muslim ancestors:

- The Muslim Assocation of Britain, 124 Harrowdene Road, Wembley, Middlesex HA0 2JF (020 8908 9108), www.mabonline.net

- The American Muslim Association of North America, PO Box 5212, Miami, FL 22014 (305-945-0414), www.al-amana.org

Fraternal organizations have long been shrouded in mystery, but the documents created by many such societies contain a wealth of information useful to family historians.

Some orders are uncommunicative about certain aspects of membership and many are open only to people who can prove blood ties to earlier members. However, fraternal organizations such as the Freemasons, the Benevolent and Protective Order of the Elks and the Ancient Arabic Order of the Nobles of the Mystic Shrine (better known as the Shriners) actually developed for mutual support and charitable purposes as a way to ensure the care of members in sickness and their families at their death. Around the world today there are scores of branches of such organizations, many of which originated in England and spread overseas during colonization and periods of emigration. While most fraternal societies initially allowed only Caucasian men as members, many have since reorganized to encourage membership for all racial and ethnic backgrounds, women as well as men.

Besides fraternal orders, other benevolent societies developed for the mutual aid of members, particularly immigrants, who shared a common ethnicity, religion, political ideology or occupation. Others, like the Grand Army of the Republic and the Sons of the Confederate Veterans, developed to tend to the needs of war veterans, while the Lions and Rotary Clubs were formed by community business leaders and more fortunate members of society specifically to serve the needy.

The Woodmen of the World is one of many fraternal organizations that publish magazines that may feature stories or photos of your ancestors.

Types of records

During your search, you may find membership records, lodge records, meeting minutes, signature books, lodge histories, society newspapers, personal correspondence, orphanage records and even published biographies. However, while most fraternal organizations maintain significant archives, societies like the Rotarians maintain relatively few records of interest to genealogists. Such records generally include where the ancestor lived, his line of work, offices

held, brief details of his tenure, his date of birth and perhaps articles written while he held the offices.

The hunt for the records may pose a challenge. Even if you know that an ancestor belonged to a fraternal order or benevolent society, the organization may no longer exist. The particular chapter may have closed, changed its name or moved away from where your ancestor lived. Records may have been lost due to fire or flood damage. Therefore, begin the process by identifying the repository most likely

to retain the records you seek. Then take a deep breath and initiate contact – preferably by written correspondence – to determine where your ancestor's records are located.

 CHECKLIST: LOCATING RECORDS FROM AN ORGANIZATION

- Try contacting the local lodge or chapter to ask where its archives are stored.

- Contact the public library, genealogical or historical society library, or a larger research facility in the town or region where the organization was located, to determine if they hold the records or know where they are stored.

- Make a list of other repositories that collect an organization's records, such as the Immigration History Research Center (IHRC) at the University of Minnesota in St Paul, the Balch Institute for Ethnic Studies Library in Philadelphia, Pennsylvania, or the Library and Museum of Freemasonry in London (which is the repository for the archives of the United Grand Lodge of England).

- Write a brief, polite and specific letter outlining your request to the secretary for the organization or the records repository.

- Specify who you are, your relationship to the person you are researching and your ancestor's full name, town or area of residence, years of residence, year of death and the records or type of information you seek.

- Request an appointment to view the records, if possible.

- Offer to compensate the organization for its time, effort and photocopies.

Establishing society membership

Problem

My parents say my great-grandfather belonged to the International Order of the Odd Fellows but I haven't been able to find any documentation to back up their claim. How do I find out more?

Solution

Even if the records you have gathered so far don't mention membership in a secret society or service organization, don't dismiss the possibility. It's the genealogist's task to determine if an ancestor belonged to a benevolent society and, if so, to then locate where relevant records are stored.

☐ **Check obituaries for organization membership.**

☐ **Look through family heirlooms and memorabilia for jewellery, emblems and items decorated with unfamiliar insignias or acronyms, which may connote membership.**

☐ **If you know where your ancestor is buried, visit the gravesite or locate a transcription. Headstones often display society insignias. Some benevolent societies provide specially designed headstones that symbolize the deceased's membership.**

☐ **Try to link the insignia or acronym to the appropriate society: Alvin J. Schmidt's *Fraternal Organizations: The Greenwood Encyclopedia of American Institutions*, (Westport, CT: Greenwood Publishing, 1980) may help.**

☐ **Read local histories, which may establish the existence of fraternal or benevolent organizations.**

☐ **Determine your great-grandfather's ethnic or religious background and then identify the benevolent organizations formed for those groups, e.g. : the Sons of Poland, the St Andrew's Society (for those with Scottish heritage) or the Knights of Columbus (founded as a Roman Catholic men's fraternal organization).**

☐ **If you know your great-grandfather's occupation, determine if a fraternal group existed for workers in that trade (e.g., the Brotherhood of Railroad Trainmen) when and where he lived.**

educational institutions

One often-neglected area of research is school records. Educational institutions all produce their own array of records.

A surprising amount of information can be gleaned from school records: family and student names, nicknames, birth dates, grades, student activities and achievements and teacher names. You may also find photos. Schools not only maintain enrolment and registration records and transcripts, they often also archive report cards, yearbooks (annuals), graduation programmes, school newspapers or magazines, alumni directories, fraternity and sorority records, board of education records, departmental records, scholastic annual reports and family census records. Each type of record can provide details or clarify conflicting information you have already collected.

Locating school records

Many educational institutions are more than willing to send photocopies of certain student files, but, because of privacy laws, items such as transcripts are normally available only to the student. If you know the name of the institution that your ancestor attended, write to it for assistance. Be brief and polite: explain who you are and that you are researching your family history, identify what records you would like to obtain and enquire about fees. Be prepared to wait a few weeks for a written response. Alternatively, contact the institution via its website for information.

Besides the individual schools, many alumni associations, student groups, fraternities and sororities also maintain Internet sites, which provide contact details to help with your research. Major genealogical websites, including the Family History Library's Familysearch and the USGenWeb Project, often contain school records, so search them as well.

Non scholastic repositories often hold school records, especially if they are old or if a school has closed. Contact the local school district or board of education, local governmental offices including some county courthouses, local record offices, state and national archives, libraries and genealogical and historical society centres. Take a look through local newspapers at the time your ancestor was a student. Read local histories and examine family documents: they may reveal unusual titbits of information about an ancestor's scholastic history, perhaps school sports records they established or theatrical productions in which they performed.

You may find old class photographs among your ancestor's treasured heirlooms. If the relative is still alive, ask them to identify classmates, the teacher and stories about that year in school. Identify the name of the school and learn as much as possible about its history and about other family members who were enrolled there.

Where did she go to school?

Problem

I would like to locate my grandmother's school records, but have no idea where she went to school or if she went to college. How do I begin?

Solution

- Ask family members for leads.

- Examine scrapbooks, family heirlooms and old photographs for school memorabilia.

- If you know the street address where your grandmother lived when she was a student, use that as a guide when making enquiries.

- Examine old town, city or county directories where she lived to identify school names and addresses.

- Contact the applicable local historical society, library or museum for information on schools that were open when she was a student.

- If your grandmother belonged to an ethnic, racial or religious group that operated its own school, contact the local branch, headquarters or responsible agency for guidance.

- Review other types of official documents for clues to her educational background, particularly census and probate records.

- Did your grandmother practice a specific craft or work in a particular type of job? If she was a teacher, nurse, seamstress or a volunteer ambulance driver, you may be able to use that information to identify the school that taught her those skills.

tip **Establish proof of relationship**

Many educational establishments will require specific proof that you are related to the student and many will be unable to issue records unless that person has died, so you will need to be able to present evidence of the former student's death.

cemeteries

Perhaps our curiosity about death and the afterlife draws many of us to cemeteries. Or perhaps it's their serenity or a wish to pay our respects to deceased relatives.

Whatever the motivation, people from all walks of life frequent cemeteries. Genealogists also understand the attraction: cemeteries are not only repositories for the dead, they also record past lives with headstone inscriptions and with sexton's records.

Although the term 'cemetery record' is woefully inadequate, it is by far the most commonly used phrase to label the records that are produced when a person dies. A better term might be records of death or even interment records, which can be interpreted to include records associated with cremations. (Headstone inscriptions are discussed in Part Five: Going Global, see pages 192–211.)

The official documents associated with the death and burial of an individual provide a wealth of information. Not only do such records specify the location of the gravesite, they also include the deceased's vital details and whatever other information the cemetery or crematorium considered essential.

Cemeteries are treasure troves of genealogical information. Not only do headstones document the past, but official records kept by sextons and burial societies provide information you might not have already located.

Locating cemetery records

Problem

I visited the cemetery where my ancestor is supposed to be buried, but as there was no full-time sexton nor an on-site records storage facility, I was unable to obtain copies of the records. What should I do now?

Solution

As with other family history research projects, it is best to make contact before visiting to determine where the cemetery (in this case) stores its records and, indeed, if it actually has your ancestor's records.

- Refer to a current telephone directory for the region. If a cemetery is listed, telephone the office number given to determine the exact location, then write a letter to the cemetery office requesting your ancestor's records. (Be sure to include the person's full name, birth and death dates, your relationship to the deceased and any other details that will point staff in the right direction.)

- Contact the local funeral director, who may know where the records are stored or be able to put you in contact with cemetery management.

- Researchers in the US may want to refer to the *American Blue Book of Funeral Directors* or the *National Yellow Book of Funeral Directors* for cemetery locations and funeral homes.

- If the cemetery is maintained by a religious group, governmental agency or fraternal organization, contact the nearest affiliated facility or check on the Internet for assistance with locating the records.

- Contact the local library, genealogical or historical society or family history centre, which may hold copies of the records.

- Check other repositories, including national archives, national libraries, county record offices and the General Register Office (in the UK).

- Search the Internet for your ancestor's cemetery records. Some websites, such as Ancestors at Rest, Interment.net and Funeralnet, provide searchable databases that may link you to the cemeteries, funeral homes or documents you need. (Remember, however, to view them with scepticism as there may be transcription errors.)

- If at all possible, obtain photocopies of original records.

Typical interment/burial records include:

- death certificates
- obituaries
- sexton's (caretaker's) records
- church burial registers
- parish registers
- burial society records
- cemetery deeds
- funeral home records

Locating cemetery records

The challenge for researchers is to find the records, which are not normally stored in central repositories. In fact, many cemeteries do not maintain offices on the property itself, so family historians have to be creative when searching for these records. Different countries also have different practices when it comes to burying the dead, so be sure to determine ahead of a visit whether or not that country produced the type of records you believe you need.

Cemeteries have never been the only burial option. For centuries, global cultures have practised cremation. In recent decades, Westerners have increasingly chosen cremation (either scattering the ashes or placing them permanently in a vault) rather than a traditional cemetery interment. Consequently, family history researchers should not limit themselves to cemetery research but should also examine other forms of burial when seeking out ancestral remains and records of death.

Most businesses create permanent records of their transactions, inventories, financial statues, employees, litigatoin and administrative details, including customer accounts. As the corporate memory of a business, these records provide evidence of past activities and are useful in legal proceedings. They also offer historical continuity, serve as training resources and aid the company's decision-making process.

Large corporations, in particular, maintain their own archives and make portions of them available to researchers. For example, The Royal Bank of Scotland Group retains more than three centuries of records in its repository in London and in its branch in Edinburgh. The archives include records of the Bank of England and other banks that have merged with the Royal Bank.

Among their holdings, the Royal Bank has partnership and corporate records, such as various committee meeting records, secretariat records, registers of members and correspondence; financial records; taxation and auditors records; legal records; staff lists, salary ledgers and applications for employment; trade union papers; photographs; property records; branch records and customer records, including customer accounts, signature and address books, passbooks, loan registers and much more. Before arranging a visit – by appointment only – Internet users should review the Royal Bank's online guide to their archives: www.rbs.co.uk/ Group_Information/Memory_Bank/Our _Archives/default.htm.

Titbits of information documented on business records, such as this invoice for meats purchased from family butcher William Welsh, can often add colour and broaden your understanding of an ancestor's daily activities.

tip Prove your heritage

Some businesses may be reluctant to allow access to their historical records. Be prepared to explain why you wish to review their archives, and, if necessary, be ready to offer some proof of identification or of your relationship to an employee.

Employment records

Family historians can find business records of great value when trying to pinpoint the nature of their ancestor's employment, when and where he or she worked, trade union membership and even his or her appearance. The first step is to identify for whom your ancestor worked. Clues can be found in the documents you have already gathered, from interviewing family members, or from researching what trades typically existed in the area and timeframe during which your ancestor lived. Depending on the actual job performed, you may find considerable information – or almost nothing.

Complete employment records are more likely to exist for managers in larger companies and skilled trade unions or captains in major shipping companies than for workers lower on the wage scale. Often you will have to closely study individual records to glean your ancestor's employment information from them. The names of men serving in the military or maritime industry may appear on a variety of record types, so diligence is the keyword here.

Locating businesses

When a company changes ownership or closes an office, a branch or its corporate headquarters, it may transfer archival materials to the new management or send them to a specific repository for storage.

The Minnesota Historical Society, for example, has collected and preserved scores of business records for financial institutions, trade associations and corporations, including 3M (Minnesota Mining and Manufacturing), the Great Northern Railway Company and the Oliver Mining Company. The society's library in St Paul holds records for the transportation, shipbuilding, farming, meat-packing, construction, milling, mining, manufacturing and other industries. It also provides an online searchable database of its collections.

Finding out about an ancestor's job

Problem

My grandfather worked on the Texas oil fields during the 1920s. I don't know the name of the oil company but would like to find out the exact nature of his job. Where do I begin?

Solution

The hunt for business or employment records pertaining to an ancestor is frequently frustrating and may result in disappointment, due to privacy laws and policies set by larger companies. But the effort is certainly worthwhile and you may learn little-known details about your grandfather's past.

- If you know your grandfather's residential address while he worked in Texas, use that as a starting point.

- Try to obtain copies of local business directories and telephone books from the 1920s to determine which companies were in business and drilling in the oil fields at that time.

- Contact the companies that are still in business to see if they are able and willing to check their archives for your grandfather's name.

- Visit or contact the local library or historical society for assistance, especially if you need information on companies no longer in business.

- Contact petroleum geologists or engineers, or petroleum-related professional societies, for assistance.

- Once you learn which company your ancestor worked for, contact their branch office or state headquarters.

- Determine where the company keeps its archives and whether it allows public access to them.

- Ask if you may obtain copies of records or other information by mail and acknowledge that you are willing to pay for any photocopies, etc.

- As always, be patient, persistent and diligent.

locating the records

There is something exhilarating about visiting an archives repository and actually touching and smelling old documents associated with your ancestors.

The degree of public access varies from one repository to another. Not surprisingly, governmental agencies are less likely than other organizations to permit personal visits to view their archives. However, they are often more than willing to send copies of certain documents by mail, usually for a modest fee. Libraries, local and regional record offices, genealogical centres, museums and other organizations are generally customer-service oriented and open their doors to the public, at least for part of most weeks during the year.

Contacting a repository

Since many repositories are understaffed and overworked, it's always wise to telephone, write or email before your visit to obtain a few basic answers. Indeed, many repositories have online catalogues and databases, which researchers who use the Internet may review from the comfort of home or the local library. Some websites offer direct access to the records or to transcriptions and, occasionally, to images of specific documents or artefacts. In any event, if possible you should first check out the cyberspace version of the repository, which will save you and staff members time, effort and, perhaps, money. Then you can decide if an on-site visit will be worth your while.

Before you walk through the main entrance and expect to examine the records, initiate contact with staff. Ask if they have any special regulations and check that they actually hold the materials you seek. Telephone the repository only to ask about

opening times, directions, booking appointments, fees and requirements for access, as staff are usually quite busy assisting other researchers or archiving records. Such questions can be answered quickly and are probably best dealt with on the telephone or, better yet, by checking the details on the facility's website, if it has one. You can also request that they post you any pamphlets or guides to doing family history research at the repository. (Such guides may be even available for download from the repository's website.) You can also telephone to ask for any official request forms and to enquire about any fees that may be required to obtain the documents.

When requesting information about specific records or ancestors, formal correspondence is preferable. Your letter, email or fax not only allows the staff to research fully and respond to your concerns, but also saves you the disappointment of reaching the repository only to discover they do not store the type of records you seek, do not allow public access to particular documents (due to privacy laws or the condition of the record) or that a different facility actually holds the materials in question. Also, if you have contacted the facility before your arrival, staff can ensure they have the information available for you, or know where to locate it when you arrive.

Before making the journey to the records repository, do as much research as possible. Make full use of the Internet. Many repositories not only provide access to their databases and actual records, they also have many of their finding aids online.

What to expect when you arrive at the repository

Protocol often requires all visitors to register and obtain a reader's ticket or admission card upon arrival. Many facilities offer day-tickets, but in some cases visitors may be able to examine only a limited range of items. In most cases, it takes only a few minutes to put together a reader's ticket, so don't worry if you don't already have one, but remember to bring identification – a passport, driver's licence or other photo-ID – or you may not be able to use the facility. Many repositories require visitors to leave handbags, briefcases, backpacks, coats and even cases for laptop computers at the security or reception desk, where they will be safeguarded while you are using the facility.

If you are a new user of the repository, ask a staff member for a brief introduction to the facility, its indexes and other finding aids, and procedures for obtaining records, photocopying and using special equipment, e.g., microfilm readers or computers. Many archives offices permit the use of pencils only for note-taking. If you want to examine precious or fragile documents, staff may require you to wear white gloves, which they will provide. Other regulations generally include no food, drink or smoking; no bags or coats on tables; no leaning on documents and only two to four documents per person at one time. Researchers are often permitted to use their own cameras to photograph individual documents, but staff normally make photocopies to minimize damage.

Writing to a records repository

Problem

I know my ancestor lived in a specific place and would like to visit the local records office to examine its archives. I have already telephoned with some general questions and now wish to write a letter. What information and questions do I need to include?

Solution

Whenever writing to a repository, be sure to keep your correspondence courteous, brief and to the point.

- Include your name, address and telephone number.

- State what records you are seeking, e.g., birth, marriage, parish or probate records, etc.

- Write down the full name (and any spelling variations you may have found) for the ancestors in question, the exact dates (or at least the time frame) when they lived, street addresses where they resided, if known, and any other identifying details. Be as accurate, specific and complete as possible.

- If you have not already asked about fees, be sure to mention that you intend to compensate the repository for any photocopies and other fee-based services and request an invoice.

- Ask what form of payment the repository accepts, e.g., personal cheque, money order or credit card.

- Enclose a self-addressed, stamped envelope. If you are sending the enquiry overseas, include enough International Reply Coupons to cover return postage.

- Keep a copy of the letter or email message and record it in your correspondence log.

- Be prepared to wait at least a few weeks for a reply.

- If the archivist writes back stating they could not find the information you requested, consider why. Review your paperwork for any transcription errors and consider if you have made mistakes in interpreting the data you have gathered.

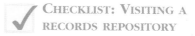

CHECKLIST: VISITING A RECORDS REPOSITORY

- Familiarize yourself with repository rules and holdings before beginning the research.

- Book an appointment and/or register for access, if required.

- Establish a plan, identifying what topics, records and names you specifically wish to research, before you arrive at the repository.

- Note any specific facts that will enable the archivist to direct you properly.

- Bring your working folder, copies of your pedigree chart and family group sheets.

- Bring your own pencils, note paper and other supplies.

- Use consistent citation procedures for each item you examine.

- Bring coins for photocopies.

- Thank staff for their assistance.

- Don't eat, drink, smoke or chew gum inside the repository.

- Remember that staff are busy – don't waste their time!

using the Internet

The Internet is a remarkable resource, but family historians can easily get overwhelmed with swarms of links when researching for the particular name of an ancestor.

When used wisely, the Internet should be the genealogist's first and best research friend. Besides reviewing articles on genealogy or searching online databases, you can download or print out free forms, including pedigree charts and family group sheets, research and correspondence logs and to-do lists from the Internet.

Genealogy websites

Websites have been established by some of the world's most well-respected authorities on genealogy. Some offer lessons for beginning researchers, articles to educate users about record types and how to use them, news items and tips for the seasoned family historian. Others post findings about specific ancestors or act as online repositories. Many hobbyist websites encourage people researching the same surname gather to share information and concerns. However, unless you obtain verifiable copies of primary records, regard the information with healthy suspicion. Don't hesitate to read 'how-to' articles, which certainly shed light on the mysterious and often overwhelming research process. But when it comes to the data itself – vital details, transcriptions and even pedigree charts – always crosscheck the details with the information you have already acquired.

The Internet top ten for family historians are:

- FamilySearch Internet Genealogy Service, The Church of Jesus Christ of Latter-day Saints: www.familysearch.org

- Cyndi's List of Genealogy Sites on the Internet: www.cyndislist.com

- RootsWeb.com: www.rootsweb.com

- The WorldGen WebProject: www.worldgenweb.org

- The USGenWeb Project: www.usgenweb.org

- GENUKI – UK and Ireland Genealogy: www.genuki.org.uk/big

- Genealogy.com Learning Center: www.genealogy.com/ genehelp.html

- Ancestry.com Library: www.ancestry.com/library/ archive.asp

- About Genealogy – The Family Tree and Genealogy Research Guide: genealogy.about.com

- Kindred Trails Worldwide Genealogy Resources: www.kindredtrails.com

Using search engines

Whether you have your own online access, use a friend's computer or log on at the nearest library, your first step should be to refer to a search engine. The Internet has both generic search engines and genealogy-specific search engines, which allow you to type in a word or phrase to identify links to relevant websites. More than likely, if you start with a generic search engine (e.g., www.google.com, www.dogpile.com, www.altavista.com or www.yahoo.com), you will have only moderate success in locating information on your particular ancestors. Although generic search engines may be able to point you in the right direction, sorting through the scores of websites can be time-consuming – and time-wasting.

Often when you enter a surname or complete name into a generic search engine, you will be directed to personal websites, online data collections or websites displaying individual genealogical charts. While these sites may confirm or add some data to what you already know about your family history, you should always double-check the information against what your family says, what other websites state and what you find in official records. Sometimes data is incorrectly transcribed, or assumptions are made about accuracy, and researchers are led off track.

Surname databases

Family historians have greater success with online surname databases and genealogy-specific search engines, which are tailored to genealogy research. After submitting a surname, the website generally directs you to specific databases, message boards or other websites that focus on the name.

> **tip** **Check whether services are fee based**
> Some websites provide fee-based services, so be sure to surf the Internet thoroughly before purchasing data you might be able to obtain elsewhere free of charge.

They may also point you to other types of genealogy resources, including searchable records databases, archives for governmental agencies and message boards where you can post enquiries.

Some of the best surname databases are:

- www.genealogyregister.com
- www.searchforancestors.com
- www.ancestry.com
- www.ancestorguide.com
- www.surnameguide.com
- www.ancestralsearch.com
- www.gengateway.com

Newsgroups and message boards

If you have access to America Online (AOL), you can subscribe to a genealogy newsgroup, a forum of sorts where members post messages relevant to their own searches or in response to other member's enquiries. Go to keyword 'Newsgroups', click on 'Search All Newsgroups', enter 'genealogy', and view the listing of newsgroups. For Internet users without AOL, head to the following link to subscribe to the same newsgroups: www.rootsweb.com/~jfuller/gen_use.html. Examples include soc.genealogy.britain, soc.genealogy.african, wales.genealogy, alt.genealogy, soc.genealogy.slavic, soc.genealogy.surnames.usa and soc.genealogy.germany.

Be cautious about posting messages on newsgroups or other types of message boards, as some people harvest the email addresses to send 'spams', those annoying, intrusive and often offensive messages that take up space on your hard drive and sometimes contain viruses. Even if you decide not to post online, you can 'lurk' in the newsgroups or website 'forums' and read the messages without posting responses.

Official records on the Internet

Problem

I would like to obtain duplicates of my great-grandmother's civil records, but the nearest records repositories are a long way from my home. Which Internet websites provide access to online data collections?

Solution

Besides the Family History Library (www.familysearch.org) and government repositories mentioned earlier, the following sampling of websites provides immediate or fee-based Internet access to official records:

The Public Record Finder offers dozens of URLs that link to agencies in the US that produce or hold records. Find links to birth, marriage and death records at www.publicrecordfinder.com/vitalrecrds.html and links to agencies that handle court records at www.publicrecordfinder.com/courtrecords.html.

Census Online boasts more than 42,000 links to websites featuring online census records and transcriptions, for the US, UK and Canada: www.census-online.com

Ancestry.com provides searchable databases for census and vital records, immigration, military, land and court records and more for ancestors from the US, UK, Canada, Germany, Ireland and the Netherlands: www.ancestry.com/search/rectype/default.aspx?rt=35

The USGenWeb Project, www.usgenweb.org, and its sister website, the WorldGenWeb Project, www.worldgenweb.org, proudly offer free access to thousands of records and other genealogical resources.

Online International Census Indexes and Records features numerous links to websites with databases for Australia, Canada, Denmark, Ireland, Norway, Sweden and the UK: www.genealogybranches.com/international.html

Interment.net Cemetery Transcription Library has links to more than three million headstone transcriptions around the world, to burial listings for some US national cemeteries and to other cemetery records: www.interment.net

Once you have made as many genealogical links to your past as you can, it may be time to consider paying someone to help move your search forward.

You have been trying your best to trace your roots, but some information simply eludes you. Perhaps you don't have enough time to devote your full attention to the project. Perhaps the records you need to review are stored across the country, or even overseas, and you have neither the time nor the finances to make a trip. Has the paperwork overwhelmed you and you can't seem to wade through it? Perhaps you lack the research skills, tools, background information or even the language knowledge to locate and properly use the records. Or maybe you have hit a brick wall and don't know what steps to take next.

Most family history researchers get baffled from time to time. Even though some decide to quit their search, many carry on. Some post questions or ask for assistance on the Internet, while others contact a local genealogical society or family history centre. Paying a professional genealogist to help you progress with your search is another option you might wish to consider.

What can a professional genealogist offer you?

Genealogical consultants help develop research plans, evaluate the information you have gathered and write family histories. They can review your work and offer guidance on where to head next. They can carry out specific, knowledgeable research on your behalf using foreign language skills or online access to databases that most family historians do not have. Many professionals have expertise in certain research areas such as particular geographic regions; ethnic, racial or religious groups; records created during specific time frames; or specific record types, for example, maritime or immigration records. Others live close enough to the repositories, or have a network of colleagues, to examine their holdings more quickly and efficiently.

Hiring a professional genealogist

If you are thinking of hiring a professional researcher, make sure that he or she has the experience to do the research you want. While amateur genealogists often have as much knowledge as full-time professionals, and certainly possess plenty of enthusiasm, they may not have the skills or access to records that you require. Although it can be expensive, hiring a full-time professional genealogist may be your best option.

Like so many other aspects of family history research, finding the right professional genealogist takes time, advance preparation and cautious consideration. Contact friends who have worked with genealogists, the local family history centre or genealogical society, and ask for referrals. Or contact a professional organization for accredited or certified genealogists and obtain a copy of their member directory.

Standards and certification

Just as worldwide interest in tracing one's roots has grown exponentially in recent decades, so has the number of people offering 'professional' research services. In response, several organizations have established a set of standards and codes of ethics for their members. Genealogists can obtain formal accreditation or certification by passing a series of fairly rigorous tests that demonstrate their competence in genealogical research. The following are some of the more commonly recognized organizations:

The International Commission for the Accreditation of Professional Genealogists (ICAPGen), located in Salt Lake City, Utah, tests individuals who wish to achieve an Accredited Genealogist credential. Originally administered by The Church of Jesus Christ of Latter-day Saints in association with the Genealogical Association of Utah, the accreditation programme is now run by a completely independent testing organization. Individuals are tested in specific subject areas. The names of researchers who pass the test are entered on ICAPGen's Accredited Genealogist list, which is available to libraries, family history centres, genealogical societies and private individuals. Accredited researchers may append the phrase Accredited Genealogist and AG after their name.

The Board for Certification of Genealogists, in Washington, DC, certifies applicants as CLS – Certified Lineage Specialist; CG – Certified Genealogist; CGRS – Certified Genealogical Records Specialist; CGI – Certified Genealogical Instructor or CGL – Certified Genealogical Lecturer. It maintains a roster of certified genealogists, which is available from its main office and also on the Internet at www.bcgcertification.org/associates/index.php.

The Association of Professional Genealogists (APG) does not formally test genealogists, but supports high standards of practice and codes of ethics to which its members adhere. Founded in 1979 in Utah, APG operates numerous local chapters throughout the US. It publishes a directory of members, which is accessible on its website at apgen.org/directory/index.php. A print version is available to private individuals for a fee and is usually held in genealogical libraries.

The Association of Genealogists and Researchers in Archives (AGRA), like the APG, does not test genealogists, but its members do abide by a code of practice and are held accountable for their work by the organization. AGRA presents itself as the only independent organization in UK genealogy that will follow up a complaint, it promotes professionalism, and membership is open only to highly qualified researchers who have worked as genealogists or researchers in archives for several years. AGRA maintains an online directory of members at www.agra.org.uk/page5.html, which features a subject index of members' special interests. The main office is in Horsham, West Sussex, England.

✓ CHECKLIST: CHOOSING THE RIGHT PROFESSIONAL

- Identify, prioritize and write down your research goals.
- Determine what you can afford.
- Identify several professional genealogists who specialize in the type of research you require.
- Interview three or four professionals to determine who best fits your needs.
- Ask each to list their number of years of experience, special skills, educational background, professional affiliations and accreditation, samples of published work and reports.
- Explain your research needs and goals and ask what their research strategy would involve.
- Ask if they are interested and available to do the work.
- Ask for their fee schedule and what work the fees cover, e.g. time, costs of photocopies, travel expenses, postage etc. Is there a retainer fee? Can they give you an estimate of the total fee?
- Obtain a list of references and contact them.
- Determine the timetable for doing the work.
- Identify the kinds of reports you will receive.
- Ask what your role will be in the research.
- Decide which researcher best fits your plans and needs.
- Make a written contract for all but the smallest, single-record projects. The contract should lay out the goals, fees, work involved, timetable, contingencies for breaking the agreement and who owns the copyright to the finished product.
- Provide the researcher with complete details about the work you have already done to prevent duplication of effort. Include copies of pedigree charts and family group sheets and a list of sources you have checked.
- Be patient – genealogical research can take weeks. Be clear when to expect to hear from the person you hire.
- Do not expect the impossible – even professional genealogists may be unable to find the records you need.
- Remember, there are no guarantees. If a genealogist claims that he or she will definitely provide the results you seek, you might want to choose someone else on your list!

If you need to find a professional genealogist, the Internet is a good place to start looking.

3 Understanding the fine print

1	Hannah	Female	23	Black	Grand Bahama	Creole
2	Joe	Male	18 Months	Black	Grand Bahama	Creole

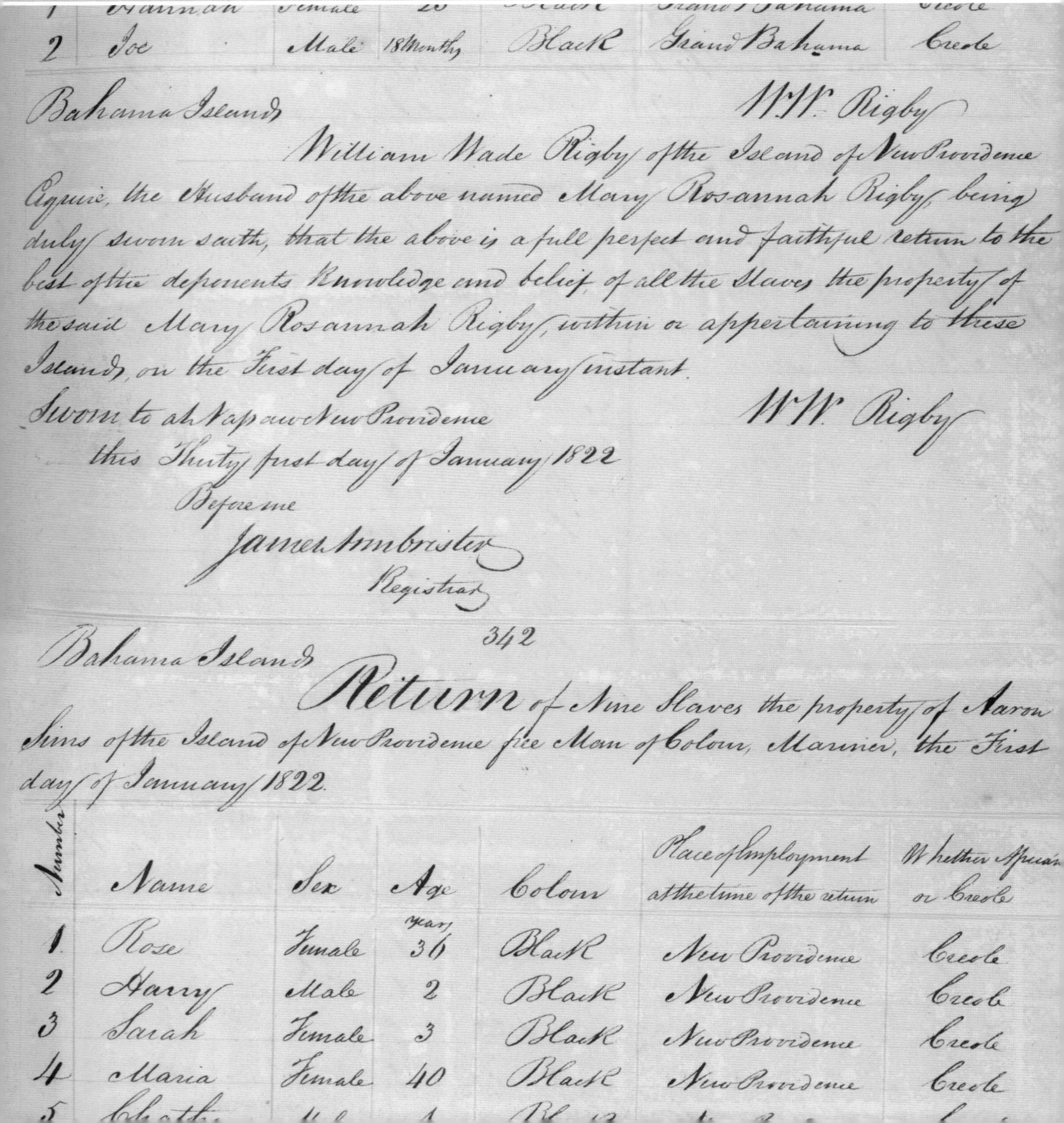

Bahama Islands W.W. Rigby

William Wade Rigby of the Island of New Providence Esquire, the Husband of the above named Mary Rosannah Rigby being duly sworn saith, that the above is a full perfect and faithful return to the best of the deponents knowledge and belief of all the Slaves the property of the said Mary Rosannah Rigby within or appertaining to these Islands, on the First day of January instant.

Sworn to at Nassau New Providence this Thirty first day of January 1822 W.W. Rigby

Before me

James Armbrister
Registrar

342

Bahama Islands

Return of Nine Slaves the property of Aaron Sims of the Island of New Providence free Man of Colour, Mariner, the First day of January 1822.

Number	Name	Sex	Age	Colour	Place of Employment at the time of the return	Whether African or Creole
			years			
1.	Rose	Female	36	Black	New Providence	Creole
2	Harry	Male	2	Black	New Providence	Creole
3	Sarah	Female	3	Black	New Providence	Creole
4	Maria	Female	40	Black	New Providence	Creole
5	[illegible]	Male	[illegible]	Black	[illegible]	[illegible]

Even though most official documents are not generated with genealogists in mind, they often contain a wealth of information that will help you fill in the gaps in your family tree and expand your knowledge about your heritage. However, it takes clear thinking to fully extract genealogical data from the records.

If you did see any such documents, you may have gaped in awe at the seemingly complicated jargon and unusual writing they contained. Over the years, you may have been curious about history and have visited museums, but you probably remained unaware of the presence of local record repositories and family history centres in your own community. You may enjoy exploring cemeteries and historic sites, but have had little or no need to review their records. And you may well have gone out of your way to avoid even glancing at the documents created by official governmental agencies.

A first glance at the records

Finally, you decide to branch out with your family history research and attempt to locate and review the records. Of course, you expect that the documents you uncover will be accurate, understandable and in good order – after all, they were created by reputable, reliable agencies and organizations. Yet when you obtain copies or head to the repositories to examine them in person, you discover records that seem to be riddled with mistakes or that are incomprehensible. Some appear to be undecipherable, even though they are in your native language, while others no longer survive or have been transferred to repositories that are far from your home. In fact, after just briefly looking at the records, you may feel that you have hit a brick wall and may decide that there's not much likelihood of you ever completing your family tree. Stay the course – the chances are that you have only reached a stumbling point!

Develop a plan

As throughout the entire research process, you should approach your examination of individual records with an orderly plan that combines common sense, organizational skills and investigative techniques to glean as much as possible from each document. Extracting pertinent details from some of the records will be a fairly straightforward process that involves identifying names, dates and places. However, most records also contain a wealth of less obvious but equally valuable genealogical information, which you will identify only by being curious, asking lots of questions and using the clues to find and review other documents. Along the way you will encounter obstacles to your search, but don't give up. As you locate and review the variety of documents that relate to your roots, take your time studying their contents. They may contain clues to your past that no one else has been able to decode.

Data protection and privacy legislation

National copyright laws, data protection legislation and freedom of information and privacy laws will affect your ability to acquire and photocopy certain official records, particularly those pertaining to people still living or those only recently deceased.

When researching your family history, the following laws (which are not intended as a comprehensive listing) may limit your access to certain official records:

United States

- The Freedom of Information Act of 1966

- The Privacy Act of 1974

- The Electronic Freedom of Information Act of 1996

United Kingdom

- The Data Protection Act of 1998 (applies to personal records within the entire UK)

- The Freedom of Information Act of 2000 (applies to the records of public bodies within England, Wales and Northern Ireland)

Canada

- The Privacy Act of 1985

- The Personal Information Protection and Electronic Documents Act of 2000

Australia

- The Federal Privacy Law of 1988

The European Union has also adopted a set of laws for the protection of individuals with regard to the automatic processing of data.

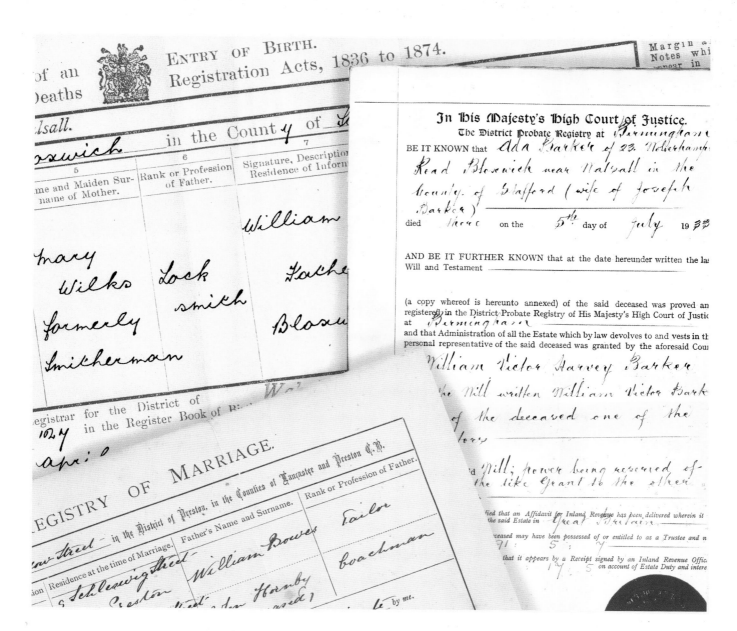

CHECKLIST: REVIEWING DOCUMENTS

Whenever you review a document, take time to examine and consider the content fully. Ask yourself the following:

- What does this mean?
- Is this accurate?
- How can I use this titbit of information?
- What other sources should I check?
- How does this all fit with the other information I have?

Closely examine the records you gather for each ancestor, and ask yourself what you actually see. Not only do they cover the vital details of key life events, these documents also provide other clues to your past.

tip  **Think creatively**

Even though most official documents are not generated with genealogists in mind, they often contain a wealth of information that will help you fill in the gaps in your family tree and expand your knowledge about your heritage. However, you first have to interpret the details in the records. Some facts are straightforward. Others must be extracted from clues hidden right before your eyes. In order to extract the less obvious details about your past, consciously ask yourself questions about what you see in each document.

When you begin your records search, first seek out vital records. Generally reliable, they provide names, dates and locations that will fill in the blanks on your family tree.

Registration of births, marriages and deaths

For centuries, countries have kept records documenting births, deaths and marriages. Yet it was not until the early 19th century, when a group of physicians concerned about public health issues advocated the collection of health-related data, that the registration of deaths and births became national policy in the United States. Even then, it took more than another century for all US states to adopt the practice of collecting records to document vital events formally, officially and consistently. Registration practices in Canada also fluctuated until later in the 19th century.

In Britain, and other parts of Europe before the 19th century, the registration of births, marriages and deaths often fell to the local parish church, chapel or other place of worship, or to town or borough authorities. In England and Wales civil registration of births, deaths and marriages began in 1837, whereas

Marvin Wesley Hull's birth certificate has three sections. The front page identifies the baby's name; parents' names; time, day, date and location of birth and doctor's name.

FAMILY HISTORY

Father's full name _Frank Earl Hull_
Birthplace _Arkansas_ — Date_____
Mother's maiden name _Mary Elma Lasley_ —
Birthplace _Colorado_ — Date_____
Residence at time child was born _Springdale, Arkansas_
Sex of child _M._ Weight at birth _6_ pounds _13_ ounces. Length _19_ inches

Baby's left footprint →

Baby's right footprint ←

Mother's left thumbprint

Mother's right thumbprint

This Certificate will always be valuable in proving the date and place of your birth and the identity of the parents. It will be useful for proving age and

For entering school + + + For beginning employment and securing work
For voting rights and jury duty + + For proving citizenship + + For mili
For obtaining passports for travel in foreign countries + For life insurance a
For social security and old age pension + + And for proving right to inheri

Official registration is at_____

Lithographed in U.S.A.

As well as revealing other important information, the reverse side of Marvin Hull's birth certificate remarkably records the baby's footprints and mother's thumbprints.

Scotland instituted registration in 1855. Ireland began registering marriages in 1845, but delayed formal registration of births and deaths until 1864.

When researching ancestors who lived during the 19th century or earlier, keep the above dates in mind. Also remember that, even after the laws went into effect, many people felt that the government was invading their privacy by requiring registration and chose either not to comply or to register vital events only sporadically. Consequently, even if you have a good idea of when your ancestor lived, you may have difficulty finding the original vital record.

Birth certificates

Birth certificates are treasure troves of information. Contrary to what some researchers believe, they can provide identifying marks or physical indicators. In fact, many display the baby's footprints and mother's thumbprints imprinted on the reverse side. Most include the child's name, gender, date and place of birth and parents' full names. Some also identify the father's or both parents' occupations. US birth certificates also contain a separate section 'for medical and health use only'. Nowadays, birth certificates are confidential and the registering agency normally retains them.

Besides the official birth certificate, states also issue a certificate of live birth. Not normally released to the public, the documents are stored by the Board of Health, or its regional equivalent.

The mother of the child was born in Colorado. Use this information and her age at the birth of the child to begin tracing her roots.

Marvin's father, Francis Earl Hull, worked in the machinery industry. What factories or other relevant businesses were in operation at the time of this birth?

ARKANSAS STATE BOARD OF HEALTH
BUREAU OF VITAL STATISTICS

ARKANSAS STATE BOARD OF HEALTH
BUREAU OF VITAL STATISTICS
CERTIFICATE OF LIVE BIRTH

Registration District No. 635
Primary Registration District No. 2379
155
9360

1. PLACE OF BIRTH
   a. COUNTY Washington
   b. CITY OR TOWN (If outside corporate limits, write RURAL and give township) Fayetteville
   c. FULL NAME (If NOT in hospital or institution give street address or location) OF HOSPITAL OR INSTITUTION Washington County Hospital

2. USUAL RESIDENCE OF MOTHER (where does mother live?)
   a. STATE Arkansas   b. COUNTY Washington
   c. CITY OR TOWN (If outside corporate limits, write RURAL and give township) Springdale
   d. STREET ADDRESS (If rural, give location) Route #4

APR 4 - 1951

3. CHILD'S NAME (Type or print)
   a. (First) Marvin   b. (Middle) Wesley   c. (Last) Hull

4. SEX M
5a. THIS BIRTH: SINGLE XX   TWIN ☐   TRIPLET ☐
5b. IF TWIN OR TRIPLET (This child born) 1ST ☐ 2ND ☐ 3RD ☐
6. DATE OF BIRTH (Month) (Day) (Year) Feb. 28, 1951

FATHER OF CHILD
7. FULL NAME a. (First) Francis   b. (Middle) Earl   c. (Last) Hull   8. COLOR OR RACE white
9. AGE (At time of this birth) 41 YEARS
10. BIRTHPLACE (State or foreign country) Arkansas
11a. USUAL OCCUPATION mechanic
11b. KIND OF BUSINESS OR INDUSTRY machinery

MOTHER OF CHILD
12. FULL MAIDEN NAME a. (First) Mary   b. (Middle) Elma   c. (Last) Lasley   13. COLOR OR RACE white
14. AGE (At time of this birth) 39 YEARS
15. BIRTHPLACE (State or foreign country) Colorado
16. CHILDREN PREVIOUSLY BORN TO THIS MOTHER (Do NOT include this child)
   a. How many OTHER children are now living? 8
   b. How many OTHER children were born alive but are now dead? 1
   c. How many children were stillborn (born dead after 20 weeks pregnancy)? 0

17. INFORMANT Mother of infant
I hereby certify that this child was born alive on the date stated above, at the hour of 12:40 P.M.
18a. SIGNATURE ~~Disco~~
18c. ADDRESS Springdale, Arkansas
18b. ATTENDANT AT BIRTH M.D. ☒ MIDWIFE ☐ OTHER (Specify)
18d. DATE SIGNED 3-1-51
19. DATE REC'D BY LOCAL REG. march 17, 1951
20. REGISTRAR'S SIGNATURE Mrs C B Paddock
21. DATE ON WHICH GIVEN NAME ADDED BY (Registrar)

FOR MEDICAL AND HEALTH USE ONLY
(This Section MUST be filled out)

THIS IS TO CERTIFY, THAT THE ABOVE IS A FULL, TRUE AND CORRECT COPY OF THE ORIGINAL CERTIFICATE WHICH IS ON FILE IN THIS OFFICE AND OF WHICH I AM LEGAL CUSTODIAN. IN TESTIMONY, WHEREOF, WITNESS MY HAND AND SEAL OF OFFICE AT LITTLE ROCK, ARKANSAS.

March 18, 1966.
STATE REGISTRAR _J C Herron, MD_ s.c. ab

The certificate of live birth lists eight living children who were born before Marvin Hull. Gather their names, vital statistics and other genealogical details.

What kind of information can you find out about the one child who predeceased the new infant?

Marriage records

Because they are so rich in genealogical information, marriage records may become your favourite tool resources. Not only are they often visually attractive heirlooms, they also contain vital information about a husband and wife, most importantly the latter's maiden name, the parents' names, witness details and other data that can fill in your pedigree chart and also lead you to further research.

Countries such as France and Germany began civil registration in the late 18th century, whereas in North America and Britain, city, town, provincial, county and state governments began registering civil marriages during the mid- to late 19th century. So always remember to look for parish registers and similar records created by the church and other religious institutions where the weddings of your ancestors may have taken place.

Types of marriage records

Although the marriage certificate may be the first marriage record you find, many other record types will also provide you with useful information.

The marriage licence is the most common type of marriage record in the US. A couple intending to marry first applies to civil authorities in the town, county, district or parish in which they wish to marry. The

The new Mrs. Bridges Webb is identified as a widow. Further research into her previous marriage may reveal other relatives on a different branch of the family tree.

Seek out the parish church for additional records related to this couple.

Was the new wife's maiden name Caroline Beatrice Boulger?

Note the different surnames for Caroline Yeats and her father, John Boulger. Was the new wife's maiden name Caroline Beatrice Boulger?

William Bridges Webb worked as a merchant. What did he trade and where did he conduct his business?

The marriage certificate of William Bridges Webb and Caroline Beatrice Yeats, dated 1878.

Gaining information from a marriage certificate

Problem

Alex Myers has a copy of her great-grandfather's marriage certificate. Some of the details conflict with his death certificate (see page 83). What should she do with this information?

Solution

- Closer investigation of William Bridges Webb's marriage certificate suggests that the curate, Henry C. Long, used generalizations – a shorthand of sorts – to fill in several of the blanks. For example, the ages of both parties are identified by the same two words, 'Full age', which means the new husband and wife were both over the age of 21 at the time of the marriage. Some marriage certificates fully identify the residences for both parties and not just the town, as is the case here. Such shortcuts point to the need for further research, while the information given in the certficate also provides several research leads. For example:

- The marriage certificate identifies Bridges Webb's occupation as 'merchant', which conflicts with his death certificate, where he is listed as a 'grain merchant'. While the two terms are not mutually exclusive, and it is possible the curate/registrar routinely simplified this information, Alex should do additional research to determine the exact nature of the business. She may also want to delve into the substance of his father's profession, also described as 'merchant'.

- Bridges Webb's 'condition' – his marital status – was listed as 'bachelor' and Caroline Beatrice Yeats was identified as 'widow'. Did the new Mrs Webb work during her widowhood? If so, what did she do? Were Webb or Yeats (or both) Alex's blood relatives? How long had Caroline Beatrice Yeats been widowed? Who was her first husband? Are there surviving children from that marriage? If so, how might they be related to Alex? Researching the widow's prior marriage may uncover a previously unknown bloodline to which Alex is linked.

- The marriage certificate indicates that the wedding occurred at the parish church after the curate announced it with banns. Alex should consider researching the couple's religion and the likely location for the church records, including the banns.

- The names of the three witnesses, two of whom are members of the Bridges Webb family while the third appears to be a relative of the bride, provide other leads. Checking their backgrounds can help Alex fill in the gaps in her family tree and perhaps clarify conflicting information she has come across.

licence signifies that they have completed all requirements for marriage. The couple's full names, ages, residences, birth dates and ages, occupations and the names and birth places of the parents are normally identified. The existence of a marriage licence does not prove a wedding took place; it only shows intent to marry.

The marriage certificate provides proof that marriage has actually taken place. The marriage certificate is presented to the couple by the officiating representative upon the completion of the wedding ceremony. Look for the couple's full names, marriage date and location, witness names and fathers' names and occupations. Other information may include the couple's current addresses and occupations, their ages and marital status (single, widowed, divorced) at the time of this marriage and whether either father was deceased.

Major Bridges Webb enjoys an outing on his private yacht. Does his marriage certificate provide leads to the two women who are also in the photograph?

The marriage register is the formal registration of the marriage after the ceremony. It normally includes the couple's names, the date and place of marriage and the name of the person who performed the ceremony.

Marriage banns are a public declaration of intent or formal announcement of a couple's intent to wed. Marriage banns are posted in public places, presented to church congregations or published in the church bulletin for two to three consecutive weeks. Anyone objecting to the marriage then has the opportunity and responsibility to present legitimate reasons why the couple should not be married. Marriage banns are located in town or church registers.

A marriage bond is an agreement to marry, which includes a sum of money posted by the groom and/or a male relative. In the event that the wedding does not take place or the marriage is voided (or annulled), the bond is forfeited. A marriage bond can be useful to the genealogist in providing clues to the financial status of a family.

A marriage contract is similar to a prenuptial agreement, whereby the terms of the marriage, including exactly what property both parties brought to the marriage, are clearly stated before the finalization of the marriage. Property descriptions can provide insight into the financial status and lifestyles of the couple and further research leads.

Marriage consent affidavits document a parent's or guardian's permission to marry when the bride and/or groom is younger than the minimum legal age for marriage.

This wedding couple and bridesmaid have just left the marriage ceremony. The couple may have also signed their marriage register to formally document the event.

Death records

Varying in format and content, death records often provide greater insights into a person's past than does his or her birth certificate. For that reason, even though you might logically choose to seek out an ancestor's birth certificate first, whenever possible study death certificates first and then marriage records, both of which contain birth information as well as other details. They can fill in many gaps in your family history and also point you to other research. Only then should you seek the birth records.

Keep in mind that grieving spouses, children or well-meaning friends may inadvertently – or even intentionally – offer inaccurate details about the deceased. So, after first recording the data exactly as shown, be sure to double-check any inconsistencies you may find on the death document.

US death certificates generally include the following information about the deceased: full name, date and place of death, age at death, birth place, last residence, occupation, marital status, parents' names and birth places, informant's name and relationship to the deceased. They may also record military service, spouse's name, name of the funeral parlour, date and place of burial. Before 1989, when confidentiality requirements changed, the certificates also included the cause of death. Nowadays, that information is recorded on a separate section of the certificate, which is not normally released to the public.

The Social Security Death Index

(SSDI) is another useful resource for family historians in the US to review. This computerized database is available on the Internet and also at the LDS Family History Centres. Established in 1962 to record the deaths of people with Social Security numbers reported to the Social Security Administration and to process survivor requests for benefits, the vast database mainly contains names of individuals who died after 1962. It also has railroad retirement board records and some names dating to 1937, when Americans first applied for Social Security cards.

Besides the person's Social Security number, the SSDI contains his or her surname, given name, birth and death dates (month and year only, before 1988), last known residence, location where survivors received the death benefit, and the date and place of issuance. The Social Security Administration has also microfilmed all original applications for cards (SS-5s) and claims files. These records contain the applicant's full name, full name at birth, present mailing address, age at last birthday, birth date, birth place, parents' full names, applicant's gender and race, current employer details and the applicant's signature.

Interpreting death records

Like other official records, death certificates, SSDI entries and SS-5s have their limitations and are prone to misinterpretation. Before 1962 many people did not have Social Security numbers, so do not give up the search if you cannot find your ancestor in the index. Also, be careful not to confuse the 'last residence' with the place of death: they are not necessarily the same. Actual places of death are not listed in the SSDI. The same applies to the place of issuance; that is, the place where the card and number were issued is not always the place of death or place of residence at the time of application.

The Inland Revenue's Death Duty Registers (DDR) in the UK span the years from 1796 to 1903 and record tax payments on the estates of the deceased. The Family Records Centre in London holds microfilm copies from 1796 through to 1858, while the National Archives at Kew holds more recent DDRs. Details of interest to family historians include the deceased's name, address and death date; executors of the will; value of the estate; legatees (names of people who received specific legacies), their blood relationship to the deceased, ages and the amount of the annuity; and the duty paid.

A page from the Rootsweb website showing how you can use the Internet to help you find ancestor's on the Social Security Death Index.

Gaining information from a death certificate

Problem

The death certificate of Major William Bridges Webb, who died in 1913, is shown opposite. What kind of information can be found on his death certificate?

Solution

UK entries of death, like the one shown for William Bridges Webb, are fairly straightforward. Details of genealogical interest include:

- the exact date and place of death

- the district and county where the death was registered

- the deceased's full name

- the deceased's gender

- the deceased's age at death

- the deceased's occupation

- cause of death

- signature, residence and relationship to the deceased of the informant who filed the certificate

- date it was filed

Besides merely recording the details, Alex should fully evaluate the data presented on the death register, for example:

- Where did a corn merchant set up business and manage his company?

- Does the business still exist?

- If so, which of its records might relate to William Bridges Webb?

- What role did Cyril E.B. Yeates play in his stepfather's life?

- Who was Cyril's mother, and did she have any children with Major Bridges Webb?

- Does 12 Mandeville Place still stand, and can descendants visit the site?

- Did Major Bridges Webb have any medical conditions that contributed to his death and that might be inheritable?

What does this address represent? Was this William Bridges Webb's final residence? Does it still exist?

A comparison between the marriage and death certificates reveals a discrepancy in the spelling of the stepson's surname. Was it Yeates or Yeats? Check for both spellings when doing research.

CERTIFIED COPY OF AN ENTRY OF DEATH

GIVEN AT THE **GENERAL REGISTER OFFICE**

Application Number G257462

REGISTRATION DISTRICT	St.Marylebone

1913 DEATH in the Sub-district of St. Mary in the County of London

Columns:–	1	2	3	4	5	6	7	8	9
No.	When and where died	Name and surname	Sex	Age	Occupation	Cause of death	Signature, description and residence of informant	When registered	Signature of registrar
340	Twenty fifth August 1913 6 G. Montagu Mansions	William Bridges Webb	Male	65 years	Corn Merchant	Cerebral Haemorrhage Asthenia 1 month 14 days Certified by E. Playfair M.B	Cyril E. B. Yeates Step son Present at the Death 12 Mandeville Place St. Marylebone	Twenty fifth August 1913	G.H. Bassett Deputy Registrar

CERTIFIED to be a true copy of an entry in the certified copy of a Register of Deaths in the District above mentioned.

Given at the GENERAL REGISTER OFFICE, under the Seal of the said Office, the .... 30th .... day of .... September 2004

DYA 443689

See note overleaf

CAUTION: THERE ARE OFFENCES RELATING TO FALSIFYING OR ALTERING A CERTIFICATE AND USING OR POSSESSING A FALSE CERTIFICATE ©CROWN COPYRIGHT
WARNING: A CERTIFICATE IS NOT EVIDENCE OF IDENTITY.

027247 7291 04/04 SPSL 007713

JB

Unlike the marriage certificate, the death certificate identifies the deceased's occupation as a corn merchant. Use this additional information to do more research into his business dealings.

Does the address at 12 Mandeville Place point to an ancestral site that should be explored? What does this address represent? Was this William Bridges Webb's final residence? Does it still exist?

William Bridges Webb's death certificate dates to 1913 and provides several interesting details.

Countries vary in their procedures for granting divorces and storing their records; consequently, divorce records are often difficult to locate.

Documents such as separation records, annulment proceedings, the divorce petition, final decree, divorce certificate and court case file provide genealogists with sources rich in information. They not only contain the names of the divorcing husband and wife, the date of the marriage and the date of the divorce (if finalized), they often also include the ages, birth dates, residences and property held by each party, names and birth dates of their living children and the plaintiff's grounds (or reasons) for the divorce.

Divorce in the UK

Before England's King Henry VIII decided he needed to rid himself of the first of his six wives in the 16th century, the Pope granted divorces from Rome. After the English Reformation, several methods were used to dissolve marriages, such as private separation, desertion, wife sale, annulment by church courts and full divorce by Act of Parliament (the first of which was granted in 1670). Look for these historical records at the National Archives in Kew, in Close Rolls, Cause Papers and Case Books, and at the Lambeth Palace Library or the Borthwick Institute of Historical Research (for the records of the consistory courts for Canterbury

Divorce records come in a variety of formats, including handwritten affidavits such as this one submitted by Barbara Seiser, plaintiff, who explains why she wishes to divorce her husband, James.

Renowned for changing the course of history when he divorced Queen Catherine of Aragon to marry Anne Boleyn, Henry VIII's quest for an heir led to several marriages, divorces and the English Reformation.

Understanding a divorce summons and petition

Problem

My parents acquired several documents from the county courthouse, including the summons and petition that relate to my great-grandmother's divorce. What details will help me complete my family tree and provide clues for additional research?

Solution

The summons reveals not only that your great-grandmother was the plaintiff in the divorce case, but also identifies the county and court where the summons was filed and the names of the serving officials.

- Note the reason why the summons was served: 'being convicted of burglary and larceny and confined in the Ohio Penitentiary'.

- Search police, court, prison and penitentiary records for more information.

The petition – though lengthy and handwritten and thus difficult to read – is also filled with details you should add to your family's history, including:

- the marriage date and location

- the child's name

- facts about the husband's conviction, including when and where it occurred and the prison sentence

- the plaintiff's request to restore her maiden name, which is stated in full

- the plaintiff's request for child custody

- the plaintiff's signature

---

and York). You will find Quarter Sessions records at the local level.

UK divorce laws changed in 1857, when the Court for Divorce and Matrimonial Causes was established to hear all divorce cases. However, it took until the 1920s for divorce to be accessible to all classes of society. In the 1960s county courts took over the task of hearing and approving divorce petitions. Researchers seeking records for divorces finalized after 1857 should contact the Principal Registry of the Family Division, Decree Absolute Section, First Avenue House, 42–9 High Holborn, London WC1V 6NP (020 7947 7015), for assistance. Alternatively, the National Archives at Kew and the Family Records Centre retain indexes for certain case files dated between 1858 and 1937. These files generally contain the petition, a copy of the divorce certificate, any affidavits and a copy of decrees.

US divorce records

In the US state legislatures or courts grant divorce, so divorce records are actually a type of court record. As such, you may find them in county courthouses, filed with circuit, superior or family courts, or in the repositories of state district courts. US researchers should first contact the courthouse in the county where they believe the divorce was granted or where the couple resided, to identify which agency had jurisdiction and where the records are held. Pre-20th century records may be stored at state level archives repositories. You may be able to order official copies on the Internet.

Australian divorce records

Divorce records created in Australia after 1863 are held by the State Records Offices or the relevant Family Court. Record types include maintenance order registers, divorce registers and divorce files, which contain petitions, counter-petitions, affidavits, decrees and even photographs. Owing to privacy laws, researchers wanting to view records less than 75 years old must obtain permission from the Principal Registrar of the Supreme Court.

This divorce record from the Circuit Court of the State of Oregon offers rare insight into the cultural values of the times, the reasons for the divorce petition and custody request, and the emotional toll felt by the plaintiff.

In the Circuit Court of the State of Oregon
for the county of Clackamas. —

Joel T. Broyles, Plff

vs

Mary Smith Broyles, Deft.

The Plaintiff Joel T. Broyles
complaining says that on the 20th day of
July 1856 the said parties were united in
marriage to wit in Linn county in the
territory of Oregon. That he the said plaintiff
has conducted himself in a proper manner
as the husband of the defendant, but that
she the said defendant disregarding her
duties towards the plaintiff has repeatedly
abandoned his home without any cause
of provocation whatever, sometimes for
months at a time

Plaintiff further says he is informed
and believes that on or about the 20th day
of July 1859 the said defendant committed adultery with one Matthew Whis-
berry, to wit in the county of Clackamas
aforesaid, and that the said crime remains unforgiven.

Plaintiff further says that during
the time the said ~~parties~~ parties lived together a
husband and wife, to wit on the 13th day
of May 1858 there was born to them a
female child named Melissa Jane which
child the said defendant has abandoned
and left to the care of the plaintiff.

Plaintiff further says that the said parties

census records

For centuries, nations have kept track of population statistics, but formal censuses were not instituted in most countries until well after the 18th century.

Denmark took its first census in 1769; the US began with the 1790 census; but, even though England and Wales had begun taking a decennial census in 1801, it took until 1841 for both countries to include individual names in their census records. Ireland began keeping track of the census as early as 1813, but the oldest surviving complete records date to 1901. Sadly, fires and governmental directives have resulted in the destruction of many decades' worth of records, not only in Ireland but in the US and other countries, too.

Locating census records

Census records are stored in US, UK, Irish, Canadian and other National Archives; the Family History Library and associated centres; the Family Records Centre in London; the General Register Office of Scotland; university and public libraries and many genealogical society libraries and centres.

Many census records are available on CD-ROM and microfilm and also on the Internet at websites such as:

- The 1901 Census of England and Wales: www.1901census. nationalarchives.gov.uk

- National Archives Census Records (UK): www.nationalarchives. gov.uk/census

- FamilySearch.org Census Records: www.familysearch.org/Eng/Search/ frameset_search.asp?PAGE=census/ search_census.asp.

Types of census record

Census records consist of population and non-population schedules. Both types of documents include extensive, detailed information of genealogical value. Early censuses generally recorded only the name of the head of each household and the number of persons in residence at the address (categorized according to age, race, gender and so forth). Over time, census records have become more detailed.

Census records typically contain the following:

- name of the head of household (HH)

- names of other family members

- street address

- each person's age or date of birth

- the state or nation of each birth

- the HH's marital status, marriage date or number of years married

- number of children

- race, ethnicity, nationality and/or citizenship

- the HH's occupation

- immigration year

- land ownership and property value (including personal effects)

- whether individuals were paupers or convicts

- military service

- level of literacy

- family members with disabilities (often listed as 'deaf', 'blind', 'mute', 'insane', 'idiotic', 'crippled' or 'maimed')

- other medical conditions.

Non-population schedules

Special census records were devised to document circumstances other than population counts and also to monitor trends over the decades. Seek out these resources, for they offer details about an ancestor's history that are not easy to find in other primary sources and may provide clues for further research.

Record types include:

- agriculture schedules

- mortality schedules

- DDD (Defective, Dependent and Delinquent Classes) schedules

- manufacturers and Products of Industry schedules

- slave schedules

- social statistics schedules

- veterans schedules

- state censuses

- other censuses, including Indian, school, church and sheriff's

Other national census records

The following is a representative sampling of census practices for nations other than the United States, Great Britain and Ireland:

Denmark: interval between censuses varies from five to ten years; after 1901 censuses occur every five years. Censuses before 1845 include names, ages, gender, marital status, occupation and relationship of each family member; after 1845 religion and birth places were added.

Finland: maintains population registration records dating back to 1634.

Greece: first census in 1828; annual censuses from 1836 to 1845, then irregularly recorded. Since 1951 censuses have been decennial and include names of all family members, ages, genders, birth places, occupations and period of residency.

Italy: first census in 1871; decennial censuses continue to present. Censuses before 1901 show the householder's name, occupation and number of people in residence; from 1911 records include all residents' names, ages, occupations, birth places and relationships to householder. Census records are stored in regional archives.

Netherlands: decennial census records kept from 1829 to 1929 and also in 1947, 1960 and 1971. Census records are stored in local municipal archives.

Sweden: earliest records date to 1652; officials counted only taxpaying people and individuals between certain ages until the 19th century, when the records became more inclusive.

Agriculture schedules are fascinating for the sheer amount of detail they cover. Like other types of census records, agriculture schedules become more complex over time. They are a boon to researchers whose ancestors, such as American pioneers, owned and worked farmland in the 19th century. Among the titbits of information, you will discover the amount of acreage and its usage, valuation, types of produce and livestock (in detail) and information about tenants and sharecroppers.

Assessing a census record

Problem

I have obtained the census record for my grandmother, Annetta De Gellecke, who lived in Wisconsin at the time of the 1930 federal census. She is listed as the head of household and was born in Wisconsin. What leads for additional research can I find on this document (see pages 90–1)?

Solution

□ When you examine this census record, first be sure to read across the line associated with your grandmother.

□ Note any details that seem particularly important. For example, the birth place for both of her parents is listed as Holland. That information may help you trace your roots overseas.

□ Of arguably even more interest is the entry immediately beneath that of your grandmother's. At the time the census was taken, Alida Houtkamp resided with your grandmother as a 'lodger'. What makes this entry notable is that Alida listed her birth place and that of her parents as Holland, just like your grandmother. Alida was also fluent in the Dutch language. The entry provides plenty of substance for further research. Was Alida related to Annetta De Gellecke, a family friend, or just another Dutch immigrant?

□ Take a look at the rest of the census record. Note that at least two other people, Arnold and Allie De Vos, also have parents born in Holland. Could they be related to your grandmother? How?

Copy of a census record (population schedule) conducted in Milwaukee, Wisconsin, on 10 April 1930.

What, if anything, does Alida's birthplace (Holland) indicate about her relationship to Annetta, whose parents were Dutch?

When examining census records, look closely for non-standard details, such as the characterization of Alida Houtkamp as a 'lodger'. Was Alida related to Annetta De Gelleke, who was the head of their household?

Check the census record for the names of other people who may be possible relatives. Look for similarities between listings, such as parental birthplaces in the same country.

Form 15-6

DEPARTMENT OF COMMERCE—BUREAU OF THE CENSUS

FIFTEENTH CENSUS OF THE UNITED STATES: 1930
POPULATION SCHEDULE

Enumeration District No. 40-240
Supervisor's District No. 10
Sheet No. 18 B

Enumerated by me on April 10, 1930, Harvey P. Jordan, Enumerator.

5264

The census record identifies a myriad of occupations for the residents of this Milwaukee neighbourhood. Try to determine exactly for whom the people worked. Who was the 'private family' that employed Fanny Anderson as a housekeeper?

Problems with using census records

While census records are among the most popular sources used by family historians, they are arguably also the most riddled with errors, so review them with a moderate degree of scepticism. Obtain an original copy whenever possible and adopt the practice of comparing consecutive census records, which will help you identify mistakes or inconsistencies, uncover all the information you can on a particular ancestor and then make a more educated decision about the validity of the details.

The following problems typically occur with census records:

- Surnames are often misspelled or have been intentionally altered (see also 'surname variations', pages 160–1). Use the Soundex system to help identify specific ancestors in US census records to avoid associating a name with the wrong person.

- Forenames often change from one census to the next: one census may record a man's forenames as 'Robert John' but, in the following census, his names may be listed as 'R.D.' or as some other variant. Always trace your roots over the course of several censuses and then check inconsistent spellings against other original records you have gathered.

- Details may be incomplete or incorrect owing to inadvertent transcription or typographical errors, illegible handwriting, evasiveness or illiteracy on the part of the person supplying the data, misinformation from neighbours or minors who acted as proxies, or inaccurate assumptions made by the enumerator. Do not presume that the information is correct: always crosscheck the data with your other sources. If there is a

conflict, it is more than likely that what you find in other primary sources is the more reliable option.

- Avoid making broad assumptions, for example, that the listed wife is the mother of all listed children. Similarly, not assume that the listed husband or HH is the father of all listed children.

- Some families or family members may have been missed altogether, or information about other family members may be on separate pages or sheets of microfilm, so check all pages of the census.

- Boundaries, place names, street names and addresses often change over time with shifting political circumstances or development; rural addresses may include the route but not house numbers; or enumerators may misinterpret boundary lines. As a result, without doing additional research, you may have difficulty locating certain census records or be unable to pinpoint the exact location of your ancestor's residence. Refer to maps from the time when your ancestors were alive to ensure you are looking at the correct records and

CENSUS

(Two Examples

RETURN of the MEMBERS of this FAMILY and their VISITORS, BO

Number.	NAME and SURNAME.		RELATION to Head of Family.	RELIGIOUS PROFESSION.	
	Christian Name.	Surname.			
1	John Stanislaus	Joyce	Head of family	Roman Catholic	R
2	Mary	Joyce	Wife	Do	
3	James Augustin	Joyce	Son	Do	
4	Margaret Alice	Joyce	Daughter	Do	
5	John Stanislaus	Joyce	Son	Do.	
6	Charles Patrick	Joyce	Son	Do.	
7	George Alfred	Joyce	Son	Do	
8	Eileen	Joyce	Daughter	Do	
9	May Kathleen	Joyce	do	Do	
10	Eva Mary	Joyce	do	Do	
11	Florence	Joyce	do	Do	
12	Mabel	Joyce	do	Do	
13					
14					
15					

I hereby certify, as required by the Act 63 Vic., cap. 6, s. 6 (1), tha foregoing Return is correct, according to the best of my knowledge and belie

Henry Hawe

(he mode of filling up this Table are given on the other side.)

FORM A.

No. on Form B. **8**

...ERS, SERVANTS, &c., who slept or abode in this House on the night of SUNDAY, the 31st of MARCH, 1901.

CATION.	AGE.		SEX.	RANK, PROFESSION, OR OCCUPATION.	MARRIAGE.	WHERE BORN.	IRISH LANGUAGE.	If Deaf and Dumb; Dumb only; Blind; Imbecile or Idiot; or Lunatic.
...hether he or she and Write," can ...d" only, ...not Read."	Years on last Birth-day.	Months for Infants under one Year.	Write "M" for Males and "F" for Females.	State the Particular Rank, Profession, Trade, or other Employment of each person. Children or young persons attending a School, or receiving regular instruction at home, should be returned as *Scholars*. [Before filling this column you are requested to read the Instructions on the other side.]	Whether "Married," "Widower," "Widow," or "Not Married."	If in Ireland, state in what County or City; if else-where, state the name of the Country.	Write the word "IRISH" in this column opposite the name of each person who speaks IRISH *only*, and the words "IRISH & ENGLISH" opposite the names of those who can speak both languages. In other cases no entry should be made in this column.	Write the respective infirmities opposite the name of the afflicted person.
...urite	51		M.	Government Pensioner	Married	City of Cork		
...o	39		F.	—	Do	Co. Dublin		
...o	19		M	Student	not married	Co. Dublin	Irish & English	
...o	17		F.		Do	do do		
...o	16		M.	Student	Do	do do	Irish & English	
...o	14		M	Student	Do	do do		
...o	13		M	Student	Do	Co. Wicklow		
...o	12		F		Do	do do		
...o	11		F		Do	do do		
...o	10		F.		Do	do do		
...o	9		F		Do	Co. Dublin		
...o	8		F.		Do	City of Dublin		

I believe the foregoing to be a true Return.

John Stanislaus Joyce

(...nature of Enumerator.)   (**Signature of Head of Family**).

---

also check censuses for towns or areas on either side of a border.

- Not all census records are complete: some have missing pages; others no longer survive, because of repository fires, warfare or intentional destruction.

- Many census records are not indexed, which can make them difficult to locate.

Clearly and legibly completed by the enumerator, this 1901 Census of Ireland return for the Joyce family provides fascinating insights into the social standards of the times. Not only are the names, genders and ages of all members of the household included, but the form also documents birthplaces, religious affiliation, education level, and employment status.

Much can be revealed about a person through a census record. The 1901 record shown here is for Major Bridges Webb and his family.

Alex Myers can use this census record to fill in the blanks in her family tree for Major William Bridges Webb.

From the number of servants listed, one can assume the Bridges Webbs family had achieved economic success at the time of the census.

Administrative County				London				The undermentioned Ho

Civil Parish of Paddington	Ecclesiastical Parish of All Saints	County Borough, Municipal Borough, or Urban District of Paddington	Ward of

Cols 1	2	3	4	5	6	7	8	9	10	11
No of Schedule	ROAD, STREET, &c., and No. or NAME of HOUSE	In-habited	In Occupa-tion	Not in Occupa-tion	Building	Number of Rooms occupied if less than five	Name and Surname of each Person	RELATION to Head of Family	Condition as to Marriage	Age last Birthday of
										Males / F
294	25 Talbot Sq	1					Arthur Lou Ellis	Head	M	43
							Mary A Do	Wife	M	
							Henry L Do	Son		6
							Marion D Do	Daur		
							Helen M Hanikel	Lady Nurse	S	
							Susan Sandy	Servant	S	
							Maria Hawkins	Do	S	
							Amelia R Spurr	Do	S	
							Suzspe Humphrys	Do	S	
295	23 Do	1					Frederick K Mitchell	Head	Widr	46
							Percy K Do	Son	S	19
							Helen M Do	Sister	S	
							Mary Foster	Servant	S	
							Isobel A Childs	Do	S	
							Lena M Do	Do	S	
296	21 Do	1					W. Bridges Webb	Head	M	52
							Caroline B Do	Wife	M	
							Cyril E B Yeates	Stepson	S	26
							John E B Webb	Son	S	19
							Violet B Do	Daur		
							Charlotte L Day	Servant	S	
							Elizabeth Harris	Do	S	
							Mary E Aldridge	Do	S	
							Emily E Wright	Do	S	
297	19 Do	1					Charlotte E Haldane	Head	Wid	
							James A L Do	Son	S	38
							Charlotte W L Do	Daur	S	
							Honey E L Hogg	Grandaur		
							Florence E Nalder	Governess	S	
							Sarah Bincham	Servant	S	
							Rosina A Robinson	Do	S	

4	Total of Schedules of Houses and of Tenements with less than Five Rooms	4						Total of Males and of Females...		8

NOTE—Draw your pen through such words of the headings as are inapplicable.

John Bridges Webb worked as a grain merchant's clerk. Was his father also his employer?

Cyril Yeates' birthplace, Westmoreland Kendal, provides a clue to the origins of the Yeates family, including Caroline Beatrice Yeates, Major Bridges Webb's wife. Her lineage should also be researched for blood ties.

are situate within the boundaries of the

	Municipal Borough / Urban District	Rural District of ____	Parliamentary Borough or Division of *South Paddington* of	Town or Village or Hamlet of

13	14	15	16	17
PROFESSION OR OCCUPATION	Employer, Worker, or Own account	If Working at Home	WHERE BORN	If (1) Deaf and Dumb (2) Blind (3) Lunatic (4) Imbecile, feeble-minded
Barrister at Law *Solicit*			Devon Exeter	/
			India	/
			London Kensington	
			Do Do	
Lady Nurse (domestic)			Lancaster Farnsworth	/
Cook Do			Kent Herne Hill	
Parlourmaid Do			Somerset Withypool	
Housemaid Do			London Paddington	
Do Do			Surrey Thames Ditton	/
Solicitor & Under Sheriff for (Court of Justice)			Cambs Sishalford	/
Undergraduate Camb:			London	
no occupation			Sussex St Leonards	/
Cook domestic			Cambs West Wickham	/
Parlourmaid do			Surrey Bisley	
Housemaid do			Do Do	/
Grain Merchant Major H.A.C Employer			Dorset Wareham	/
Living on own means			London Brompton	
Grain Merchants' Clerk	Worker		London Nottinghill Gate	
			Do Do	
Lady's maid (domestic)			Herts Waltham Abbey	
Cook domestic			Carmarthenshire Llanydd	/
Parlourmaid do			Norfolk Pulham St Mary Magdalen's	/
Housemaid do			London Bayswater	
Living on own means			Notts Misterton	/
Army Captain Infantry			Scotland	/
			Do	/
			Bangoon Burmah	/
Governess *School*			St George Barrow-in-Furness *Lancs*	
Lady's maid domestic			Kent Sevenoaks	/
Cook (dom)			Herts Ware	/

Census records: finding out more

Problem

Alex Myers has a copy of the census record for her ancestor William Bridges Webb (see pages 94–5). What clues point to further research?

Solution

◻ This record is filled with genealogical details. Not only does it state the exact location of the residence occupied by William Bridges Webb (listed as HH) and his household at the time of the 1901 census, it also lists individual residents by name, their relationship to the HH, marital status and ages (by gender). The document also indicates each person's occupation and birth place.

◻ Individual names contain abbreviations: try to identify these secondary names. Are they maiden names or names taken from other relatives? If so, who were they?

◻ William Bridges Webb's occupation is identified as 'Grain Merchant Major H.A.C.' and he was an 'employer'. Where did he work? What is the H.A.C.? Did he work at both professions at the same time? Where and how? What kind of career did he have with the H.A.C.? Do any records of his military service survive?

◻ His birth place is also identified. Try to locate records from that area.

◻ A 'stepson' is identified. Whose son is this? Have you identified the other parent? Does his birth place provide a clue to the whereabouts of other relatives or other records?

◻ A 'son' worked for William Bridges Webb as a 'Grain Merchants' Clerk'. Did he progress within the company after this census was taken? What other positions or occupations did he have? Did he marry and have children?

◻ The record also lists several servants. What does that tell you about Bridges Webb's financial and social status? What can you interpret about the family's lifestyle from this information?

◻ Does the house still exist? Are there property or probate records related to this residence?

Old photographs, like this one of Major William Bridges Webb, can help to bring documents such as census records to life.

England, Wales and Scotland Census Records Highlights by Decade

- **1801** (first census): basic population count tallied according to who was at home on the night of the census.

- **1811 to 1831**: basic population counts.

- **1841**: first census to record individual names of all present; also lists street address and house name, family members by gender, occupation, age (people over the age of 15 had their ages approximated to the nearest five years, e.g., a person aged 27 was recorded as age 25) and if members were born within the county.

- **1851**: records exact ages, relationships between family members, marital status and birth place. A separate census of places of worship was also taken.

- **1891**: adds the number of occupied rooms in the house; Welsh speakers were also noted specifically.

- **1931**: destroyed during World War II.

- **1941**: no census; national registration initiated with the issue of identity cards.

US Census Records Highlights by Decade

- **1790** (the first census): lists HH by name, notes numbers of free white males aged 16 and older, free white males under age 16, free white females, other free persons, slaves.

- **1800 to 1840**: as 1790, but further divides categories to include, for example, number of free white males and females in different age groups; also states the number of 'Indians taxed' (or those who did not live on reservations).

- **1850 & 1860**: identify each member of household by name and note places of birth (state or country); identify race, gender, disabilities and other details.

- **1870**: first census to identify former slaves by full name; addition of 'Indian' as a racial category.

- **1880**: relationships between family members identified; this special census counts all 'Indians not taxed' (those living on reservations) and documents tribal name, number of people in each household, type of dwelling, Indian name and translation, relationships, physical descriptions, occupations and much more.

- **1890**: nearly the entire census was destroyed by fire when the Commerce Building in Washington, D.C., burned in 1921; only fragments survive.

- **1900**: immigration information first reported, i.e., year of immigration and citizenship status of individuals aged over 21.

- **1910**: adds military status during Civil War.

- **1920**: also notes whether individual owns or rents house, his or her native language, ability to speak English and business status.

- **1930**: adds present employment and veteran status. This is the most recent census currently accessible to the public.

Ireland Census Records Highlights by Decade

- **1901** (earliest surviving census): includes each family member's full name, age, gender, relationship to HH, occupation, marital status, religion, county or country of birth, literacy and whether individual spoke Irish.

- **1911**: adds number of years a woman was married to present husband, total number of children and number of living children.

- **Post-1911** censuses not yet available to the public.

Long before civil registration, the task of recording vital details fell to the clergy, who recorded (not always accurately) names, dates and places of major life events.

The widespread civil registration of births, marriages and deaths did not come into effect in Europe and the United States until the latter part of the 19th century and in many countries was adopted only as recently as the mid-20th century. Nevertheless, family history researchers should not despair about locating ancestors' vital details. Centuries before the advent of civil registration, clergy were recording the details surrounding major life events. Religious records provide the ideal complement to civil registrations, particularly during times when civil records were not kept or have been destroyed by fire, flood or warfare.

The 24th session of the Council of Trent in 1563 first formally required parish priests to document the particulars of marriages and baptisms in a book, but Roman Catholic clergy in many European countries had long maintained such records. In fact, parish registers in France date back to 1334. In England and Wales parishes began recording births, marriages and burials at least as early as 1538 and made the practice obligatory under an Act of Parliament passed in 1597. By then, the Church of England had become the official religion and, like their Roman Catholic counterparts, Anglican priests maintained parish records, which were used to prove legally an individual's right to an inheritance and social standing, the ability to hold public office or eligibility to obtain poor relief.

Baptism Solemnized in the Parish of *Bloxwich in the County of Staff.*					
When Baptized.	Child's Christian Name.	Parents' Name.		Abode.	Quality,
		Christian.	Surname.		
1870 May 29 No. 75	*Ada.*	*William and Mary*	*Wilkes.*	*Bloxwich*	*M*

The above is a true Copy of the Baptismal Register of the Parish aforesaid, extracted this ___ *22nd*

in the Year of our Lord One Thousand Eight Hundred and *Seventy five*

By me, C

London: Shaw & Sons, Law Publishers, Fetter-lane.

Baptismal records, such as this one for Ada Wilkes, are often simple in format but contain a wealth of information. This record not only identifies the parents' names and the date of baptism, it also reveals that William Wilkes worked as a machinist.

Marie Clayton's ancestor, Ada Barker, the daughter of William and Mary Wilkes, was baptized in 1870 in Bloxwich, Staffordshire.

Looking at baptismal registers

Problem

Marie Clayton has gathered numerous records for her ancestors, including those for her great-great grandfather, William Barker and his wife, Ada. She is particularly proud of Ada's baptismal register and wonders what clues the document contains for additional research.

Solution

☐ Interestingly, Ada's baptismal register fails to indicate where the ceremony took place. However, the name of the parish, Bloxwich, in the county of Staffordshire, is listed.

☐ Marie should look in a local directory or on the Internet or contact the applicable county or town council for the name of the parish church that existed when the baptism took place in 1870.

☐ Marie may then decide to visit the church in person, perhaps to do research on the Wilkes family in the archives in the adjoining cemetery or inside the church itself. She should focus both on William and Mary, Ada's parents, and on Ada herself.

☐ Noting the discrepancy between the dates when the baptism actually took place and when it was registered – a gap of five years, Marie should also try to clarify whether the family continuously lived at the same address in Bloxwich or moved around the parish during those five years.

☐ William Wilkes identified his occupation as 'Machinist'. Did he work for himself or for a local or distant business? Identifying the names and locations of businesses employing machinists in the 1870s can help Marie determine the nature of her ancestor's trade and possibly provide insight into the family's lifestyle and role with their community.

Types of religious records

- baptismal and christening registrations

- marriage records and religious contracts

- deaths, funerals and burials

- Holocaust records

- tombstones and memorials

- parish and diocesan registers

- confirmation records and communion books

- church books and minutes

- membership lists or rolls

- parish census and family registers

- household examination rolls

- bar and bat mitzvah records

- pew rentals

- newsletters

- published congregation histories

- local histories

- ordination records

- clergy and member biographies

- clergy papers, personal correspondence and writings

Locating parish records

An excellent starting point when researching parish records is the Family History Library or one of its branch Family History Centres. The LDS centres store microfilm copies for many countries, including Denmark, Eastern European nations (such as Hungary, Slovakia and the Czech Republic), Greece (Greek Orthodox diocesan records), Portugal, Spain, Sweden and the UK. However, FHL microfilm records are not necessarily complete, so if you cannot find records of your ancestor, your next step should be to contact the church your ancestor attended (assuming it still exists) or the denomination's archives repository.

Churches and other houses of worship often store the records they create to mark the key events in member's lives. Contact staff prior to a visit, and take the opportunity to enjoy the setting.

Although the details vary from country to country, most parish registers include the participants' names, the date of the event and the names of parents or witnesses. In order to locate these records, you need to know at least a few key details, such as the full name of the person you are researching, their religious affiliation (not always as obvious as it first seems), the country of origin (which can provide a clue to the religious affliation) and the exact dates of the event or the approximate time period.

As always in family history research, it takes a bit of sleuthing to determine which repository maintains church records. Depending on the nationality of your ancestor, you should try the following repositories first:

- **England and Wales** – records may be stored in the relevant county record office rather than the church.

- **Scotland** – stored centrally in the General Register Office.

- **Northern Ireland and Republic of Ireland** – records may be located in the public record offices in Belfast and Dublin.

- **France** – records may be held by the church, but also check the archives départementales for records created before 1792, when civil registration was instituted.

- **Portugal** – the church, but records may also have been transferred to the district's archives.

- **Spain** – the relevant parish church, which may still hold the records or may have passed them on to the Bishopric Archives for that region.

- **Canada** – much like their European counterparts, Canadian parishes produce registers for births, baptisms, marriages, deaths and burials. Today, these parish registers may be held at the church or in denominational or regional (provincial) archives. The earliest surviving Canadian parish register dates back to 1621.

Settling the New World

Beginning in the 1620s, European emigrants fleeing religious persecution began settling in North America, organizing parishes and other religious communities, constructing churches and synagogues and creating new religious records well before the governmental bodies took on the task of civil registration. Today, scores of religions coexist in the US and Canada; the most common are Protestantism (in its myriad denominations), Roman Catholicism and Judaism. Each produces a variety of records, which keep track of membership, the day-to-day management of the place of worship and congregational activities.

The Roman Catholic and Protestant religions document key events in members' lives, such as baptism or christening, confirmation, marriage and burial. Marriage records created by a church generally include the names of the couple (including the bride's maiden name), witnesses' names, the name of the officiating clergyman and the date and location of the wedding. They often also contain the couple's ages, birth places and current residences. Baptismal or christening documents usually include the names of the child and parents, their residence(s), baptism date, the name of the minister or priest conducting the baptism and godparents' or sponsors' names. Baptismal records may also indicate the child's birth date and the father's occupation. Burial records routinely list the name of the deceased, the date and cause of death, the clergy person overseeing the funeral and/or burial, the names of the spouse and surviving children and the burial place.

Churches also create records about the history and practices of the religious community, the clergy and church committees and even the building itself. These documents can give researchers great insights into their ancestors' lives and the religious beliefs that guided them.

Using synagogue records

Religious records for life events occurring before marriage, including birth and the bar/bat mitzvah, are rare in the Jewish religion. However, family historians researching Jewish ancestry will find genealogical information in a variety of resources, such as marriage contracts (ketubot) and divorce records (gets) and on synagogue memorials known as 'yahrzeit plaques' and tombstones. These sources normally document the date of the event (according to the Hebrew and secular calendars), the place where the event occurred and the religious names of the participants or the deceased.

Clues to an ancestor's background come from interpreting the religious names, the shemot ha'kodesh, which include the name of the person and that of his or her father (ben indicates 'son of'; bat indicates 'daughter of'). Ketubot also contain the signatures of the couple and of the rabbi performing the ceremony. Once the contract is signed, it is presented to the bride for safekeeping; so, when seeking out marriage records, your first stop should be your family's own archives or filing cabinets. Synagogues do maintain listings of individuals and their death dates, but you will need to know to which congregation the deceased or a close relative actually belonged to locate the records.

Holocaust records

One of the 20th century's greatest tragedies, the Holocaust entailed the genocide of more than six million Jews and took the lives of Europeans of other ancestry as well. Essentially, every individual of Jewish heritage has relatives who died during this horrific human disaster, which is also referred to as the Shoah. The calamity produced an array of records, which family historians will find of considerable use.

Concentration camp records ('death books') include photographs, identity cards, documents about prisoners and the management of the camp, and detailed lists of victims, with their full names, parents' names, spouse's name, date and place of birth, date and circumstances of death, nationality and former occupation.

Some 46 million concentration camp documents are stored at the International Tracing Services Archives in Bad Arolsen, Germany. The American Red Cross Holocaust and War Victims Tracing and Information Service acts as liaison. Contact it at: 4800 Mt. Hope Drive, Baltimore, Maryland 21215 (410-24-2090), URL: www.redcross.org/services/intl/holotrace. The US National Archives also holds some concentration camp registers.

Yizkor books, which were written or produced in Yiddish or Hebrew with the help of survivors, memorialize specific Jewish communities in Eastern and Central Europe and their Holocaust

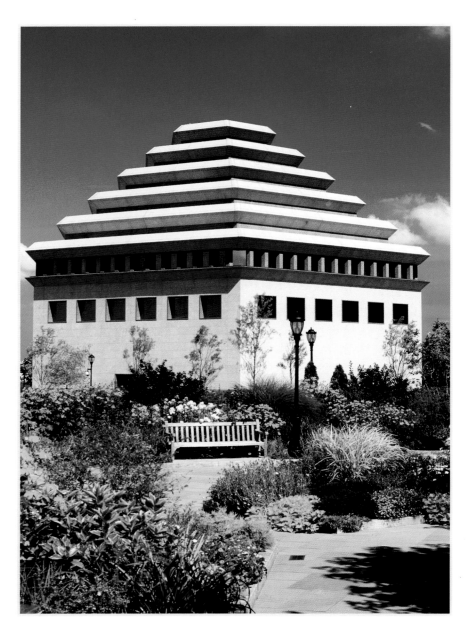

Specialist museums, such as the Museum of Jewish Heritage located in New York City, not only educate visitors about the religious, ethnic or racial group they honour. They often store archival information which the public may access.

victims. They contain biographies, personal remembrances, information on families with no survivors, necrologies (victim lists), photographs, maps and local histories. The world's largest collection of yizkor books is held by Yad Vashem, The Holocaust Martyrs' and Heroes' Remembrance Authority, in Jerusalem. Major collections are also held by libraries and other repositories around the world. Internet researchers can find details at: www.jewishgen.org/Yizkor/yizlibs.html. Begin by searching for people's names.

Hall of Names and Pages of Testimony

are among the most important projects of the world's largest and most comprehensive repository of Holocaust material, Yad Vashem, The Holocaust Martyrs' and Heroes' Remembrance Authority, which has played a key role in the acquisition, conservation and display of millions of records. The Hall of Names houses documents submitted by survivors with details of relatives killed during the Holocaust. Known as the Pages of Testimony, the acid-free papers identify the full name of each victim, his or her date and place of birth, the place of residence and occupation

A page from the death books produced at the Mauthausen concentration camp and seized by American soldiers during its liberation in 1945. The prisoners listed in this excerpt, written in German, were identified by their full names and as Jews.

before the war, parents' and spouses' names and where and when they died. Records sometimes include photographs of the deceased. Access to the records is possible by visiting the Hall of Names in Jerusalem or via the Central Database of Shoah Victims' Names on the website. Contact Yad Vashem at: PO 3477, Jerusalem 91034 Israel (972-2-6443400) URL: www.yadvashem.org.

The Benjamin and Vladka Meed Registry of Jewish Holocaust Survivors documents lives of survivors who went to the US after World War II. The registry includes more than 185,000 records related to survivors and their families and gives names of survivors from all backgrounds living all over the world. The registry is co-ordinated by the United States Holocaust Memorial Museum, 100 Raoul Wallenberg Place SW, Washington, DC 20024-2126 (202-488-6130) URL: www1.ushmm.org/remembrance/registry.

Unpublished documents and other artefacts, such as passports, diaries, correspondence and deportation lists, are housed in repositories such as Yad Vashem, the United States Holocaust Memorial Museum and the Museum of Jewish Heritage in New York City.

Family historians who visit ancestral gravesites often neglect interment and funeral home records, which may be located well away from the cemetery.

Certainly, headstones offer a range of vital details about the deceased and provide pointers, in the form of words or symbols, for further research. They also allow us to honour the dead, acknowledge the fact of their existence and feel a spiritual bond to our ancestors. But the value of interment and funeral parlour records to family history research is at least as crucial.

Interment records

Often called cemetery or sexton's records, records of interment not only document the site and circumstances of a burial but also identify the history of ownership of each plot. Types of interment records and their general contents include:

- **cemetery plot deeds** – name of owner, exact location, plot price.

- **interment registers or records** – name of deceased, birth place and dates, doctor's name, cause of death, place of death and date, sexton's name, gravesite location, names of parents, marital status, spouse's name.

- **interment cards** – in addition to the information listed in the interment register, the cards annotate the deceased's religion and type of coffin.

Funeral parlour files

The sensitive nature of their occupation requires undertakers to obtain several different types of official documents, which give them permission to handle and transport a deceased person.

WALTER CRAVEN LIMITED   FUNERAL DIRECTORS

D. W. CRAVEN
D. R. CRAVEN

CRAVEN LODGE
BROADGREEN ROAD
LIVERPOOL L13 5SG
Tel: 051-228 3900

Mrs F.M.Kilbride,
127 Queens Drive,
Liverpool 13.

18th Spet. 1978

To furnishing the funeral of the late:

	£	
Sarah Flaherty	225	00
Disbursements		
Grave charges, Allerton Cemetery	43	00
Priest's fee, Allerton Cemetery	2	00
Death Notice, Liverpool Echo	13	78
£	283	78

RECEIVED
WITH THANKS
18.9.78.
WALTER CRAVEN LTD
D.R. Craven

Also at
HUYTON HOUSE, LIVERPOOL ROAD, HUYTON
Telephone: 051-489 1212

Funeral parlour records often provide leads for further research. Look beyond the deceased's name and burial place, and record other items, such as the name of the person who paid for the funeral expenses, which is shown on the accompanying invoice. Is Mrs. F.M. Kilbride another relative who should be researched?

Using cemetery records

Problem

I have obtained cemetery records for a relative from the funeral directors who handled the burial. What key information should I note for further research?

Solution

- In addition to the deceased's name, the cemetery record lists the exact location of the gravesite and when the relative was actually buried there. Note these carefully.

- Note the the name of the individual to whom the receipt was made. What is the relationship of this person to the deceased?

- Note the reference to 'Death Notice, Liverpool Echo'. Seek out a copy of this obituary to see if it will provide additional family details.

- Note the reference to the 'Priest's fee'. Do additional research on this entry.

While they are not aimed at genealogists, these records are an often-neglected but valuable resource for research. They include the following types of records:

Death certificates, which include the deceased's full name, birth place and date, death place and date, age at death, burial place, marital status and spouse's name, date of marriage, parents' full names, residence at death, former occupation and military service. The responsibility for completing a death certificate will often fall to the undertaker.

Burial or cremation permits grant the undertaker permission for burial or cremation of the deceased. These permits are generated by the Board of Health and are also stored in cemetery files. Besides vital details, the permits include cause of death, occupation, burial site or crematorium, plot number and owner.

Transit permits are required to transport a deceased person. Details are similar to burial permits, but transit permits also identify the means of transport, e.g. train, aeroplane.

Other information in the records may include: list of children, siblings, other relatives, former residences, educational background, memberships, religion, interests and achievements.

Other documents found in funeral parlour files include: copies of birth and marriage certificates, wills, insurance records, military service records and photographs.

WHEN RESEARCHING FUNERAL HOME RECORDS…

 Do

- contact the mortuary by written correspondence before a visit.

- specify the information you are seeking and include the deceased's full name, the record type and the burial date or time frame.

- offer to pay the expenses you incur if the funeral parlour can meet your request.

- ask funeral parlour staff for assistance in identifying the names of other mortuaries if you determine they do not hold your ancestor's records.

- be patient: staff are often busy and records are not necessarily located on site so it may take some time for staff to obtain them.

 DON'T

- assume that all funeral directors will willingly open their files to the public, especially if they contain sensitive or confidential information.

- expect to view the records without an appointment.

- assume that the funeral parlour presently located in the town where your ancestor lived is necessarily the one that arranged his or her burial. Owners change over time and funeral parlours do go out of business.

- neglect to check with other local organizations, such as historical societies or the public library, which may hold copies of the relevant interment records that you can view.

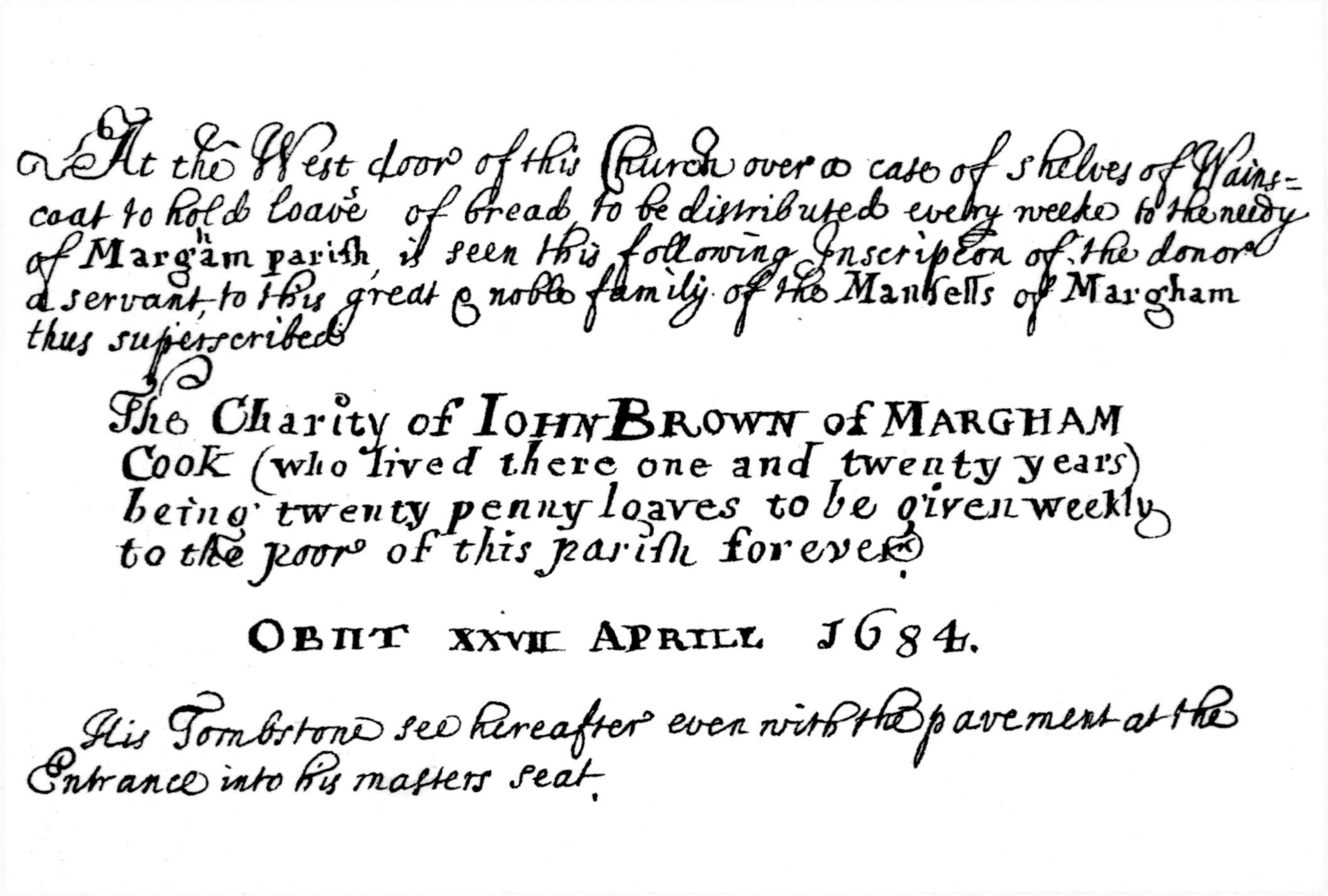

At the West door of this Church over a case of shelves of Wainscoat to hold loaves of Bread to be distributed every weeke to the needy of Margam parish, is seen this following Inscription of the donor a servant to this great & noble family of the Mansells of Margham thus superscribed

The Charity of IOHN BROWN of MARGHAM Cook (who lived there one and twenty years) being twenty penny loaves to be given weekly to the poor of this parish for ever.

OBIIT XXVII APRILL 1684.

His Tombstone see hereafter even with the pavement at the Entrance into his masters seat.

An inscription honours the memory of John Brown of Margham, deceased cook for the Mansell family, in whose name loaves of bread were given each week to the poor.

Other burial records

Parish registers are among the best resources for UK burial information. In these registers researchers can find the deceased's full name, date and place of death, age, cause of death, occupation and details about the person who registered the death.

Besides being held by the Anglican churches themselves, parish registers are also stored and accessible to the public in county record offices. Burial records for other religious groups are generally kept at cemetery offices. The Family Records Centre and the National Library of Wales maintain collections of Nonconformist records. Larger town councils and local authorities also store interment records.

National Burial Index (for England and Wales)

Arguably the best starting point when seeking UK burial records is the National Burial Index (NBI), a computerized index of burials produced by the Federation of Family History Societies. Proposed in 1994 but not begun until 2001, the NBI is a work continuously in progress. It presently contains well over 5.4 million entries spanning the time period from 1538 to 2000. Derived from parish registers, bishops' transcripts and other relevant records, the NBI database includes the full name of the deceased, burial date, age at death, where the record is located and the name of the person or organization who transcribed the record. For more information, visit the FFHS website at: www.ffhs.org.uk/ General/Projects/NBI.htm.

Available on CD-ROM, a second edition of the NBI was released to the public in late 2004, bringing the total number of entries to more than 13.2 million records. A similar project is underway for Scotland.

The burial record shown here lists individual burials by year and then subdivides them by month, date and the name of the deceased. As shown here, a person's status ('Sir Richard Baker Knighte') may also be noted, and one entry records the circumstances of death.

Aprill anno Domini 1594

1	Bur:	Alexander Tayler sergeant to mr Docter Jeremie
14	Bur:	a pore Twitte
16	Bur:	a Chile wid of Twitte
18	Bur:	Alis Colle uxor Johannis
21	Bur:	Alexander Sneade

Maye 1594

2	Bur:	Alis Twitte uxor Abrahami
7	Bur:	Nathaniell Twitte
26	Bur:	Margret Foster uxor Thoma

June 1594

5	Bur:	Widdowe Foster
10	Bur:	Chrystopher Paynetres
18	Bur:	Sir Richard Baker Knighte
21	Bur:	Richard Aborrewes killed in a ffray
21	Bur:	Richard Coole

July 1594

| 22 | Bur: | Thomas Seberry |

August 1594

2	Bur:	Thomas Lillie
26	Bur:	Mr william Fowle his Talorer
30	Bur:	Alis Hide uxor Roberti
30	Bur:	John And

September 1594

6	Bur:	Margery Boyer
8	Bur:	Mary Milles
11	Bur:	Craters wide or wyfe

October 1594

| 20 | Bur: | Richard Tarrante |
| 26 | Bur: | Joan Towe |

Novemb Nulli

December 1594

2	Bur:	Paynetee Larrin
2	Bur:	Elizabeth Nash
10	Bur:	Rebecca Drawlor
16	Bur:	Thomas Christeden Smyly
21	Bur:	Richard Lewes
22	Bur:	Chas Woodland
27	Bur:	Joan Dowtopp uxor willmi a godly & good woman

Willm Eddy Vicar
James Ange

Your ancestor's land records can provide a variety of details that you might not come across when searching other record types.

Land records are concerned with the sale and purchase of real property. Depending on who sold the land (e.g. a governmental entity or a private individual), the document recording the transaction will be in the form of either a patent or a deed. Historically, transfer of land ownership has been a complex process. In many countries, including Ireland and Scotland, private individuals have only recently been allowed to purchase the lands they and their ancestors worked and occupied over a period of time.

These extensive, highly specific documents often cover a lengthy period. From them, you should be able to identify the chain of ownership over the years, place an ancestor in a location at a specific time and trace your family's movement within or through an area. Even more importantly, land records also contain property descriptions and detailed locations, lists of residents, slave information (slaves were not emancipated throughout the US until 1865) and information about female ancestors (who owned 'dower rights', or one-third of their husband's land. Before a man could sell the land, his wife – or widow – had to agree to the sale). They also enable you to interpret relationships between the persons identified in the records – and, therefore, their links to you.

US land records

Land records in the US can be distinguished by whether or not the property is located within a 'State-Land State' or a 'Public-Land State' and also by the county in which the sale of land occurred.

State-Land States include the 13 original colonies (i.e., Connecticut, Delaware, Georgia, Maryland, Massachusetts, New Hampshire, New Jersey, New York, North Carolina, South Carolina, Pennsylvania, Rhode Island and Virginia), along with Hawaii, Kentucky, Tennessee, Texas and Vermont. Here, the original seller (or grantor) was the colony, territory or state that had legal control over, and authority to sell, the lands.

Begin your search for these records in state archives or county offices. Deeds are generally recorded in deed books and filed with the state or county. When beginning your research, review the grantor and grantee indexes, which should point you to any other deeds that are associated with your ancestors' property. Then, find the deeds you want in the relevant deed book and make a copy or transcribe the data exactly as it appears.

Record types include:

- warrant – identifies the tract of land, original owner and value.

- survey – details the boundaries of the property as measured in 'metes' and 'bounds', often with a map or written statement.

- patent – the title certificate, which identifies the 'grantee', the first private owner of the site.

- deed – confirms any subsequent sale of the property.

Public-Land States were created by the US federal government with land acquired either by purchase or treaties following wars with other nations (such as France or Spain) or by legal claim after a period of intentional settlement (Florida, Oregon and Washington). Later sales of the land are recorded in deed books, which are held at county courthouses.

Deeds for Public-Land States normally include:

- names of the seller and buyer

- sale price

- description of the property, including a plat map (see page 157)

- residences of the seller and buyer

- signatures of the seller and his wife (as applicable)

- witness signatures

Tract books include records of the initial transfer of land from the government to private individuals and are stored at the National Archives. Of particular interest to family historians, these books contain abstracts for individual properties and the chain of ownership, which lists the names of all of the property's owners over time, starting with the original grantee. When doing your research, be sure to look at the deeds held by these other owners, who may also be related to you.

As pioneers made their way across the North American continent, they staked land claims and began new lives with the construction of log cabins.

Using a land claim record

These three land claim records date back to February 1847 and relate to property then located in what became the states of Oregon and Washington.

Problem

I have a land claim record for my great-great grandfather, who migrated to what is now Washington State in the mid-19th century. How do I find the exact location of the property?

Solution

Samuel Hancock, the grantee, probably settled the large parcel of land before US government ownership. Therefore, he had a strong and valid claim to the property, which (you should note) is in a Public-Land State. This land claim record uses general landmarks to describe the location of the parcel (at the time, this description would have been quite specific). So, in order to locate the actual property, you will have to do some further investigation, as follows:

You will see from the land claim record that you already have the date, the county name and a neighbour's name, Al Simmons. You also know that the site was alongside Puget Sound. Since the Puget Sound covers a large swathe of landscape, your first step should be to contact the Lewis County Courthouse in Washington State to see if it holds land-entry case files dating to 1847. If it does not, contact the National Archives in Washington, DC, which stores tract books for the Western States.

Next, use the appropriate index to find the entry for Samuel Hancock and any entries for Al Simmons.

Record whatever information you find, including the location, acreage and price and the date and place of the land entry.

Obtain a road atlas and topographical map. Plot the details you have extracted from the records.

Identify other landmarks in the area, e.g., churches, cemeteries and houses, which may be associated with your ancestor or contain information about him.

Also check the records for his age, place of birth, citizenship, military service, literacy, economic status and information about family members.

Document the above details so that you can use them as leads for further research.

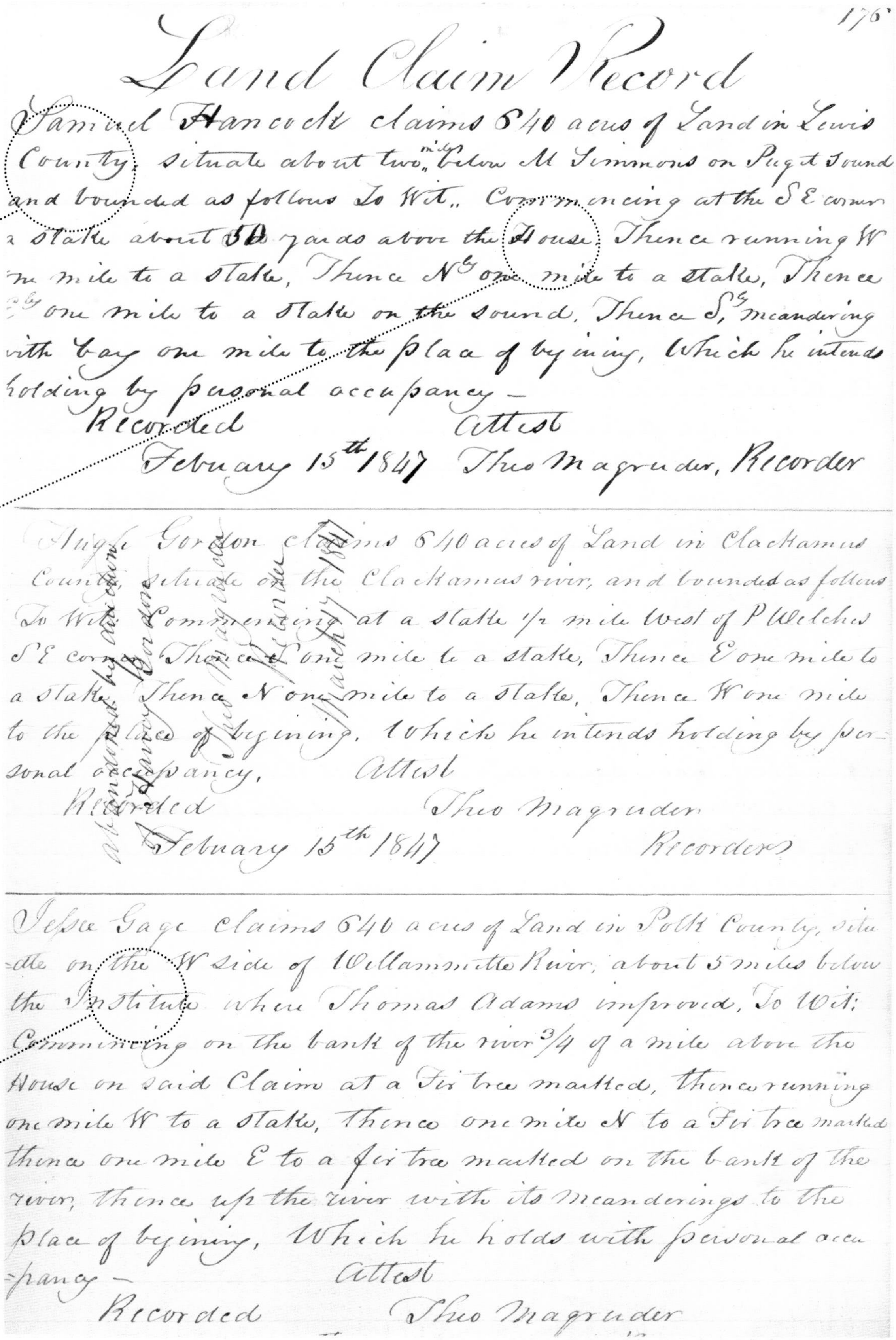
176

Land Claim Record

Samuel Hancock claims 640 acres of Land in Lewis County, situate about two miles below M Simmons on Puget Sound and bounded as follows To Wit,, Commencing at the S E corner a stake about 50 yards above the House, Thence running W one mile to a stake, Thence Nly one mile to a stake, Thence Ely one mile to a stake on the sound, Thence Sly meandering with bay one mile to the place of begining, Which he intends holding by personal occupancy –

Recorded Attest

February 15th 1847 Theo Magruder, Recorder

Hugh Gordon claims 640 acres of Land in Clackamas County, situate on the Clackamas river, and bounded as follows To Wit Commencing at a stake 1/2 mile West of P Welches S E corner Thence S one mile to a stake, Thence E one mile to a stake, Thence N one mile to a stake, Thence W one mile to the place of begining, Which he intends holding by personal occupancy, Attest

Recorded Theo Magruder

February 15th 1847 Recorders

Abandoned by Hugh Gordon ... Theo Magruder Recorder March 1847

Jesse Gage claims 640 acres of Land in Polk County, situate on the W side of Willammette River, about 5 miles below the Institute where Thomas Adams improved, To Wit: Commencing on the bank of the river 3/4 of a mile above the House on said Claim at a Fir tree marked, thence running one mile W to a stake, thence one mile N to a Fir tree marked thence one mile E to a fir tree marked on the bank of the river, thence up the river with its meanderings to the place of begining, Which he holds with personal occupancy –

Attest

Recorded Theo Magruder

Determine to which state the land claim record belongs: is it a Public-Land State or a State-Land State?

Try to pinpoint the location of the 'House'. Look for the stakes when attempting to identify the site if the house no longer stands.

What is the 'Institute' mentioned in relationship to Thomas Adams? Who was Thomas Adams?

The Family History Library also holds microfilmed deed records, so, in addition to contacting the applicable county courthouse, you may want to check the local family history centre as well. In due time, you may need to turn to the National Archives or the Bureau of Land Management (BLM) for assistance in locating original land grants. Internet researchers should visit the BLM General Land Office Records website at: www.glorecords.blm.gov.

Other types of US land record include:

- Deeds of sale, deeds of gift, deeds of mortgage, deeds of trust, quit claim deeds and deed releases.

- Deed books also include bills of sale, slave sales, powers of attorney, wills, voter lists and prenuptial agreements.

- Bounty land warrant applications – used as enlistment inducements during wartime, bounty land warrants were granted to soldiers who served during the Revolutionary War, the War of 1812, the French and Indian Wars and the Mexican War. If the service member before the end of the war, his widow or heirs acquired the right to the land grant.

- Homestead applications document the names of the applicant and spouse, family size, present residence, the applicant's birth date or age, the location of the land and the date acquired, and often include as well an immigrant's naturalization or citizenship papers and other documents.

- Donation land entries.

- Land entry case files and individual land claims.

Land records in Great Britain and Ireland

The dramatic changes in land ownership that have occurred since the Middle Ages have resulted in a veritable gold mine of documentary information for family historians tracing their roots in Great Britain and Ireland. Land records vary depending on the era and whether the ancestor was the actual landlord or a tenant, a freeholder or leaseholder, held a position of political power or assumed some religious status.

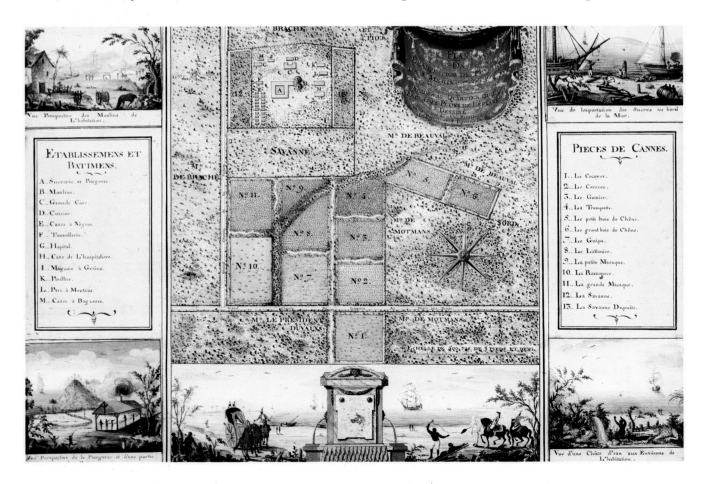

Meticulously hand-drawn, estate maps are historical documents that accurately depict the layout of a property, including the buildings and associated fields. This early 19th century water colour by engineer De Beauvernais shows Chateau de Blerancourt, the estate of Charles B. Fevret of St. Mesmin, Saint Domingue (part of Hispaniola), West Indies.

Mortgage records often provide extensive details of a property, including the legal description, physical layout, types of buildings, previous owners and present buyers.

The Registry of Deeds is one of Ireland's most important genealogical resources. The Registry, which was created in 1708 and is located in Dublin, is comprised of a Surname Index of grantors and a Lands Index identifying the exact locations of properties being sold. The Registry also features copies of registered deeds of sales, leases, marital settlements and wills. The person who submitted the registration information retains the originals and microfilm copies are held by the Family History Library.

Estate and manorial records are among the most fascinating and informative kinds of land records that genealogists will encounter for Britain and Ireland. Created to document virtually every aspect of an estate's management, they relate the entire tenancy history for a property.

These records are located in local record offices, the National Library of Wales, the National Archives at Kew, the National Library of Ireland, the National Archives of Ireland and other repositories. The Family History Library holds some microfilm copies.

Information contained in estate and manorial records includes:

- detailed, hand-drawn estate maps
- rent rolls and leases
- freeholder registers
- lists of tenants, their tenancies and how long they held them
- relationships between tenants
- death dates
- family movement between farms of different sizes
- leases, including those granted for life
- estate surveys, which include tenants' names, farm lists, rents and lease terms
- marriage settlements
- wills
- title deeds, which include the name of the previous owner, the location and date of sale
- account books
- written correspondence

- servant records, which document names of servants, their wages, details of employment and years of service

Other types of British and Irish land records include:

- Domesday Book – the historic survey of William the Conqueror's kingdom in 1086
- Land Registry (England and Wales) – as the governmental department responsible for maintaining the Land Register for England and Wales, the Land Registry provides an online database (Land Register Online, at: www.landregisteronline.gov.uk) for the general public to search for documents for properties in England and Wales that can be identified by an address. Details include a property description, owner's name, the mortgage lender, sale price, rights of way, and any other restrictions.
- Land Registry (Ireland) – located in several county offices, holds folios with land titles and other relevant information.
- Land Commission records (National Archives in Dublin or the Public Record Office in Northern Ireland) – 'topographical index' and 'names index'.
- The Scottish 'general register' – documents land transactions involving more than one county and those associated with Scottish interests overseas.
- Scotland's 'particular register', also known as sasine records, documents changes in land ownership within a single county or city. It is stored at the National Archives of Scotland.
- 'Services of heirs' documents
- Inquisitions post mortem

military records

Virtually every one of us has had a relative or ancestor who served in a branch of the military, as a volunteer or conscriptee, at home or abroad, in peacetime or war.

In order to make the most out of your search for an ancestor's military records, read about the history behind the war in which he or she participated. Learning about specific battles and skirmishes and the state or region's military history will better enable you to place the information you find in its true context.

At some point during your research you will probably want to refer to military records to add more detail to your past. Not surprisingly, each of the world's military branches creates a plethora of records suited to their specific needs and priorities. Not only do these records provide the vital details of service men and women and information about their family members, but they also document the regiments in which they served, where they were stationed and much more.

Service records

The most common type of military record is the service record. As well as vital details, such as age and place of birth, service records typically contain the following information:

- where the person served (duty stations, ships, squadrons)
- performance evaluations and advancement
- training and other qualifications
- awards, medals and letters of commendation
- disciplinary actions
- emergency information/next-of-kin
- type of discharge
- place and date of discharge
- place of intended residence
- information about family members, including next-of-kin and siblings
- religion
- medical history and mention of any service-related injuries.

Some service records also describe the person's physical description and cover some of the family history, such as the names and ages of siblings and parents.

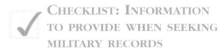

CHECKLIST: INFORMATION TO PROVIDE WHEN SEEKING MILITARY RECORDS

In order to determine if a repository holds your ancestor's military records, you must provide the following information, as completely as possible:

- the service member's full name
- the branch of the military (army, navy, marines, coast guard or national guard) and the regiment, unit, ship or squadron in which he or she served
- the time period or war in which the service member served
- his or her enlisted or officer rank and rating (job type)
- whether or not he or she received a pension
- specific duty stations, as available

US military records

In order to make the most out of your search for an ancestor's military records, read about the historical setting of the war in which he or she participated. Learning about specific battles and skirmishes and the state or region's military history will better enable you to place the information you find in its true context.

Types of US military record include:

- service records
- pension records
- bounty land warrant applications
- enlistment, draft and conscription records
- muster rolls
- navy deck logs
- payroll records
- discharge papers, including the DD-214
- medical cards and medical records
- court martial records
- desertion records
- national military cemetery records
- records from veterans' hospitals and veterans' homes
- registers of lighthouse keepers and records of the Lifesaving Service (predecessors to the US Coast Guard)

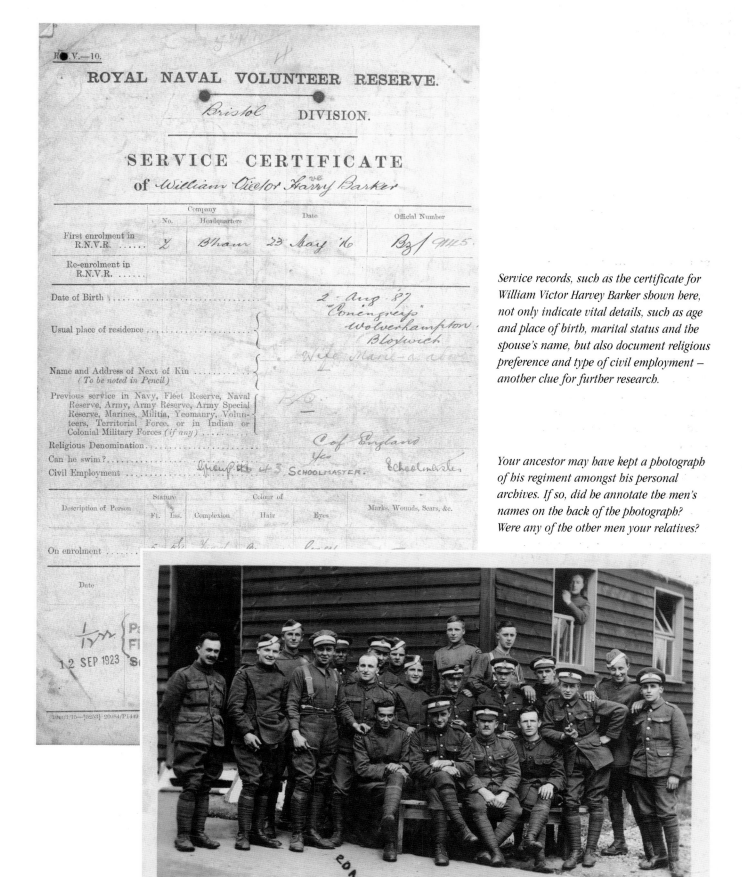

Service records, such as the certificate for William Victor Harvey Barker shown here, not only indicate vital details, such as age and place of birth, marital status and the spouse's name, but also document religious preference and type of civil employment – another clue for further research.

Your ancestor may have kept a photograph of his regiment amongst his personal archives. If so, did he annotate the men's names on the back of the photograph? Were any of the other men your relatives?

Pension records

If you know your ancestor received a pension, begin your research with pension records, as they are often, albeit unintentionally, filled with genealogical data and include supporting documents, such as birth, marriage and death certificates, personal correspondence, affidavits and other informative paperwork.

In the US the NARA holds pension records for military members who served in the armed forces between 1775 and 1916. An invaluable resource for genealogists, military pension records contain an incredible amount of information and clues to further research, as the pension records shown here for Matthew Dowling and his widow, Lee Ann, reveal. This set of documents features the veteran's name, birth date and place, unit and rank, time served, discharge date, discharge papers and even when the veteran died, his residence when making the application, other residences after discharge, the widow's name (including her maiden name, Neal), the place and date of marriage, religion, their marital status when the veteran died and the widow's death date. (NOTE: Pension records often document children's names and whether they are living or deceased.)

MILITARY SERVICE.

NAME OF SOLDIER: Matthew Dowling

Bureau of Pensions, June 4, 1892

SIR:

It is alleged that the above-named man enlisted 11 July, 1864, and served as a private in Co. A, 192 Reg't Pa Inf.

and was discharged at Philadelphia Pa on Nov 11, 1864

No. of prior claim

The War Department will please furnish an official statement in this case, showing date of enrollment and date and mode of termination of service.

War Department,

Record and Pension Division,

JUN 10 1892

Respectfully returned to the

COMMISSIONER OF PENSIONS.

The rolls show that Matthew Dowling

PENSION OFFICE JUN 11 1892

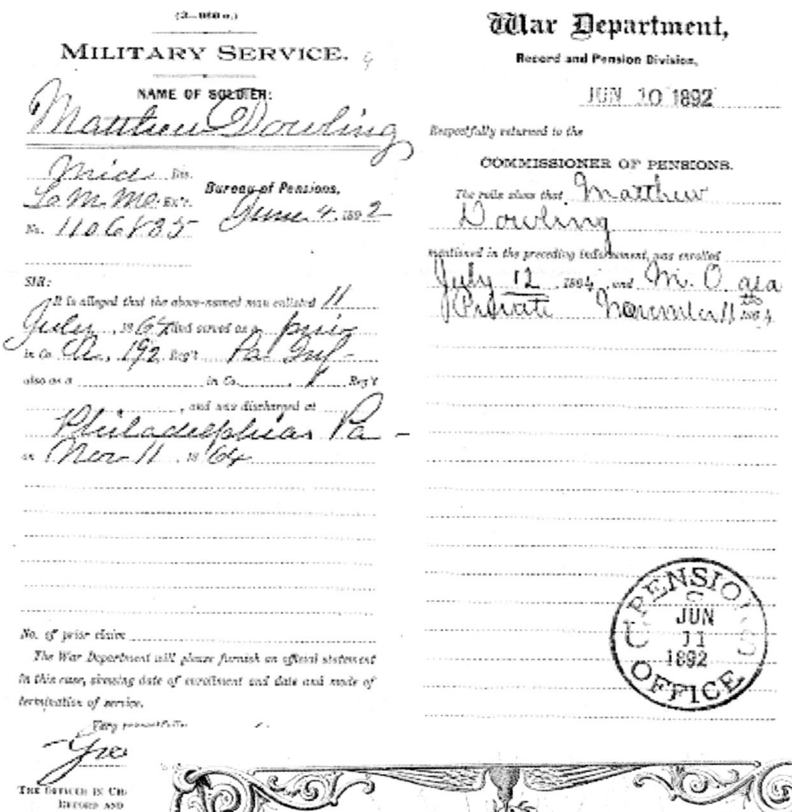

Matthew Dowling's pension certificate features a handwritten number, which is difficult to read. Compare this number to the widow's declaration to ensure its accuracy.

"MARRIAGE IS HONORABLE IN ALL."

This is to Certify that

Mathew Dowling of Grafton W.Va and Lee Ann Neal of Grafton W.Va were united in

HOLY MATRIMONY

on the 23rd day of July in the year of our Lord, One Thousand Eight Hundred and 79 in accordance with the Laws of the State of West Virginia and the usages of Church

J. H. Flanagan
Pastor Pres Ch. Grafton

Witnesses:

H.M. Crider, Publisher, York, Pa.

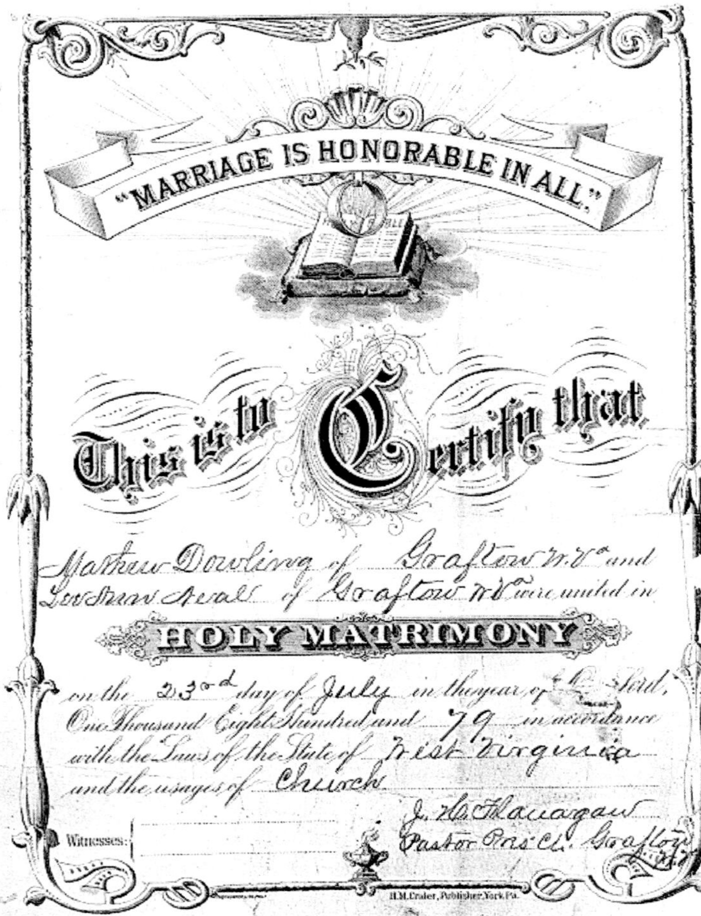

Pension records often include a copy of the service member's marriage certificate, which documents the place and date of the wedding and the wife's maiden name.

3—015.

DECLARATION FOR WIDOW'S PENSION.

Act of April 19, 1908,
Amended by Act of September 8, 1916.

STATE OF *Maryland* COUNTY OF *Allegany* ss:

On this *14th* day of *April* 19 *2?* personally appeared before me, a *Notary Public* within and for the County and State aforesaid, *Lee Ann Dowling* who, being duly sworn by me according to law, declares that she is *60* years of age and that she was born *May 4* *1859* at *Brownsville Pennsylvania*

That she is the widow of *Matthew Dowling* who enlisted *July 11 1864* at *Philadelphia, Pa*, under the name of *Matthew Dowling* as a *Private* (Rank.), in *Co. A, 192 Regiment Pennsylvania Infantry* (Here state company and regiment, if in the Army; or vessels, if in the Navy.) and was honorably discharged *Nov. 11,* 18 *64*, having served ninety days or more during the CIVIL WAR.

That he also served *none*

(Here give a complete statement of all other military, naval, or coast guard service, if any, at whatever time rendered.)

That otherwise than as herein stated said soldier (or sailor) was _____ employed in the United States service.

That she was married to said soldier (or sailor) *July 23*, 18 *79*, under the name of *Lee Ann Neale*, at *Grafton, W. Va.* by *Rev. J. H. Flannagan*, that she had *not* been previously married; that he had *not* been previously married *that she was never divorced from said Matthew Dowling, her late husband*

(Here state all prior marriages of either, naming the names and dates and places of death or divorce of all former husbands or wives.)

and that neither she nor said soldier (or sailor) was ever married otherwise than as stated above.

(If any former husband rendered military or naval service, here describe same and give number of any pension claim based thereon.)

That said soldier (or sailor) died *March 9* 19 *20* at *Westernport, Md.*; that she was *not* divorced from him; and that she has *not* remarried since his death.

That the following are the ONLY children of the soldier (or sailor) who are NOW living and under sixteen years of age, namely:

(If he left no children under sixteen years of age, the claimant should so state.)

| _____ born _____ l. _____ at _____ |
| _____ born _____ l. _____ at _____ |
| _____ born _____ l. _____ at _____ |
| _____ born _____ l. _____ at _____ |

That the above-named child _____ of the soldier (or sailor) {is} {are} now receiving a pension, and that such child _____ {is a} {are} member _____ of her family and _____ cared for by her.

That she has *not* heretofore applied for pension, the number of her former claim being _____ ; that said soldier (or sailor) was _____ a pensioner, the number of his pension certificate being *1106939*

That she makes this declaration for the purpose of being placed on the pension roll of the United States under the provisions of the ACT OF APRIL 19, 1908, as amended by the ACT OF SEPTEMBER 8, 1916.

(1) *W. W. Uhl* (Signature of first witness.)
Westernport, Md. (Address of first witness.)

(2) *T. J. Gilmore* (Signature of second witness.)
Westernport, Md. (Address of second witness.)

Lee Ann Dowling (Claimant's signature in full.)
Westernport, Md. (Claimant's address in full.)

Subscribed and sworn to before me this *3rd* day of *April* 19 *2?*, and I hereby certify that the contents of the above declaration were fully made known and explained to the applicant

Take note of Matthew Dowling's rank and the regiment to which he belonged. His brief enlistment occurred during the American Civil War, prior to his marriage. Why did he only serve for four months?

Another source of marital information, the declaration for widow's pension reveals not only the place and date of the wedding but also the widow's maiden name.

Pension certificates are identified by a number, which is clearly recorded on the widow's declaration. If the certificate has been mislaid, the number can help locate the original.

The date and location of Matthew Dowling's death are clearly recorded.

One of the best starting places when researching your ancestor's military career is the pension record.

Locating US military records

Depending on the time frame and the military branch, US military records created during or after the Civil War may be stored in state archives, the National Archives and Records Administration (NARA) in Washington, D.C., or the National Personnel Records Center (NPRC) in St. Louis, Missouri. Some state archives also hold Confederate Army records.

Before the Civil War, local military units, known as militia, were organized on a voluntary basis. You will find militia records in county courthouses, state archives or libraries and held by some historical societies. After the Civil War, many militia units evolved into the National Guard.

Requesting recent US military records

Privacy and data protection laws now require US repositories to restrict access to living veterans or next-of-kin, or to authorized representatives such as attorneys, doctors and researchers who can provide written authorization from the veteran or next-of-kin. You will need to submit a formal, written request to the appropriate facility in order to obtain copies of military records.

The NPRC requires you to submit a written request, accompanied by the signed authorization of the living veteran, or, if deceased, by his next-of-kin. Be sure to determine exactly what official request forms and any other paperwork you need to prepare so that your request is complete at the time of submission. Send your request to: National Personnel Records Center, Military Personnel Records, 9700 Page Avenue, St. Louis, Missouri 63131-5100.

This field and staff muster roll, prepared for Colonel Theodore Roosevelt, records highlights of two months of military service based at Camp Wikoff, Long Island, New York.

Then expect to wait up to eight weeks for a response from repository staff. They will inform you whether or not they hold the records and what charges you will incur for copies. Internet researchers will find forms and more than ample information on how to request veterans' records on the NARA website (www.archives.gov).

Military records held at the NARA:

- Volunteers – both enlisted and officers who served during federal emergencies from 1775 to 1902

- Regular Army – enlisted: 1789 – 31 October 1912; officers: 1789 – 30 June 1917

- US Navy – enlisted: 1798–1885; officers: 1798–1902

- US Marine Corps – enlisted: 1798–1895; officers: 1798–1895

- The Revenue Cutter Service, the Lifesaving Service and the Lighthouse Service (predecessors of the US Coast Guard): 1791–1919

Military records held at the NPRC:

- The NPRC stores military records created after 1900, as follows:

- US Army – enlisted members who left military service after 31 October 1912; officers who left after 30 June 1917

- US Navy – enlisted members who left military service after 1885; officers who left after 1902

- US Marine Corps – enlisted members who left military service after 1904; officers who left after 1895

- US Coast Guard – enlisted members who left the military after 1914; officers who left military service after 1928; civilian records of predecessor agencies: 1864–1919

- US Air Force – enlisted and officers who left after September 1947

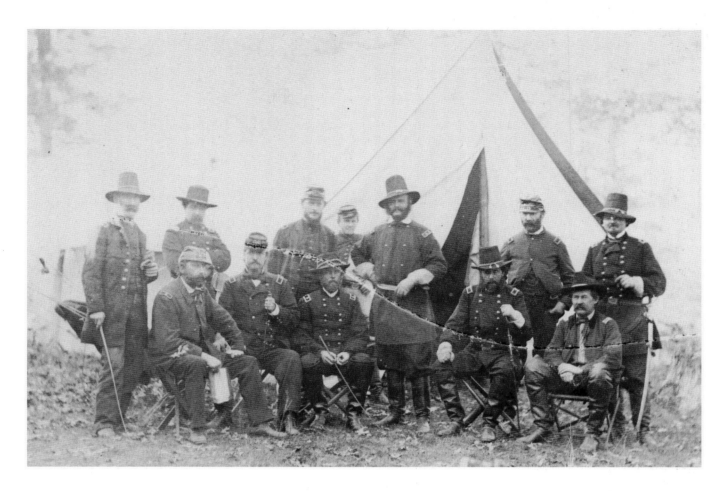

When searching for early wartime records, use any information you can glean from a photograph of your ancestor and his military companions to guide you to the appropriate documents, which in this case will be stored at the National Archives.

Attestation papers

Included among US service records you will find attestation papers (completed at the time of enlistment), like those shown on page 120 for William McCormack, which identify the soldier's full name, age at enlistment, birth place and prior occupation, and give a physical description as well.

Apparently, George William Warr, alias William McCormack, had a colourful military career, which is reflected in the changes made to his attestation papers, the originals of which are held at Kew. Further research into Warr's background uncovered a letter (not shown here) from Commodore James E. Erskine

relating information on the status of several deserters from HMS Nelson (including Warr), stationed at Sydney, Australia, in 1884 and a summary of Warr's service. Stored at Kew, the documents provide a vivid insight into Warr's military career, including his assignment to the *Nelson*, his desertion, the term and place of imprisonment, the date of court martial and several character assessments.

Warr's attestation papers also document the branch of the military he joined, his physical description, the lack of any known medical conditions, the place and term of enlistment and what he received for his enlistment – 'A Free Kit'.

UK military records

When researching UK ancestors who served in the military before 1913, first try to locate discharge documents, issued for soldiers who received a pension upon leaving the army.

Types of UK military records include:

- discharge documents
- pay lists
- muster rolls
- pension records (medical or service pensions)
- description books
- registers of service, service certificates
- returns of service
- chaplains' returns
- regimental records
- Army Lists for commissioned officers
- Navy Lists for commissioned officers
- Militia Lists (dating back as early as 1297)

R.—105.

ENLISTMENT AND ATTESTATION PAPER.

NO made

356

Questions to be put to the Recruit before Enlistment, under the 60th Section of the Marine Mutiny Act, 1860.

1.—What is your Name? .... *William Mc Cormack*

2.—In what Parish, and in, or near what Town, and in what County, were you born? .... { In the Parish of *Islington* / in or near the Town of *London* / in the County of *Middlesex* }

3.—What is your Age? .... *17* Years *10* Months

4.—What is your Trade or Calling? .... *Laborer*

5.—Are you an Apprentice? .... *No*

6.—Are you Married? .... *No*

7.—Are you Ruptured, or Lame; have you ever been subject to Fits; or have you any Disability or Disorder which impedes the free use of your Limbs, or unfits you for ordinary Labour? { *No* }

8.—Are you willing to be attested to serve in the Royal Marine Forces for the term of* *Twelve Years and Two Months* provided Her Majesty should so long require your services; and also for such further term, not exceeding two years, as shall be directed by the Commanding Officer on any Foreign Station? { *Yes* }

* This blank to be filled up with "twelve years," if the person enlisted is of the age of eighteen years or upwards; but if under that age, then the difference between his age and eighteen is to be added to such twelve years.

9.—At what place, on what day, at what hour of the day, and by whom, are you enlisted?† .... { At *Woolwich* on the *24th* day of *June* 187*8*, at *11.30* o'clock *A.* M. by *Sergt Thomas Logan of The Royal Marines* }

† The Recruit must be attested within four days (any intervening Sunday, Christmas Day, or Good Friday not included), but not sooner than twenty-four hours after enlistment, before a Justice not being an Officer in the Marines residing in the vicinity of the place, or acting for the division, district or place where such Recruit shall have enlisted, or where the Head Quarters of the Recruiting Party shall be stationed.

10.—For what Bounty do you enlist? .... *A Free Kit*

11.—Have you any objection to make to the manner of your Enlistment? { *No* }

12.—Do you now belong to the Militia or to the Naval Coast Volunteers? { *No* }

13.—Do you belong to any Regiment or Corps in Her Majesty's Army, or to the Marines, or Navy, or to Her Majesty's Indian Forces? { *No* }

14.—Have you ever served in the Army, Marines, Ordnance, Militia or Navy, or in Her Majesty's Indian Forces, or in the Forces of the late East India Company? ‡ { *No* }

‡ If so the Recruit is to state the particulars of his former service, and the cause of his discharge, and is to produce the Certificate of his discharge if he has it with him.

15.—Have you ever been rejected as unfit for Her Majesty's Service, or for Her Majesty's Indian Forces, or the Forces of the late East India Company, upon any prior Enlistment? { *No* }

NOTE.—The Recruit should be warned by the Recruiting Party, before any of the above questions are put to him, that if the Recruit, by means of any false answers, obtains enlistment money, he will be liable, if in England, to be punished as a Rogue and Vagabond; or if in Scotland or Ireland, to be imprisoned as the 65th Section of the Marine Mutiny Act directs.

Description of *William Mc Cormack* .

Age, apparently _____ *17 10/12* Years

Height _____ *5* Feet *6 1/4* Inches

Complexion _____ *Fresh*

Eyes _____ *Blue*

Hair _____ *Light Brown*

Any distinctive Mark _____ *Nil*

MEDICAL CERTIFICATE ON ENLISTMENT.

I have examined the above-named Recruit, and find that he has no Rupture nor Mark of any old Wound or Ulcer adhering to the Bone; he is free from Varicose Veins of the Legs, and has the full Power of Motion of the Joints and Limbs. He is well formed, and has no Scrofulous Affection of the Glands, Scald Head, or other inveterate Cutaneous Eruptions; and he is free from any trace of Corporal Punishment, and not marked as a Deserter with the letter D. His Respiration is easy, and his Lungs appear to be sound. He has the perfect use of his Eyes and Ears. His general appearance is healthy, and he possesses strength sufficient to enable him to undergo the fatigue to which Soldiers are liable. I consider him fit for Her Majesty's Service. He has § _____ particular Marks or Scars :

Dated at _____ this _____ day of _____

Signature of }
Surgeon. }

§ This blank to be filled up with the words "the following" or "no"—as the case may be.

Even though the recruit's name was registered as William McCormack, another name – George William Warr – appears alongside this name. What, if anything, might that indicate about McCormack?

The recruit joined the Royal Marines. Use this information and the date he enlisted to search for other military records.

McCormack's reward for enlistment: a free kit.

Confusion over the recruit's signature may have foreshadowed the problems he would face during his military service, which ultimately led to a court martial. Who were William McCormack and George Warr?

Locating UK military records

British military records are stored in several locations, so you will need to know your ancestor's army regiment or naval ship in order to contact the appropriate facility. Records detailing service prior to and during World War I are held at Kew, whereas service records created after World War I are generally held by the relevant branch of the Ministry of Defence (MoD).

Military records for members on active duty, retirees or individuals meeting other specifications are located with the relevant branch of the armed forces. To gain access to service records, former service members must submit written requests, known as Subject Access Requests (SARs), and include personal details such as the veteran's full name, service number, rank, birth date and service dates (and the name of the regiment or corps for Army personnel, e.g. Artillery, Cavalry, Engineers, Guards, Infantry) plus proof of identity. Replies take about 40 days to process. If you are not the veteran but wish to request a military record, you must first obtain the service member's written authorization (or, if he or she is deceased, the written authorization of his or her next-of-kin) and send that with the SAR. Internet researchers should review: www.veteransagency. mod.uk/service_recs/service_recs.htm for further guidance.

Military records held at National Archives, Kew:

- Army records for officers and soldiers who enlisted before 1920.

- Royal Navy records for officers who enlisted before 1914.

- Royal Navy records for ratings who enlisted before 1924

- World War I records for the Women's Royal Naval Service.

- Royal Marine records for officers and non-commissioned ranks who enlisted before 1926.

- Records of the Royal Flying Corps and Royal Naval Air Service (predecessors of the Royal Air Force).

- Royal Air Force records (service during World War I) for officers who enlisted before 1922; airmen who enlisted before 1924.

Other UK repositories:

- General Register Office for Scotland.

- Military museums, including the Imperial War Museum, the National Army Museum, the Fleet Air Arm Museum, the Royal Artillery Museum and the Tank Museum. Many have their own archives, which they make accessible to the public.

- Regimental museums and archives, such as the South Wales Borderers & Monmouthshire Regiment Museum, the Fife and Forfar Yeomanry Collection, and the Royal Inniskilling Fusiliers Regimental Museum.

- The Commonwealth Graves Commission, 2 Marlow Road, Maidenhead, Berkshire SL6 7DX (01628 634221), URL: www.cwgc.org.

- The British Library holds some records for the Royal Indian Air Force, the Royal Air Force in India, the Indian Navy and the Royal Indian Marines and Navy.

Records for other countries

These are stored in a variety of repositories. For example, French military records are held by the Army and Navy Historical Services in Vincennes. Depending on their content, you may find Australian military records stored in state government or national archives, with the Department of Defence, Department of Veterans' Affairs and even the Attorney-General's Department. The National Archives of Australia (www.naa.gov.au/ Publications/fact_sheets/default.html#de fence) provides several useful fact sheets to guide your search.

maritime records

Information about seafaring ancestors who served as ship's captains or crew members in merchant navies, commercial shipping or fishing fleets can be invaluable.

Maritime records can be divided into two categories: records of seamen and records of ships. Records of seamen, such as crew lists, have long been kept for both merchant and commercial seafarers. They include vital details; the town, parish or country of birth; dates of entry and discharge from particular ships; when and where paid and any desertions. Crew lists also show actual signatures. Crew agreements specify terms of service, monthly wages, provisions, primary destinations, assignment lengths and ratings and types of assignment. Some maritime documents chronicle daily activities and eating habits, other records provide a man's physical description. Records of ships contain a ship's particulars, including vessel number, port of origin or date of construction.

Countless numbers of men and women have sailed the open seas, commandeering ships, seeking their fortunes, battling for power and creating all sorts of maritime records.

Polyphemus at sea off Gorce 28th July 1805

Yours of the 13th Inst and 9th of May, dear Jamie you may believe was received with much pleasure when I found all my friends were in perfect health, yourself excepted which I was sorry to hear but I trust before this reaches you that you will be in your former state of good health — Admiral Graves is on board here at present and has been most of the passage home from the Baltic as all the seven fours left us off the Naze of Norway for Ireland and his ship among the rest — The day after our arrival they sent

This letter from Captain Alexander Nairne to his brother James, both ancestors of Alex Myers, discusses the seafarer's life and historic events in which he took part.

Types of maritime records

- Captain's diaries, journals, correspondence, personal papers
- Registers of Seamen, agreements, accounts of crew, crew lists, log books, muster rolls
- Registers of Apprentices
- Registers of Seamen's Tickets
- Seamen's Protection Certificate Records and applications
- Registers of Certificates of Competency and Service
- Seamen's service records (Norway)
- Seamen's house records (Finland)
- Trinity House petitions
- Vessel registers, certificates of registry, port certificates
- Shipping lists and registers
- Crew lists and agreements for fishing vessels
- Customs records
- Shipping company records
- Trade manifests
- Lloyd's Lists
- Lloyd's Captains' Registers and Registers of Shipping, of Masters, of Yachts, Survey Reports, War Loss Books
- Admiralty and other court records

When researching maritime records...

 Do

- read maritime histories to gain an understanding of the time period you are studying, before you probe the records.

- visit maritime museums and historical archives, if possible.

- obtain copies of the actual records and double-check transcriptions.

- compare details from more than one record to confirm accuracy.

 Don't

- begin researching without some notion of the kind of information you wish to find.

- rush your efforts.

- expect to find what you're looking for easily: maritime records are more difficult to research than others.

During your research you may come across a photograph of the ship's crew to which your ancestor belonged. He may even be amongst the men in the picture. Try to identify their names from associated records.

To search maritime records, you need to know your ancestor's full name, the approximate dates he or she served and the name or official number of the vessel(s) he or she sailed on. Then follow these steps:

- Identify the official name and/or number of the ship by checking Lloyd's Register of Shipping, the Mercantile Navy List, Merchant Vessels of the United States and other lists of registered ships.

- Check the Registers of Merchant Seamen and Registers of Seamen's Tickets, which have alphabetical lists of seamen's names, ship's service and other vital statistics.

- Review crew lists, muster rolls, crew agreements and Registers of Masters' Tickets, some of which are now online. Others are stored in the National Archives at Kew, the National Maritime Museum in Greenwich, England, and the Maritime History Archive at Memorial University of Newfoundland, Canada URL: http://www.mun.ca/mha/research/principalrecords.php; www.mun.ca/mha/research/principalrecords.php).

- Contact the Registrar General of Seamen and Shipping, Ground Floor, Anchor Court, Keen Road, Cardiff CF24 5JW for crew lists, agreements, registers of masters mates and engineers, certificates of competence and service and other maritime records.

- Some obituaries, parish records, probate records and even gravestone inscriptions identify a person's association with the sea, ship names, shipwreck dates and locations or death in a specific port. Look for and record that data accurately.

Deciphering a ship's register

Problem

What do I do if I can't find my ancestor's name on the register for the ship I believe he worked on?

Solution

☐ **Registers of Merchant Seamen and Registers of Seamen's Tickets may be inaccurate because some mariners were suspicious of the registration scheme and deliberately falsified their names.**

☐ **Some men's names were spelled phonetically, so be sure to read the names closely.**

☐ **Examine handwriting closely: sometimes poor penmanship alters the look of the signature. Transcriptions may also be faulty and misleading.**

☐ **Make a list of spelling variations (e.g., Johns for Jones) and look for those names.**

☐ **Determine if your ancestor used a nickname and check the records for that name.**

☐ **Locate other records for the same ship and check them for your ancestor's name or a variation of it.**

☐ **Review records for other ships built at or departing from the same port near the same date.**

☐ **fill another bullet or two if poss**

☐ **fill another bullet or two if poss**

☐ **fill another bullet or two if poss**

Note: Military records for the world's navies are not classified as maritime records for genealogical purposes.

Waves of people have moved across continents and sailed the seas since the dawn of humankind and reasons for changing residences and homelands have varied.

Some population movements result from conquest, religious bigotry or the need for new food sources. New nations, new cultures and new societies have emerged as a consequence of migration. Some resettlement was voluntary, while other people were forced to move home. In either case, records of movement were often created and family history researchers will find these of special interest.

This section focuses on those documents traditionally categorized as immigration records – such as ship's passenger lists, port records and ship's manifests – and on naturalization records, which developed as immigrant settlers acquired citizenship in their new homelands. Slavery records, which document the movement of masses of people from Africa to the New World, and records of convict transport, which played a key role in the foundation of Australia and New Zealand, and are examined in detail in Part Four: Special Circumstances (see pages 180–3 and 184–7 respectively).

If your ultimate goal is to retrace your ancestors' steps back to their original homeland, you will need patience and a methodical approach to migration records. Tracing immigrant ancestors can be quite time-consuming, and often more than a simple challenge, but, as you extend the branches of your family tree to foreign shorelines, not only will you discover

Countless men, women and children have migrated by ship to the US and other destinations over the course of history and there are many documents that record their passage.

the cultural traditions and lifestyles that influenced your ancestors, you will also begin to comprehend more fully the legacy they left behind – you!

Immigration records

While millions of immigrants have entered the US and other countries by ship, others have crossed national boundaries on foot or by some form of land transportation. Consequently, when attempting to locate immigration records for a particular ancestor, your first step should be to determine whether he or she arrived as a ship passenger or by some other means.

Immigrant ancestors arriving by ship landed at specific ports of entry. Once you have identified the means of arrival, then determine the port of entry and the ship's name, if possible. The most commonly used ports for immigrants sailing from Europe to the US were New York City, which was served by Castle Garden from 1855 to 1890 and after then by Ellis Island; Boston, Massachusetts; Philadelphia, Pennsylvania; Baltimore, Maryland; New Orleans, Louisiana; Galveston, Texas and San Francisco, California. Since each of these ports compiled its own records, it is vital that you know where your ancestor landed – and when. Then you have a starting point for your research. You should also try to determine where the records for that location are stored.

Before 1820 ship's masters were not required to maintain lists of passengers, and, sadly, relatively few immigrant records survive from that time. In 1891 a new US law required ship's masters to create passenger lists

(known as customs passenger lists), which they had to submit to the collector of customs for the district where the ship landed. Besides official documents, information on ship arrivals and departures regularly appeared in print, so researchers should also attempt to locate newspaper archives for the port city and relevant date.

Types of immigration records

- ship's manifests and passenger lists
- ship's logs
- border arrival records
- immigrant visas
- passport applications and issued passports
- alien registration records
- port registers of monthly departures and arrivals
- certificates of aliens
- special certificates of nationality
- Ministry of Labour Vouchers
- records of the UK Colonial Office

Before contacting specific repositories for immigration records, try to establish answers to the following questions:

- Did your ancestor arrive by land or sea?
- If by land, where did he or she cross the border?
- If by sea, what was the port of entry?
- Where are the records for that location stored?
- What was the name of the ship?
- When did it dock?
- Can you also locate newspaper archives for the port city and time period?

Online repositories

Thanks to the ever-expanding Internet, immigration records are fairly easy to locate. Many websites offer online searchable databases of all sorts of records, and immigration records, in particular, are becoming increasingly available. In order to utilize the Internet records, you should know your ancestor's full name (remember to research alternative spellings), the port of entry (POE) and the arrival date (be as specific as possible).

Arguably the best place to begin your search for US immigration records is the National Archives and Records Administration (NARA), which maintains port records dating from 1800 to 1959. Copied onto microfilm, these records are available at the main repository in Washington, D.C., at some NARA regional facilities, the Family History Library, local family history centres and libraries with substantial genealogical collections. The NARA also holds Border Crossing Records and Chinese Immigration Records and has excellent finding aids to help researchers. Family historians with Internet access may purchase copies of immigration records from the NARA website at: www.archives.gov/ global_pages/inquire_form.html or obtain paper copies by post using one NATF Form 81 for each person or family group travelling together.

Now part of the US Citizenship and Immigration Service, the Immigration and Naturalization Service (INS) also maintains original immigration arrival and naturalization records, copies of which may be obtained for a fee by submitting the appropriate request forms. For INS records, begin at: uscis.gov/graphics/aboutus/history/ index.htm to find information on ordering copies.

Using passenger lists

Perhaps the most important type of immigration record for genealogical purposes, passenger lists contain a variety of data, including name, age, gender, occupation, nationality, port and date of departure, port and date of arrival, destination, medical condition, ship's name and registry number and type of ship. Other information you might find on these records are the passenger's last residence before immigration and even physical descriptions, which were added in later lists.

In addition to the US and UK National Archives, US Citizenship and Immigration Services (uscis.gov/ graphics/aboutus/history/NatzRec/NATR EC.htm) and the Library and Archives of Canada (www.archives.ca), organizations such as the Immigrant Ships Transcribers Guild (www.immigrantships.net), Ancestry.com, the Ships List (www.theshipslist.com), the American Family Immigration History Center (webcenter.ellisisland.netscape.com/def ault.asp) and the Canadian Genealogy Centre (www.genealogy.gc.ca/ 10/1008_e.html) have painstakingly transcribed and uploaded scores of passenger lists. Use these websites as your first ports of call when researching immigrant ancestors.

Passenger lists are also available in book form and on CD-ROM. Check the National Archives, Family History Library, local family history centres and even university and larger public libraries (such as the Allen County Public Library in Fort Wayne, Indiana) for published or microfilm copies.

US passenger records are categorized by arrival date as follows: pre-1820, 1820–1890 ('Customs Passenger Lists', maintained by the US Customs Service) and 1891–1954 ('Immigration Passenger Lists', maintained by the US Immigration and Naturalization Service).

Only after 1820 were passenger lists recorded in any sort of systematic way, which means that family history researchers may have difficulty in finding information for immigrant ancestors who sailed to the Americas before that date.

tip **Check border-crossing records**
If your ancestors arrived in the US from Canada or Mexico, don't forget that you will also need to identify where they crossed the border. Records for those sites of entry also exist and are equally valuable resources for the family history researcher.

A gift from France, Lady Liberty has welcomed immigrants to the shores of North America since the statue's installation on Ellis Island in 1886.

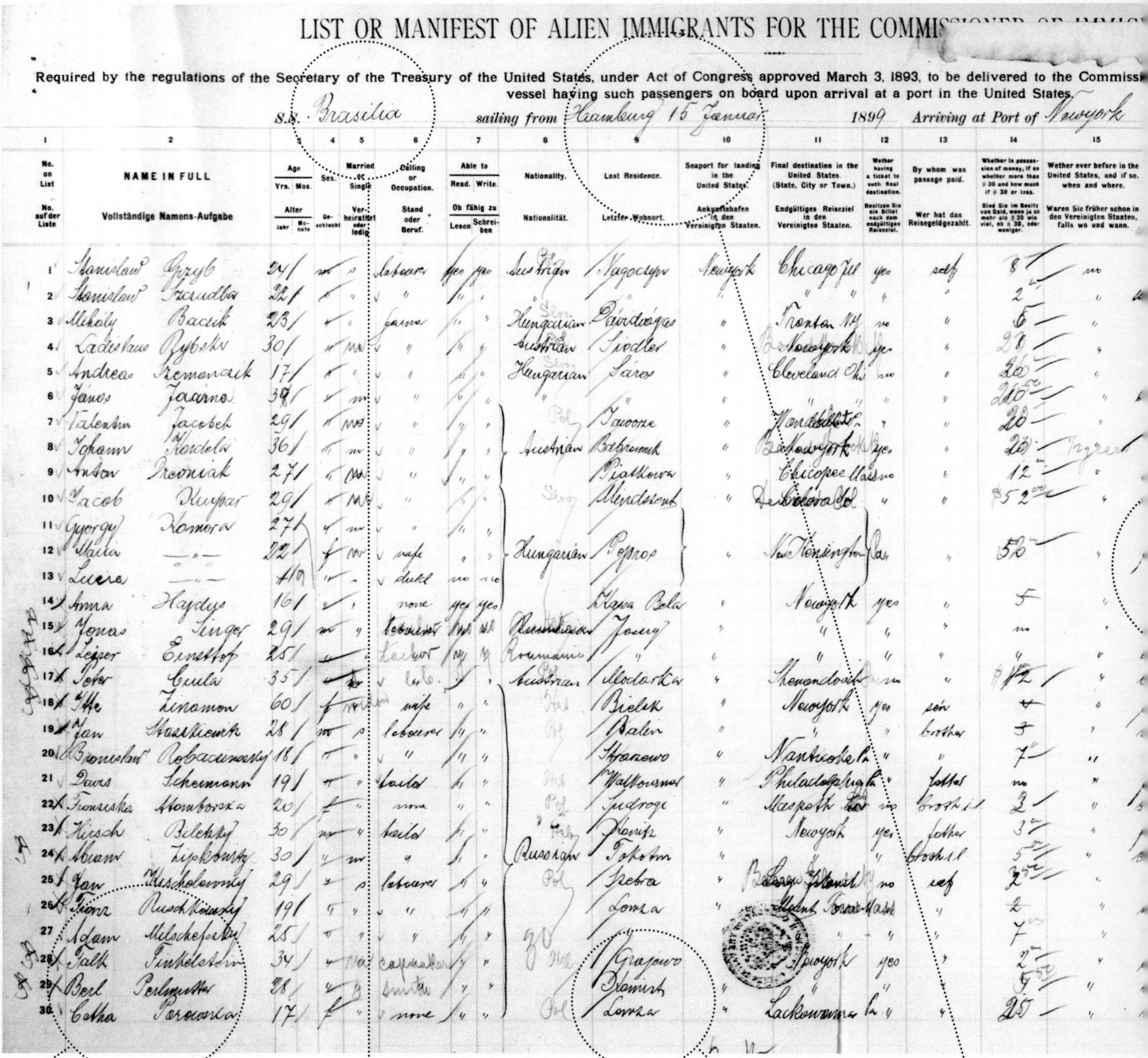

LIST OR MANIFEST OF ALIEN IMMIGRANTS FOR THE COMMIS[…]

Required by the regulations of the Secretary of the Treasury of the United States, under Act of Congress approved March 3, 1893, to be delivered to the Commissi[…] vessel having such passengers on board upon arrival at a port in the United States.

S.S. Brasilia sailing from Hamburg 15 Januar 1899 Arriving at Port of New York

1	2	3	4	5	6	7	8	9	10	11	12	13	14	15
No. on List / No. auf der Liste	NAME IN FULL / Vollständige Namens-Aufgabe	Age Yrs. Mos. / Alter Jahr Monate	Sex. / Geschlecht	Married or Single / Verheiratet oder ledig	Calling or Occupation. / Stand oder Beruf.	Able to Read. Write. / Ob fähig zu Lesen Schreiben	Nationality. / Nationalität.	Last Residence. / Letzter Wohnort.	Seaport for landing in the United States. / Ankunftshafen in den Vereinigten Staaten.	Final destination in the United States. (State, City or Town.) / Endgültiges Reiseziel in den Vereinigten Staaten.	Whether having a ticket to such final destination. / Besitzen Sie ein Billet nach dem endgültigen Reiseziel.	By whom was passage paid. / Wer hat das Reisegeld gezahlt.	Whether in possession of money, if so whether more than $30 and how much if $30 or less. / Sind Sie im Besitz von Geld, wenn ja ob mehr als $30 wie viel, ob $30, oder weniger.	Whether ever before in the United States, and if so, when and where. / Waren Sie früher schon in den Vereinigten Staaten, falls wo und wann.

Look closely at adjacent entries, such as those for Berl Perlmutter and Falk Finkelstein. What connections might these people have?

The SS Brasilia was one of many ships that carried immigrants from Europe to the United States. Knowing the name of the ship you ancestor sailed on may help you locate other records related to your immigrant past.

Handwritten records can be difficult to decipher. Check modern maps and maps dating to the late 19th century to verify place names.

Hamburg was one of the key European ports from which immigrants sailed to New York. Consider searching for port records originating in Hamburg.

This handwritten document is difficult to read, but close scrutiny will yield results. It's easy to understand how an immigrant's name may have been changed inadvertently owing to pronunciation misunderstandings, simple misspellings or mistranscriptions. Other documents you have may spell your ancestor's name differently from what the ship's captain recorded on the passenger list. Don't discount what you see. Spelling variations offer clues for further research.

Immigrat... by the Commanding officer of any

January 1899.   267

16	17	18	19	20
to join a relative, and if what relative, name and address.	Ever in Prison or Almshouse or supported by charity, if yes, state which.	Whether a Polygamist.	Whether under contract, express or emplied, to labor in the United States.	Condition of Health, Mental and Physical.
andten gehen, zu welchen, Wohnort derselben.	Ob jemals im Gefängniss od.Armenhaus gewesen oder Armenunterstützung genossen, An geben, was derf'all.	Sind Sie Polygamist.	Haben Sie einen festen Arbeitscontract für die Vereinigten Staaten ab-geschlossen.	Gesundheitszustand, Geistig und Körperlich.

Relationships identified on passenger lists can provide clues to further research, and also fill in the gaps in your family tree. Here, the father-in-law's surname may also be the wife's maiden name, which is not identified on this record. Do additional research to verify this relationship.

Using information from passenger lists

Problem

My Russian great-grandfather came to the United States around the turn of the 20th century. How do I find the relevant passenger list and what kind of information will it have that might help me trace my family back to their homeland?

Solution

☐ Immigration records created between 1891 and 1954, such as the one that would have been created for your great-grandfather, are filled with genealogical information. Microfilmed copies are available through the National Archives in Washington, D.C., and the Family History Library. To obtain a copy, you need to know the passenger's full name, port of entry and approximate arrival date.

☐ Take a close look at the example shown here, which lists Austrian, Hungarian, Romanian and Russian passengers sailing on the SS *Brasilia* from Hamburg, Germany, who arrived in New York City in January 1899.

☐ Once you believe you have identified your great-grandfather (for example, Berl Perlmutter), look across the line, column by column, to see what other information is listed.

☐ Here we see that Berl was 28 years old, worked as a smith and intended to stay with his brother-in-law, Leib. (Ask yourself, is his surname Furhermann or Finkelstein? Is it a coincidence that the name on the line immediately above Leib Furhermann is Leib Finkelstein? Dig deeper into the relationship between Berl Perlmutter and Falk Finkelstein.)

☐ Berl Perlmutter's last residence was apparently a town or village named [Komish or Komist or ....?]. In order to pinpoint the location, you will need to identify the exact spelling of the town as it is nowadays, as it was in 1899 and also as it is in the native language.

☐ After you've identified the place name – or at least have leads for a couple of possibilities – determine what kind of records might be held for that community and where they are stored. Remember that the boundaries of Russia and Eastern Europe have changed dramatically over time, so you will need to look at historical atlases and place names as well as modern ones. You may also need to do research in more than one country.

Naturalization records

Depending on when they were created, the documents issued to immigrants (also known as 'aliens') who wish to acquire citizenship in their new country can lead you back to your ancestral homeland. Early naturalization records generally contain the immigrant's full name, country of origin and date and port of arrival. US records created after 1906 also include the applicant's date and place of birth or nationality and age; marital status; spouse's and children's names, ages and places of birth; occupation; last residence before immigration; date and port of departure; ship's name; place of naturalization; names, occupations and addresses of witnesses and a physical description of the immigrant (sometimes including a photograph).

Family history researchers often have difficulty locating naturalization papers. Nevertheless, when you do manage to find them, you will discover a valuable source of genealogical information. Repositories include the US and UK National Archives, US Citizenship and Immigration Services (formerly the Immigration and Naturalization Service), individual state archives and county courthouses.

Since applicants were required to file the documents with the court system, US naturalization records may also be classified as 'court records'. Frustratingly, because of the nature of immigration and movement over time, you may have to search in more than one location for these court records.

Applicants often filed their 'first papers' at the courthouse nearest their port of entry but then submitted 'second papers' at the courthouse near where they finally set up residence.

Before 1844, when the Home Office took over responsibility for naturalization, 'denization' was the favoured means for achieving a measure of British citizenship. Immigrants to the UK could apply to become 'denizens' and pay for letters patent, which designated them as British subjects but without the full rights allotted to citizens. Although protected under the law, denizens paid higher tax rates and were prevented from voting, holding public or military office or inheriting land. An Act of Parliament was required to grant full citizenship to individual immigrants.

Types of naturalization records

- declarations of intent (US: also known as 'first papers')

- petitions for naturalization (US: also known as 'second' or 'final' papers)

- certificates of naturalization (UK: as early as 15th century; US: also known as 'C-files')

- certificates of citizenship

- certificates of aliens (UK: 1836–1852)

- records of denization (UK: as early as 15th century)

- certificates of British Nationality

Enrico Fermi's occupation is listed as physicist. What does that tell you about his educational background and his present work situation?

You will have to search other records to identify Laura Fermi's maiden name.

The names and birth dates of the Fermi children provide leads to other branches of the family tree.

Seek out records from the port of Southampton, England, which may point you to Fermi ties in Italy.

Other immigration records for Enrico Fermi may be stored at the Bergen County courthouse in Hackensack, New Jersey. Contact staff for assistance.

---

tip Tracing UK immigrants on the Internet

Internet users seeking Caribbean, Irish, Jewish or South Asian ancestors who immigrated to the UK should also visit the 'Tracing your Roots' gallery on the Moving Here website (www.movinghere.org.uk) for the history of immigration to the UK and research tips. For example, passenger lists for immigrants from India not only include details about British passengers, but also note if they brought with them native servants. Names of free native passengers are recorded, but not those of servants.

Petitions for Naturalization, such as this one submitted by Enrico Fermi, contain personal information, including skin, hair and eye colour.

ORIGINAL
(To be retained by Clerk of Court)

UNITED STATES OF AMERICA

No. 300812

PETITION FOR NATURALIZATION

[Under General Provisions of the Nationality Act of 1940 (Public, No. 853, 76th Cong.)]

To the Honorable the ___DISTRICT___ Court of ___THE UNITED STATES___ at ___CHICAGO, ILL.___

This petition for naturalization, hereby made and filed, respectfully shows:

(1) My full, true, and correct name is ___ENRICO FERMI___
(Full, true name, without abbreviation, and any other name which has been used, must appear here)

(2) My present place of residence is ___5537 Woodlawn Ave., Chicago, Ill.___ (3) My occupation is ___Physicist___
(Number and street) (City or town) (State)

(4) I am ___42___ years old. (5) I was born on ___Sept. 29, 1901___, in ___Rome, Italy___
(Month) (Day) (Year) (City or town) (County, district, province, or state) (Country)

(6) My personal description is as follows: Sex ___male___, color ___White___, complexion ___dark___, color of eyes ___grey___, color of hair ___black___
height ___5___ feet ___5___ inches, weight ___155___ pounds, visible distinctive marks ___None___, race ___white___
present nationality ___Italy___ (7) I am ___ married; the name of my wife or husband is ___Laura___
we were married on ___July 19, 1928___, at ___Rome, Italy___
(Month) (Day) (Year) (City or town) (State or country)
he or she was born at ___Rome, Italy___, on ___June 16, 1907___
(City or town) (County, district, province, or state) (Country) (Month) (Day) (Year)
and entered the United States at ___New York, N.Y.___ on ___Jan. 2, 1939___ for permanent residence in the United States
(City or town) (State) (Month) (Day) (Year)
and now resides at ___with me___ and was naturalized on ___not___
(Number and street) (City or town) (County and State) (Month) (Day) (Year)
at ___ certificate No. ___ or became a citizen by ___
(City or town) (State)

(8) I have ___2___ children; and the name, sex, date and place of birth, and present place of residence of each of said children who is living, are as follows:

Nella (F) Jan. 31, 1931   Both born in Rome, Italy and both reside in
Giulio (M) Feb. 16, 1936   Chicago, Illinois

(9) My last place of foreign residence was ___Rome, Italy___ (10) I emigrated to the United States from
(City or town) (County, district, province, or state) (Country)
___Southampton, England___ (11) My lawful entry for permanent residence in the United States was
(City or town) (Country)
at ___New York, N.Y.___ under the name of ___ENRICO FERMI___
(State)
on ___Jan. 2, 1939___ on the ___SS Franconia___
(Month) (Day) (Year) (Name of vessel or other means of conveyance)
as shown by the certificate of my arrival attached to this petition.

(12) Since my lawful entry for permanent residence I have ___not___ been absent from the United States, for a period or periods of 6 months or longer, as follows:

DEPARTED FROM THE UNITED STATES			RETURNED TO THE UNITED STATES		
PORT	DATE (Month, day, year)	VESSEL OR OTHER MEANS OF CONVEYANCE	PORT	DATE (Month, day, year)	VESSEL OR OTHER MEANS OF CONVEYANCE

(13) I declared my intention to become a citizen of the United States on ___Dec. 2, 1939___ in the ___COMMON PLEAS___
(Month) (Day) (Year) (Name of court)
Court of ___COUNTY OF BERGEN___ at ___BERGEN COUNTY, HACKENSACK, N.J.___ (14) It is my intention in good faith to become a
(City or town) (State)
citizen of the United States and to renounce absolutely and forever all allegiance and fidelity to any foreign prince, potentate, State, or sovereignty of whom or which at this time I am a subject or citizen, and it is my intention to reside permanently in the United States. (15) I am not, and have not been for the period of at least 10 years immediately preceding the date of this petition, an anarchist; nor a believer in the unlawful damage, injury, or destruction of property, or sabotage; nor a disbeliever in or opposed to organized government; nor a member of or affiliated with any organization or body of persons teaching disbelief in or opposition to organized government. (16) I am able to speak the English language (unless physically unable to do so). (17) I am, and have been during all of the periods required by law, attached to the principles of the Constitution of the United States and well disposed to the good order and happiness of the United States. (18) I have resided continuously in the

United States of America for the term of 5 years at least immediately preceding the date of this petition, to wit, since ___Jan. 2, 1939___
(Month) (Day) (Year)
and continuously in the State in which this petition is made for the term of 6 months at least immediately preceding the date of this petition, to wit, since
___Sept. 1, 1942___ (19) I have ___not___ heretofore made petition for naturalization: No. ___
(Month) (Day) (Year)
on ___ at ___ in the ___
(Day) (Month) (Year) (City or town) (County) (State) (Name of court)
Court, and such petition was dismissed or denied by that Court for the following reasons and causes, to wit: ___
___ and the cause of such dismissal or denial has since been cured or removed.

(20) Attached hereto and made a part of this, my petition for naturalization, are my declaration of intention to become a citizen of the United States (if such declaration of intention be required by the naturalization law), a certificate of arrival from the Immigration and Naturalization Service of my said lawful entry into the United States for permanent residence (if such certificate of arrival be required by the naturalization law), and the affidavits of at least two verifying witnesses required by law.

(21) Wherefore, I, your petitioner for naturalization, pray that I may be admitted a citizen of the United States of America, and that my name be changed to ___

(22) I, aforesaid petitioner, do swear (affirm) that I know the contents of this petition for naturalization subscribed by me, that the same are true to the best of my own knowledge, except as to matters therein stated to be alleged upon information and belief, and that as to those matters I believe them to be true, and that this petition is signed by me with my full, true name: SO HELP ME GOD.

___Enrico Fermi___
(Full, true, and correct signature of petitioner, without abbreviation)

Form N-405
(Old 2204 L-B)
U.S. DEPARTMENT OF JUSTICE
IMMIGRATION AND NATURALIZATION SERVICE
(Edition of 3-1-42)

c16—19120-1

1244

No. 743

UNITED STATES OF AMERICA

DECLARATION OF INTENTION
☞ **Invalid for all purposes seven years after the date hereof.**

State of Oregon
County of Marion } ss:

In the _Circuit_ Court
of _Marion County Oregon_

I, _Knute Anderson_, aged _34_ years, occupation _Fruit Grower_, do declare on oath that my personal description is: Color _White_, complexion _Medium_, height _5_ feet _8_ inches, weight _155_ pounds, color of hair _Dark_, color of eyes _Brown_, other visible distinctive marks _None_

I was born in _Brufladt, Norway_ on the _30th_ day of _March_, anno Domini 18_89_; I now reside at _Salem, Oregon - R. 3_
(Give number, street, city or town, and State.)

I emigrated to the United States of America from _Liverpool England_ on the vessel _Celtic_; my last
(If the alien arrived otherwise than by vessel, the character of conveyance or name of transportation company should be given.)
foreign residence was _Brufladt, Norway_; I am _____ married; the name of my wife is _Hilda Peterson_; she was born at _Duandahl, Iowa_ and now resides at _Salem, Ore - R. 3_

It is my bona fide intention to renounce forever all allegiance and fidelity to any foreign prince, potentate, state, or sovereignty, and particularly to _Haakon VII_
King of Norway, of whom I am now a subject;
I arrived at the port of _New York_, in the State of _New York_, on or about the _2nd_ day of _April_, anno Domini 19_05_; I am not an anarchist; I am not a polygamist nor a believer in the practice of polygamy; and it is my intention in good faith to become a citizen of the United States of America and to permanently reside therein: SO HELP ME GOD.

Knute Anderson
(Original signature of declarant.)

[SEAL.]

Subscribed and sworn to before me in the office of the Clerk of said Court this _24_ day of _August_, anno Domini 19_21_

U. G. Boyer

Clerk of the _Circuit_ Court.
By _R. E. Wallace_, _Deputy_ Clerk.
14—56

Immigrants arriving at Ellis Island enjoy views of their new homeland. Their names, vital statistics and ports of departure can often be found on passenger lists and other ship records, which are increasingly available on the Internet. Begin your search online and do not give up if you cannot immediately find your ancestor's record.

Naturalization papers, such as this Declaration of Intention signed and sworn to by Norwegian Knute Anderson and filed in the local county courthouse, often provide a wealth of personal information on immigrant ancestors, including the person's age, occupation, race and physical appearance, birth place, marital status, and other pertinent details, such as that the applicant was 'not an anarchist'.

One of the most informative but often overlooked resources available to genealogists is the probate record, which often provides details that other record types may not include.

The term 'probate' comes from the Latin word for 'to prove' and describes a fairly simple judicial proceeding intended to verify the authenticity of a person's will. These documents specify how the testator's (the person making the will) property will be disposed.

When tracing your roots, try to obtain a copy of your relative's probate file, or at least a will. These documents contain a wealth of information. Some, such as spouse's and children's names, you may already have uncovered, but they also document citizenship, financial status, property locations, household furnishings, cultural and religious preferences and the quality of the testator's relationships.

Probate files may contain the following:

- wills
- signed affidavits of witnesses to the completion of the will
- codicils (amendments to the will)
- inventories and sales of the testator's assets
- minutes of the court proceedings
- a list of heirs, creditors and debts
- receipts from heirs
- petitions for guardianship in the case of minor children

The will of Vivian Edward Burrows not only lists family members and their addresses, but also identifies his passion for tramways and UK transport systems, about which he wrote extensively.

This is the last Will and Testament

of me VIVIAN EDWARD BURROWS of 80 Bridge Avenue Upminster in the County of Essex.

1. I HEREBY REVOKE all former Wills and Codicils made by me AND DECLARE this to be my last Will.

2. I APPOINT my Brother ALFRED LEONARD BURROWS of "Little Thatch" Blackmore End Near Dunmow Essex GEORGE SYDNEY WALTER ATKINS of 85 The Ridgeway St. Albans Herts and JOHN BRENNAN NORRIS of 3 Adur Road Burgess Hill Sussex (hereinafter called "my Trustees") to be the Executors and Trustees of this my Will.

3. I GIVE:-

(a) To the Mayor Aldermen and Burgesses of the London Borough of Newham for preservation in the Library under the title of "The GRATWICKE-BURROWS Tramway Collection" all my transport records consisting of photographs colour slides negatives books relics files personal memoranda and any other miscellania relevant thereto

(b) To the Mayor Aldermen and Burgesses of the London Borough of Newham all copyrights and interests in copyrights to which I am entitled in photographs created by me by the late Walter Gratwicke and by the late G. N. Southerdon.

4.(a) I GIVE to JOAN BERYL CLAYTON of 289 Blandford Road Hamworthy Poole Dorset all my books photographs and colour slides and negatives other than those referred to in Clause 3 hereof

(b) I GIVE to my niece CAROL MARIE CLAYTON of 135 Perryfield Way Ham Near Richmond Surrey absolutely all "personal chattels" as defined by Section 55(1)(x) of the Administration of Estates Act 1925 belonging to me and not otherwise specifically bequeathed

(c) I GIVE all copyrights and interests in copyrights of my published works and all my manuscripts to which I am entitled other than those referred to in Clause 3 to such of them the said George Sydney Walter Atkins and the said John Brennan Norris as survive me and if both survive me in equal shares absolutely

(d) I GIVE to PAULINE THEOBALD of 84 Bridge Avenue Upminster aforesaid

Evaluating a will

Problem

I have obtained a copy of my grandfather's will, which is filled with unfamiliar names and information. How do I evaluate this document?

Solution

Wills not only contain straightforward facts, such as the deceased's name, they also offer many clues for further research. Vivian Edward Burrows's last will and testament, shown opposite, is a case in point.

- In addition to identifying two brothers, a niece and the name of his wife, who predeceased him, Mr Burrows named 13 other individuals but not their relationship to him. Two other names, those of the witnesses, are also noted in the will. Who were they? Are they still living? What were their occupations? Were they business associates, friends, members of the same organization?

- At the end of the will, Burrows identified the cemetery and exact location of the burial plot for his wife and himself. Such detailed information will enable you to obtain cemetery records and also to visit the gravesite in person.

- Burrows took great pains to bequeath a series of transport records he identified as 'The Gratwicke-Burrows Tramway Collection' and related copyrights to the Mayor, Aldermen and Burgesses of the London Borough of Newham. Why? What is in the collection and where is it now? What role did he play in the transport industry? What works did he write?

- What items comprised the 'personal chattels' Burrows bequeathed to his niece? Does the probate file include an inventory of these assets? Where are they now? What do they reveal about the deceased's financial status and lifestyle?

Locating UK probate records

Before 1858, when a secular Court of Probate was created to handle the proceedings, the responsibility for proving wills in England fell to the Prerogative Courts of Canterbury and York (ecclesiastical courts). Consequently, pre-1858 probate records for southern England are now held at the National Archives at Kew (copies available at the Family Records Centre), while those for northern England are stored at the Borthwick Institute at the University of York.

Probate records created in Wales before 1858 are located at the National Library of Wales in Aberystwyth. Wills and other probate documents dating from 1858 to the present are held at the Probate Record Centre, 65 Egerton Road, Erdington, Birmingham, or at one of the regional probate registries located throughout England and Wales. Contact details can be found at: www.courtservice. gov.uk/cms/3798.htm.

The National Archives of Scotland hold Scottish probate records created from the 16th century to 1991. Records up to 1901 are available on the Scottish Documents website (www.scottish documents.com) for a small fee.

Locating US and Canadian probate records

County-level courts are the first places to check for probate records in the US and Canada. In many cases, older records may have been moved from the local courthouse to a larger repository. Be sure to contact the county clerk's office to find out where the documents are being held before a visit.

tip Family relationships and wills

Be cautious about drawing conclusions about relationships based on a will. Sometimes the eldest son or a married daughter are not included in the will, as provisions for them have already been established (i.e. inheritance based on primogeniture or a dowry). Moreover, some relationships are mislabelled in such documents, for example, in-laws being described as stepchildren.

Governmental bodies have levied taxes on populations for centuries. In the process, they have created countless documents that family history researchers will find of value.

Especially useful as substitute census records (but only when census records do not exist for a particular locality or time frame), taxation records contain a combination of straightforward details, such as the names of heads of households, and also information that can be used for additional research.

Poll Tax Lists

Poll taxes were important sources of revenue in the UK and the US into the 19th century, but this is no longer the case. (Other famous poll taxes in history include one introduced briefly in the UK by Margaret Thatcher in 1990.)

Poll (or head) taxes consist of lists of individuals, usually males, who had

reached a taxable age (16, 18 or 21, depending on location and also whether the person was a slave or free), regardless of whether they actually owned property. Once a male reached the age of 50 or 60, he was normally removed from the poll tax list. Those exempt from paying poll tax included women, children, slaves,

Property tax records not only identify the legal description, with section, township and range, of land owned by specific individuals, but they also offer insight into the economic background of people who may be your ancestors.

indentured servants, paupers, veterans, clergymen and even tax assessors.

Poll tax lists and other tax records can be used to identify a man's wife; his children (at least, the fact of their existence if not their individual names or birth dates); other males over the age of 16; specific property items, such as livestock, carriages or slaves; the acreage owned; a man's annual income; and the approximate size of his house. The presence or absence of certain individuals over time may indicate that they moved, died or finally achieved taxable age and were removed from the list. By comparing lists from several years, you can estimate the approximate date of a man's death or the birth years of his children. By comparing lists from more than one locality, you can track the migration of a family over time. You can use tax records to pinpoint if and how men with the same names are related, and some records contain descriptive words that may distinguish individuals with the same names.

US taxation records

The most common types of US tax records, the majority of which have been created after 1782, include personal property and real estate tax records and poll tax lists (also known as tithables).

Other US taxation records

- quitrent rolls or lists
- real estate tax records
- personal property tax records
- income tax records
- tax assessment lists and appraisal records
- rent rolls
- delinquent tax lists
- federal direct taxes (1798–1917)
- federal income taxes (beginning in 1917)

Locating US tax records

When seeking your US ancestor's tax records, start with the relevant county courthouses and state archives. You may also find the records you need at the tax collector's or tax assessor's office in the area where your ancestors resided, or where you believe they lived. Federal tax records may be stored at the National Archives in Washington, D.C., the Family History Library in Salt Lake City, or one of its branch Family History Centres.

UK taxation records

The earliest UK tax records still in existence are known as Lay Subsidy Rolls, the creation of which began in earnest in 1290 and continued until 1324. Imposed by Edward I to fund his assaults on the Scots and French, lay subsidies were levied on the 'laity'. The rolls documented the name of every taxpayer, who was required to pay taxes on his 'movables', or personal possessions.

Other types of UK taxation records

- poll (or head) tax
- land tax assessments (after 1692)
- apprenticeship tax records
- hearth tax records (1662–88)
- marriage tax records (1695–1706)
- window tax records (1696–1798)
- tithe apportionments
- poor rate assessments (parish taxes)

Locating UK tax records

UK taxation records may be stored at the National Archives in Kew, the National Archives of Scotland, the National Library of Wales, or the applicable county record office. Microfilm copies of some British tax records are also held by the Family History Library in Salt Lake City or the branch Family History Centres.

electoral records

Known as voting records, voter registrations, electoral registers, these official documents can serve as reliable census substitutes.

Even though voting has occurred for decades, changing regulations and changing attitudes have had a direct impact on whose names appear in the records. Consequently, researchers should always review the history of suffrage for the country of their ancestors before looking for voter registration records.

US electoral records

In the US only men were allowed to vote until 1920, when women received the same right by constitutional amendment.

Types of US electoral records

• voter registration records

• affidavits of registration

• naturalized voter registrations

• great registers

Great registers are a special type of voter registration record produced by local governments primarily in Arizona, California and Hawaii. They date from as early as the 1860s and contain voters' names, ages, birth place, occupation, residence, naturalization and date of registration.

Locating US electoral records

Contact the relevant county courthouse or bureau of elections, city or state archives or libraries, local or state historical societies, or the Family History Library or nearest branch centre for US voting records. Since some states retain voting records for only a limited time, enquire by written correspondence, email or telephone to

determine whether or not the records you want still survive and if the repository actually holds them.

UK electoral records

Until 1832 only UK property owners had the right to vote. From 1832 to 1885, 'householders' and 'lodgers' were also granted the right; women who qualified as householders could vote in local elections after 1872. From 1918 men over the age of 21 and women over 30 could vote, but women aged 21–30 could vote only from 1928.

Types of UK electoral records

• poll books

• registers of electors (also known as electoral registers, voters' lists, or burgess rolls)

• ward rolls

Poll books include the voter's name, parish and how he or she voted (until 1872, when secret ballots were instituted). They may also list the registrant's address. (Remember that only men voted in parliamentary elections until the 1920s.)

Electoral registers, on the other hand, list the names of people entitled to vote, but not who they voted for.

Locating UK electoral records

If you do not have easy access to the county records office, town hall or local library near where your ancestors lived, contact the British Library when seeking UK voter records. The British Library has a complete set of electoral registers for the entire UK, dating back as early as 1947. It also holds registers created before 1947, but does not carry the complete collection. Remember that electoral registration halted during World Wars I and II, so no registers exist for those years.

In order to use electoral registers to trace UK ancestors, you will need to know not the person's full name, their address and the constituency where they voted. Even with this information, you may have difficulty pinpointing the records because constituency boundaries may have changed over time.

Irish electoral records

Religious affiliations as well as age and gender differences should be taken into account when searching Irish electoral

tip Use the Internet

Increasingly, electoral records of all types are creeping onto the Internet. Some websites feature finding aids, which will help you find out where records are located and how to gain access to them. Others offer limited searchable online databases. Check the Internet to determine if your ancestor's records have been transcribed into a particular database, which will probably be organized by location and time period.

records. From 1727 to 1793 only Protestants claiming a 40-shilling or greater freehold could vote. Between 1793 and 1829 Roman Catholics meeting the same qualifications were also allowed to vote. In 1829 the required value of the freehold was raised to £10. In 1918 all men over age 21 acquired the vote, and in the 1920s it was extended to women 21 and older.

Freeholders registers are similar in content to poll books. They contain a freeholder's name, place of residence, the location and value of the freehold, and, sometimes, the freeholder's occupation and names of tenants and the landlord. Unlike poll books, however, the registers do not reveal how an individual voted. An inventory of Irish freeholder records and their locations is accessible online at: www.ireland.progenealogists.com/ freeholdersdata.asp.

Other types of Irish voting records

- freeman records
- voters' registers or lists
- poll books

Locating Irish electoral records

When seeking Irish voting records, check county record repositories, the National Archives of Ireland and the Public Record Office of Northern Ireland. Even though their contents vary from locality to locality, the records generally feature the voter's name, address, age, birth date and place, residency status, race and naturalization information.

Voting records such as this Official Register of Electors dating from 1900 can help fill in the gaps in your family history. Registrant names, occupations, ages, birth place and naturalization status are documented. Charles Arnold's French heritage and immigration records (see entry 10) could be topics for further research.

other court records

For millennia, human behaviour has been regulated by informal and formal legal systems with different methods of enforcing communal policy and law.

Types of court

Different types of courts deal with the array of disputes that commonly arise between individuals, their communities and larger jurisdictions. Types of courts and court systems vary from one country to another.

In the US courts exist at the federal, state and county levels. They include small claims, municipal, family, traffic, juvenile, appellate, district, circuit, trial and supreme courts.

Canadian laws fall under the provenance of municipal, provincial or territorial and federal jurisdictions.

In the UK England and Wales operate High Courts (Family, Chancery and Queen's Bench Divisions), crown, county and magistrates courts, administrative courts, coroner's courts, ecclesiastical courts and various tribunals. The House of Lords is the final appeals court for matters of national civil law and criminal cases in England, Wales and Northern Ireland.

Scottish courts include the Court of Session, High Court of Justiciary, sheriff and district courts and tribunals. Northern Ireland maintains a supreme court, crown and magistrates courts, county courts and high courts.

Besides using the records from these courts, researchers should also make use of historical documents produced from the Middle Ages until 1971 by Quarter Sessions, Great Sessions and Assize Courts in England and Wales, which are primarily stored at county record offices or the National Archives at Kew (see the Resource Directory for further details).

What you can find

Each type of court mentioned above – and others around the world – deals with either criminal or civil cases, and, in doing so, produces a multitude of records that family historians will find useful, including those relating to:

- adoption
- appellate cases
- bankruptcy
- bastardy
- citizenship and naturalization
- copyright, trademarks and patents
- corporate matters
- criminal proceedings
- divorce
- guardianships
- homestead and land ownership
- incidents at sea
- inheritance and partitions
- inquisitions post mortem
- insanity and commitment
- insurance claims
- court minutes, docket books and case files
- libel and slander
- mortgage
- poor law
- probate
- slavery
- small claims
- taxes

Obtaining and using court records

Governmental agencies and other organizations now often provide the public with free access to official documents. Since many repositories are now placing their records on the Internet, you should first check to see whether the agency has a website and whether they maintain online records databases. If not, contact the repository by telephone or written correspondence, not only to ensure they carry the records you need but also to be sure staff can grant you access upon your arrival. You may be able to obtain certified copies by letter or telephone.

> **tip** **Check who received the final judgement**
> Because cases often take several years to finalize, the records may actually be indexed under a surviving family member's name. So, if you are having trouble locating your ancestor's court records, look past the obvious – your ancestor's name – and check the index for the names of other family members who may have been involved in the case or who actually received the final judgement.

Be sure to do a complete search, which includes reviewing court packets and record books. In the US court records are generally indexed by the names of the parties involved: one index lists cases by each plaintiff's name and another by defendant. To use the indexes properly, you need to know the full name of at least one of the parties involved in the case.

Court records can be difficult to use – not only does the format vary from region to region, but so does the subject matter and the specific content covered. And, depending on the type of case, its location and the date it took place, the records may be stored at courthouses, in archive repositories or even in libraries.

However, because court records often hold clues to your past that no other records contain, you should be particularly persistent when looking for these documents.

Types of court record

Knowing whether the case was a criminal, civil or equity action will point you in the right direction to begin your search. Then look for the following types of document:

- case files – contain evidence, testimony, correspondence, depositions and other details

- dockets – identify the names of the plaintiff and defendant, the date of the hearing, the case file number (also called the docket number) and document titles

- court minutes – a synopsis of all court action for each day

- court orders – summarize the proceedings and detail the final outcome

Besides the basics …

Court records can provide important insights into the extent and quality of your ancestors' relationships, their finances, their problems and struggles

and their roles within a community or corporation. Two of the many record types you may encounter are:

Slavery records

Many researchers tracing African roots use records created for free persons – former slaves who acquired certain rights upon receiving their freedom, such as the right to own property – yet they fail to do additional research for records documenting their ancestors' history as slaves. Since slaves were considered the private property of their

owners, you may find information on them in legal documents related to the sale or acquisition of property (probate records) or to civil cases that transpired between the slaves and their owners. There may also be records of criminal cases to which they were party – because they had knowledge of or participated in the crime or because they were victims of illegal trade or crimes perpetrated upon them by whites. When reviewing these records, always record the slave's full name and also the full name of the owner.

African-ancestored researchers will find slave returns from the Bahamas and Caribbean Islands of particular interest. Family relationships can be identified.

Petitions to sell slaves, bills of sale and records of transfer (which were produced with the sale or inheritance of an estate – to which slaves belonged) are excellent primary resources. They can include the slave's name, the former and new owners' names, the date and place where the sale occurred and the purchase price. Civil cases are particularly valuable, as they often describe the nature of the relationship between the parties and the conditions in which the slaves lived and laboured.

Inquisitions post mortem

Literally meaning 'inquiries after death', inquisitions post mortem are a type of probate record, the purpose of which was to determine what property (particularly land) the deceased (a lord or individual of status) owned, its value and what lands and income should revert to the monarchy.

Implemented in Britain with feudalism during the Middle Ages and originally written in Latin, these documents often provide detailed information about the lord of the manor (the tenant-in-chief), his tenants and the local communities associated with the manor.

Use them to identify the heirs and to gain insight into the financial status (they list the property held by the lord), the rights and holdings granted to the widow (the assignment of dower) and the lifestyle enjoyed by the family.

tip **Family stories**
These often have a sound basis in fact. Pay attention to your relative's tales of intrigue. An ancestor's bankruptcy, insanity and commitment, or the impact of poverty and life in a workhouse may be documented in official records stored in a local records office or in a historical society library that acts as a repository for a long-closed institution.

Birth certificate amendment

Problem

My grandmother applied to the Wyandot County, Ohio, Probate Court to amend her birth certificate. I have obtained copies of the court records. In addition to her full name, what genealogical information can I glean from these papers?

Solution

This birth certificate amendment application contains genealogical details such as your grandmother's true name, actual birth date, birth place and gender; her parents' names, marital status, race, birth places, ages at time of child's birth and occupations; and the name of the attending doctor. These records also provide several clues to your past:

- The city listed as the place of birth, Bellevernon, was crossed out twice on the application – was this a mistake or misinformation? Try to verify this place name.

- The midwife's surname indicates she was related to the baby, but only her initials, rather than forenames, are listed. Try to establish this person's identity.

- The names, addresses, ages and relationships of the two witnesses provide leads for further research.

- Also note the applicant's current address and the number of months of pregnancy before the birth.

- Crosscheck the details with other records you have gathered. Notice the inconsistent spelling of the surname (some records state 'Seiser' while others use 'Seizer' for the same family members) – which is correct?

A typical court record, this change of birth certificate filed by Nina Marie Stoner, the author's grandmother, actually confounds the research process, as the spelling of her maiden name (Seizer) conflicts with her birth records and parents' divorce records (Seiser). Further research is necessary in such cases to determine the correct surname. Spelling errors are a common problem with official documents.

APPLICATION
This Application must be Typewritten
All Facts must be given as of Time of Delivery of this Child

No. _____ Doc. _____ Page _____ Filed _____ 19 ___

Probate Court, _____ Wyandot _____ County, Ohio

In the Matter of

(1) Correction of Birth Record _____ Case No. 1422

of Nina Maude Seizer (Stoner) _____ APPLICATION

Your applicant respectfully represents that she was born in

Wyandot County, Ohio; that she now resides in Millbury, Ohio

R.R.#1 : and that the following are the available facts with relation

to her birth as of the date of delivery:—

2. USUAL RESIDENCE OF MOTHER (At time of Deliv.)

(a) State	Ohio
(b) County	Wyandot
(c) Belleverannen	Tymochtee Twp.
	(City) (Village) (Township)
(d) Street No.	-----

Nina Maude — 4. Date of birth Jan. 14, 1895
First Middle (Month) (Day) (Year)

15. Full maiden name Stover, Barbara Ethel
Surname First Middle
16. Color or race White 17. Age at time of this birth 21 yrs.
18. Birthplace R.D.# Sycamore, Ohio
(State or foreign country)
19. Usual occupation housewife
20. Industry or business
22. Attending Physician or Midwife
Name Dr. Wickham
Address Sycamore, Ohio
Mrs. A. D. Stover - Midwife

represents the registration of her birth

ly and accurately recorded in Volume 1891,
irth Records of Wyandot County, Ohio.

omplete in that it gives only the name of
t or middle name. Also the record states that
orn on Jan. 4, 1895, when in reality it was Jan.
makes application for an order of the Court directing

er birth record.

Nina Maude Seizer Stoner
(Present full name of applicant)
Nina Maude Seizer Stoner

int, being duly sworn, says that the facts stated in the
ue, as she verily believes.

Nina Maude Seizer Stoner
P. O. Address R#1, Millbury, Ohio
Sworn to before me and signed in my presence
this 3rd day of April 19 63.
R. H. Stansbery
R. H. Stansbery, Notary Public

Probate Court, _____ County, Ohio

In the Matter of
(1) _____

of _____ AFFIDAVIT OF PHYSICIAN

The State of Ohio, _____ County: ss.

I _____, do hereby certify that I was the
physician in attendance at the birth of _____
the applicant herein, and that the facts in the application are true, as I verily believe.

P. O. Address _____ Attending Physician
Sworn to before me and signed in my presence this _____ day of _____ 19 ___

NOTE: If the affidavit of the attending physician cannot be secured, the application must be supported by the following affidavits of two persons, relative or non-relative, having personal knowledge of the facts.

The State of Ohio, Wyandot County: ss. AFFIDAVIT
I, Lottie Hannum, Age 70 Years, (4) Cousin of Applican
do hereby certify that I have personal knowledge of the facts stated within application, and that the facts stated therein are true, as I verily believe.
P. O. Address Upper Sandusky, Ohio Lottie S. Hannum
Sworn to before me and signed in my presence this 3rd day of April 1963
Russell H. Kear Judge
(Official Title)

The State of Ohio, Wyandot County: ss. AFFIDAVIT
I, Charles D. Stubbs, Age 87 Years, (4) Not related
do hereby certify that I have personal knowledge of the facts stated in the within application, and that the facts stated therein are true, as I verily believe.
P. O. Address Upper Sandusky, Ohio Charles D. Stubbs
Sworn to before me and signed in my presence this 3rd day of April 1963
Russell H. Kear Judge
(Official Title)

FILED
COMMON PLEAS COURT
Probate Division
APR 3 1963
Russell H. Kear
JUDGE, WYANDOT COUNTY, OHIO

JOURNAL ENTRY

Probate Court, _____ Wyandot _____ County, Ohio

In the Matter of the _____ April 3 19 63

(1) Correction of Birth Record _____ Case No. 1422

of Nina Maude Seizer Stoner (1) FINDING AND ORDER
Correction of Birth Record

This day this cause came on to be heard on the application of
Nina Maude Seizer Stoner for an order of the Court
requesting the correction of her Birth Record

On consideration of the evidence submitted, this Court finds that the facts stated
in the application are supported by (2) the testimony of Lottie Hannum and
Charles D. Stubbs credible witnesses; also, Marriage record showing
given name to be "Nina Maude" and birthday to be Jan. 14, 1895;
that notice of the hearing on the said application has been (3) dispensed with

: and that the facts stated in the application
are true, viz:— correction of the
It is therefore ordered that the registration of the birth of said applicant be
recorded in accordance with the findings of the Court herein
and that a summary of the finding and order of this Court, duly certified, be forthwith transmitted as provided by law.

Russell H. Kear
xxxxxx Judge.

(1) "Correction of Birth Record" or "Registration of Birth."
(2) "The Affidavit of the Physician in Attendance" or
"The Testimony of _____ and _____ credible witnesses"
"Clear and convincing documentary evidence."
(3) "Duly given by publication" or "Dispensed with."

town and borough records

While many official documents provide specific details about an individual's life, town and borough records add depth to family history research.

Like larger governmental bodies, towns, boroughs and villages compile all sorts of records that document the activities, policies, traditions and relationships carried out by community, religious and political leaders, councils and governmental departments, tradesmen and other dignitaries. They also record historical events and their impact on the community and its residents, document financial transactions, and relate much more. Reviewing town and borough records can offer insights into the social and cultural conditions that influenced ancestors, place their lives in the context of the times in which they lived, and, quite possibly, present ideas for additional research.

Types of town and borough records include:

- town and city council meeting minutes
- proprietor's records
- historical borough records, which document the community's earliest history
- records of earmarks (for tracking cattle)
- records of freemen's oaths
- petitions
- documents dealing with the care of the poor and the management of workhouses

The repositories

Not surprisingly, the best place to begin your search for a town or borough's records is the town hall or local library.

In the US many town records are maintained by town clerks, whom you should contact first when delving into the documents. State and university libraries and archives and local and state historical and genealogical societies often retain copies as well. Some genealogical societies publish the records in their journal or in local history books.

In the UK search the applicable county records office or public library, which may not store the actual records but may hold published compilations.

The Family History Library (FHL) in Salt Lake City also has town records on microfilm for some states and also for countries such as England and Canada. Nova Scotia, for example, produces township books, copies of which are held at the FHL and also in Nova Scotia's Public Archives.

WHEN SEEKING TOWN RECORDS...

 DO

- contact the town clerk, librarian or archivist before a visit to establish if they hold the records you seek.
- review the history of the region to be sure you have identified the correct placename.
- look closely for the names of your ancestors; these records can be quite lengthy and you can easily skip over a titbit of information about your relative.
- identify and copy any lists of names and comments about the characters who lived in and influenced the community .

 DON'T

- rush through the records; important information may be found when examining the minute details.
- ignore details about daily life, trade and commerce, occupations, poverty, religious activities and crises; they can fill in the gaps in your history.
- expect to find extensive histories of particular individuals, but rather bits and pieces of information that you will need to fit together.

A case in point

The borough records of Haverfordwest have a reputation for completeness and are touted as the best of their kind in Wales. As such, they provide a useful reference for family historians: even if you do not have ancestors from Pembrokeshire, they can be helpful as models for understanding other town/borough records.

Published in book format by the University of Wales Press, the Calendar of the Records of the Borough of Haverfordwest 1539–1660, edited by B.G. Charles, provides readers with an in-depth look at the borough and the personalities who shaped the course of its history. The main strength of these records is the extensive documentation of the day-to-day administration of the borough by its mayors, aldermen, common council and burgesses.

Among the most intriguing details are statements about who sat with whom in which pews at church, which reveals class and gender distinctions. Particulars on who may trade, when trade may occur, who may not trade, market regulations, guilds and apprenticeships are also featured. The impact of the devastating plague of 1652 is especially fascinating.

The Haverfordwest records do have their limitations, however. In particular, the roles of women and families in the borough are almost completely omitted, as are discussions on the agricultural communities that supported the borough.

Borough records such as these encourage researchers to gain a sense of the times in which their ancestors lived. Best of all, they may provide direct and indirect references to the ancestors themselves.

You may find details about your ancestor's life in unusual places, such as the Winchester City Order Book, 1717–1787, *which includes orders to prevent galloping in the High Street (1716), to be whipped for forging a pass (1717) and not to entertain strangers who have small pox (1719). Scour the records for your ancestor's name.*

business records & trade directories

Business records are produced in so many forms that you'll need to be patient as you decide which ones might be useful for your family history project.

As mentioned in Part Two, sometimes you may have to contact a business or corporation to request access to its archives – some businesses will allow the public to visit in person and to make copies of their records. But you may also discover business records stored in your family's own in-house archives. Whether they include private correspondence, customer records, business accounts, donations or bankruptcy files, business records can provide fascinating insights into your ancestor's trade, financial status, community role and, perhaps, their business reputations as well.

Finding out about your ancestor's business activities

Be sure to examine local business, community and old telephone directories and newspaper advertisements. Look for information about a family member's commercial activities, for details such as the individual's residential address and occupation, and also for maps pinpointing the locations.

Often held by state or public libraries, state archives, local historical societies, museums or local newspapers, these publications provide details about the location and type of business, its practices and its traditions – and may even offer clues about your ancestor's personality.

The community's chamber of commerce might know where the records are located, what company took over the business you are researching or how the name of your relative's business changed over time, so contact the staff for assistance.

US city directories

During the 19th century, US city directories often listed an individual's occupation and the company for which he or she worked. Later city directories featured separate sections for business entries, which included advertisements and items of interest to family historians, such as photographs of the business or staff members.

Locating city directories

In addition to the aforementioned repositories, which generally hold only directories specific to their region or locality, other facilities that store city directories include:

- Library of Congress
- Family History Library and branch centres
- Newberry Library
- Allen County Public Library
- New York Public Library
- Library of the Daughters of the American Revolution
- New English Historic Genealogical Society and the American Antiquarian Society in Worcester, Massachusetts

In the UK the British Library and National Library of Wales maintain a large selection of city directories.

Trade directories

Contact trade guilds or professional associations to which your ancestor may have belonged. They often maintain business and member directories that list names, addresses and even the birth, marital and educational details of their members.

Don't be surprised if you come across misspellings, typographical errors or what appear to be incorrect addresses. Review directories from consecutive years to confirm the details, as necessary. Record or photocopy even the most seemingly trivial titbit of information, which could lead you in a new direction or help paint a clearer, more colourful and comprehensive image of your past.

For example, what can you discover in the Sissinghurst advertisement shown opposite that points to further research?

Advertisements like this one for the revival of the well at Sissinghurst Castle are filled with titbits of historical information, including the dispersal of ancestral property.

tip Think beyond a company's archives

In addition to searching for the specific name of the business or company associated with your ancestor, try broadening your research. Research the type of business and even the area where he or she worked. British family historians should visit the relevant county record office, which indexes information by subject name, place name and family name.

<h1 style="text-align:center">Thefe are to give Notice,</h1>

That the Old Admired

<h1 style="text-align:center">WELL</h1>

IS

<h1 style="text-align:center">REVIVED,</h1>

For the Publick Good.   With the Caufes why

DEMOLISHED and now REVIVED.

Shewing the Excellency of the Water, the Scituation of the Place, the Variety and Plenty of the Country, the Diftance from *LONDON*, the Way and the Rates thereunto.

THE Water often try'd by Eminent Phyfitions, and Approved of to be better, and heavier than *Tunbridge*; and does Operate by Urine to admiration, Curing moft Diftempers: The Wells at *Tunbridge* being of little Ufe before this was Demolifhed.

This Well is in *Siffinghurft Park*, in the Parifh of *Cranbrook*, in the County of *Kent*, but by Reafon of the great concourfe of Perfons of Quality and others to this Well, caufed fuch a Refort to the place in the Park where the Lady *Baker* then Lived, that fhe caufed the Stones and Bafon to be taken up, and the Gates of the Park to be Locked to Obftruct the fame.

But now the Lady being Dead, and her Heirs Marryed into other Counties, they have been prevailed with to admit the Stones and Bafon to be fet in again, and the Walks, &c. made convenient for any Perfons of Quality and others to refort thereunto.

The *Scituation* of it is in a very good Healthy Aire, there are feveral Hills in the Park, from which you have a Profpect of 20 or 30 Miles about. The Park is very large, being 7 Miles in compafs, with very great plenty of Strawberys in and about it. The Growth of the Wood in it is moft Birch, which is much in ufe for Birch-Wine. Adjoining to the Park is a great Common, much in ufe for Horfe-Racing. Near adjoining to the *Park* is a great Street of Houfes, called *Milk-Houfe-Street*, with many large and pleafant Dwellings, and 3 good Inns, 'tis a great *Poft Road* to many Market Towns: Alfo near adjoining to the Wells is very good *Chery-Gardens*, and great plenty of Fruit: The beft Sider is but Six Pence the Bottle. Two Miles Diftant from the Wells is that great Market Town *Cranbrook* aforefaid, a great *Poft Town*, Fifteen or Sixteen Miles from the Sea, which is many Miles nearer than *Tunbridge*; and much fupply'd with Fifh, there being much Gentry in the Parifh, and many great Ponds of Frefh Fifh. Near the Town is a larg Bowling-Green, and more will foon be made near the Wells.

There is alfo great plenty of all Provifions and Wood, at a Reafonable Rate.

The Buildings are very Many, Large and Pleafant, exceeding moft places in *England* for Timber; they were formerly Inhabited moftly by Cloathyers, but now the Trade is Decay'd, which caufes them to be Lett Cheap. The Road is very broad and pleafant.

The Gentry, unto whome the place doth belong, are willing to accomodate perfons of Quality with a great part of the place, Furnifhed or Unfurnifhed; and alfo the Chappel.

There is alfo Mr. *Bafden*, a Merchant in *London*, hath feveral good Houfes in the faid Street, is willing to Lett fome, or Lodgings Furnifhed or without: With good *Fating Pafture* for Horfes, &c. He is to be Spoken with on the *Turky* or *Jamaica Walk* at *Change Time*, after *Change* at *Batfon's* Coffee-Houfe againft the *Exchange*, or at the *Artichoke* in *Finch-Lane* near the *Exchange*, when not at his Houfe aforefaid near the Wells.

There is alfo many in the faid Street and Parifh are willing to Accomodate any Gentry, &c. with Lodgings Furnifhed at Reafonable Rates.

This Well is Forty Miles from *London*, but there is a Coach that goes from *Tho. Cropper's* in *Bifhops-gate-ftreet*, near the *Great James Tavern*, to thefe Wells in One Day, for Ten Shillings a Paffenger. But if any defire a cheaper and pleafanter paffage, they may go from *Billingfgate* to *Gravefend* for 1s. then prefently by Coach to the City of *Rochefter* for 1s. fome times 1s. 6d. from thence by water to *Maidftone* for 6d. which is ten Miles from the Wells, to which you may go be Coach or Horfe as you pleafe.

A requisition for a certified copy of an entry of birth

Problem

Chantal Glover has obtained the 'requisition for a certified copy of an entry of birth for the purpose of [The Factory and Workshop Act, 1901], or for any purpose connected with the employment in labour or elementary education of a young person under the age of sixteen years, or of a child' (see opposite), which was submitted when her grandfather began his apprenticeship in a factory at Preston, England. She also has the certified copy of his entry of birth (see overleaf), issued for the same purpose. She wonders if this is her grandfather's actual birth certificate and what information she should pay close attention to.

Solution

The Factory and Workshop Act of 1901 required all children under the age of 16 to produce a certified copy of their birth certificate in order to work in a factory or workshop. A parent or guardian submitted the requisition to the Superintendent Registrar (SR) of the district where the child was born, who in turn issued the certified copy of the entry of birth, which verified the child's eligibility to work.

■ This requisition form shows Chantal's grandfather's 'Christian name and surname', her great-grandparents' forenames, the child's birth place and date, the reason for the requisition, the date (which allows Chantal to calculate how old her grandfather was when he first sought employment – just under 14 years old! – and her great-grandfather's signature, current residence and occupation. (Does the smudging indicate that Fred Bowes was unaccustomed to signing his name?)

■ As this is Chantal's grandfather's first employment record, she should try to learn more about the apprenticeship, what trade he acquired, who his employers were, etc.

■ The addresses and her great-grandfather's occupation also provide clues for further research.

■ The certified copy of the entry of birth details when and where the boy, John William, was born, his parents' names, his mother's maiden name, his father's occupation (note that it differs from what is listed on the requisition – here's another lead to chase up) and district, subdistrict and 'count(ies)' where the birth took place.

■ Notice the discrepancy between the two records: the requisition lists two different addresses for John William's birth place and his father's present residence, whereas the certified copy of the entry of birth states that they are the same. Chantal should question this conflict and make a note in her log to do follow-up research.

■ These documents were produced purely to prove the child's age and availability for work. The actual birth certificate can be traced using the number listed in the first column, which indicates the entry number for the register where it was recorded.

■ Contrary to what some researchers speculate, these records are not indirect evidence of illegitimacy or of any problem with the child's parentage. They are standard business records for the times.

When searching for an ancestor's employment history, educate yourself about the regulations and conditions of the times. Knowing the relevant laws can point you to documents that you may not be aware of, such as the Factory and Workshop Act of 1901, which regulated child employment practices.

[This FORM of REQUISITION is furnished gratuitously. The applicant must fill in the required particulars in ink, sign his or her name at the foot, and either take the form to the SUPERIN-TENDENT REGISTRAR of the DISTRICT in which the Birth occurred, or send it to him, together with the fee of 6d. and 1d. for postage.]

The Form must NOT be sent to the Registrar-General.

The Certificate is not available for purposes of Secondary Education.

SCHEDULE.

THE FACTORY AND WORKSHOP ACT, 1901.

REQUISITION for a CERTIFIED COPY of an ENTRY of BIRTH for the purposes of the above-mentioned Act, or for any purpose connected with the EMPLOYMENT in LABOUR or ELEMENTARY EDUCATION of a Young Person under the age of Sixteen years, or of a Child.

To the **Superintendent Registrar** or **Registrar of Births and Deaths** having the custody of the Register in which the Birth of the under-mentioned Young Person or Child is registered:—

I, the undersigned, hereby demand, for the purpose mentioned below, a Certificate of the Birth of the Young Person or Child named in the subjoined Schedule.

Christian Name and Surname of the Young Person or Child of whose Age a Certificate is required.	Names of the Parents of such Young Person or Child.		Where such Young Person or Child was Born.	In what Year such Young Person or Child was Born.
	FATHER.	MOTHER.		
John William Bowes	Fred	Agnes	Leskswig St. Preston	March 1st 1903

The Certificate is required for the following purpose, namely:—

Employment

Dated this _____ 19th _____ day of _____ March _____ 1917

Signature _____ Fred Bowes

Address _____ 71 Grimshaw Street Preston

Occupation _____ Chauffeur

WHEREAS by Section 134 of the Factory and Workshop Act, 1901, it is enacted as follows:—"Where the age of any young person under "the age of sixteen years, or child, is required to be ascertained or proved for the purposes of this Act, or for any purpose connected with the "employment in labour or elementary education of the young person or child, any person shall, on presenting a written requisition, in such "form, and containing such particulars as may be from time to time prescribed by the Local Government Board, and on payment of a fee of "sixpence, be entitled to obtain a certified copy under the hand of a registrar or superintendent registrar, of the entry in the register, under "the Births and Deaths Registration Acts, 1836 to 1874, of the birth of that young person or child; and such form of requisition shall on "request be supplied without charge by every superintendent registrar and registrar of births, deaths, and marriages." NOW THEREFORE, We, the Local Government Board, in pursuance of the powers given to Us by the Statutes in that behalf, hereby Order as follows:—

ARTICLE II.—The requisition to be made to entitle any person to obtain a certified copy of an entry of a registry of birth under the section above-cited shall be in the Form set forth in the Schedule to this Order.

ARTICLE III.—This Order shall come into operation on the Fifteenth day of April, One thousand nine hundred and ten.

GIVEN under the Seal of Office of the Local Government Board, this Fifteenth day of March, in the year One thousand nine hundred and ten.

(Signed)   JOHN BURNS, *President.*
(Signed)   WALTER T. JERRED, *Assistant Secretary.*

CERTIFIED COPY of an ENTRY of BIRTH.

(Issued for the purposes of the Factory and Workshop Act, 1901.)

Registration District of _____ Preston

Sub-District of _____ Trinity _____ in the Counties of _____ Lancaster and Preston C.B.

Columns:—	1	2	3	4	5	6	7	8	9
No.	When and Where born.	Name (if any).	Sex.	Name and Surname of Father.	Name and Maiden Surname of Mother.	Rank or Profession of Father.	Signature, Description and Residence of Informant.	When Registered.	Signature of Registrar.
453	Twenty fourth March 1903 9 Schleswig Street U.D	John William	Boy	Fred Bowes	Agnes Bowes formerly Hornby	Coachman	Fred Bowes Father 9 Schleswig Street Preston	Twenty seventh April 1903	Edward Ambler Registrar

I hereby certify that the above is a true Copy of an Entry of Birth in a Register Book in my custody.

Witness my hand this _____ 19th day of _____ March _____ 1917

Superintendent 1

[NOTE.—_The word "Superintendent" to be s_
Certificate is given by the Regist

25ª Winckley Square,
Preston.

Frederick Bowes has been in my Employ as Coachman for seven years, v during that time I always found him honest v sober. He is a good groom, an excellent driver, v has a good all-round knowledge of horses.

J.R. Dunn.

May 5th 1905.

Many companies required proof of age in order to legally employ young workers. John William Bowes' Certified Entry of Birth is not his actual birth certificate. This document was issued to verify his employment eligibility in accordance with the 1901 child-labour laws. Use it as a substitute for the birth certificate, but always double-check the accuracy of the details.

Letters of recommendation from employers offer insights into the daily life and reputation of an ancestor.

Further leads from a letter of reference

Problem

Chantal has copies of letters of reference written by the employers of her grandfather, Fred Bowes, which were stored in a tin in his tallboy. What do they tell her?

Solution

These interesting letters describe, albeit briefly, the content and quality of the work performed by Mr Bowes as a groom and later as a coachman who had broad experience with horses and an excellent character. The letterheads provide address details for the two employers, whose signatures are also indicated. The envelope for the 1905 letter is a valuable record indicating where Chantal's great-grandfather lived at the time. For further research, Chantal could pursue the following leads:

Family heirlooms often include photographs, such as this one of Fred Bowes and his co-workers. They also provide visual clues to an ancestor's past. What is the significance of the badges worn by the men in this photograph?

- Study the places where Fred worked – what kind of workday did he experience? What were his job responsibilities? With whom did he interact?

- Try to identify his co-workers – they may be related to her.

- Look into the histories of the houses where Fred Bowes lived.

museum collections

Most of us recognize the value of museums as repositories of national and regional artefacts. Don't overlook them when tracing your family roots.

If you have traced your family to a locality or, perhaps, you know something about their livelihood – were they pioneers, political leaders or fishermen? – or their hobbies – did they make quilts, nets or lovespoons? – there may just be a local museum that has artefacts or personal items made or used by them. Such artefacts, photographs of events or street scenes that depict your ancestors, or archives with information about historical – or quirky – events in which your ancestor participated, can all increase your knowledge of your ancestors and the times in which they lived.

Filling in historical details

Even if a museum does not store items specifically known to have been your ancestor's, examining similar artefacts and photographs can bring you closer to them, in spirit if not in physical proximity. And, even if you are not certain that a relative has donated memorabilia or a private collection accumulated over the course of his or her lifetime, exploring the collections of a museum located in or near where you believe an ancestor once lived, worked, fought, or died can reveal

much about your heritage. You can learn about the times in which they lived, the social and cultural traditions in which they grew up, and the factors that influenced their lives and, ultimately, yours as well.

Thinking creatively

If you do gain access to artefacts directly related to an ancestor, examine them closely. Was she a skilled weaver or porcelain painter? Did he live a comfortable life or labour in backbreaking conditions? Did he or she receive any medals for military service? Use your imagination and seek out clues to further research. Perhaps you recognize the name of someone in a photograph who you know knew your ancestor. Perhaps the type of artefact offers clues to the kind of work they did or places they visited.

The key to using museum resources successfully is to think creatively and to ask lots of questions, which can prompt new research leads or spark the curator's memory of an object in the collection dating to the time when your ancestor lived. Just maybe, the item will turn out to have some direct tie to your personal past.

WHEN VISITING A MUSEUM TO DO FAMILY HISTORY RESEARCH

 Do

- know the names and/or occupations of the ancestors you wish to research before arriving at the museum.

- set up an appointment with the curator to receive his or her undivided attention and assistance with research.

- confirm whether special permission is required to handle or photograph objects in the collections.

- handle all objects with care and reverence.

 Don't

- expect the museum to have something of your ancestor's just because he or she lived in the town.

- demand too much of the curator's time, as they tend to be understaffed and overworked.

- ignore folklore and tales you may hear from local residents volunteering their time in the museum – they can hold clues to your past.

- assume that, just because the museum does hold a collection donated by your ancestor, they will automatically grant you unlimited access.

tip Accessing museum collections

Increasingly museums are using the Internet to share their collections with the world. Family history researchers should check relevant websites to determine if images of items within a museum's collections related to an ancestor are available online or if they can be requested for online access. Though not comprehensive, websites such as Gathering the Jewels, at www.gtj.org.uk/en/index, might just connect you with a piece of your past.

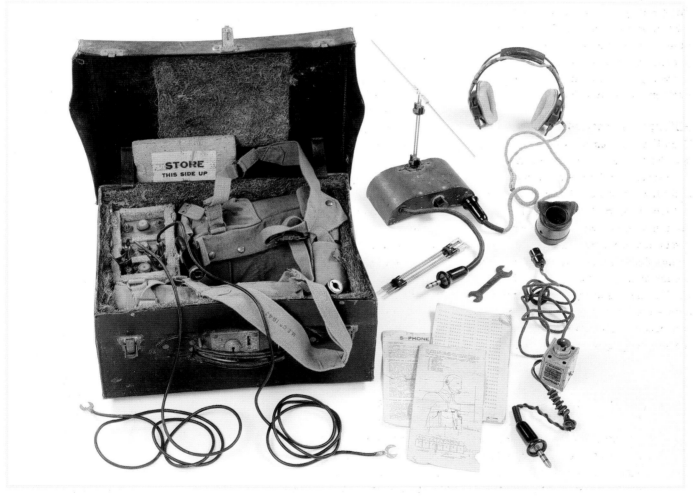

Military museums are filled with memorabilia from both war and peacetime. Items such as this mobile communications device may have been used by your ancestor. Even though you cannot take the artefacts home, you can gain a real sense of the job from such artefacts.

maps

Genealogists value all sorts of maps. The information you can extract from them will not only fill in research gaps but can also lead to your past.

Types of maps

From road maps, street guides and gazetteers, which route you around the countryside, county atlases and historical town maps to parish, railway, highway and land ownership (plat) maps, maps can help you locate ancestral homes, farmsteads, cemeteries and businesses.

Some governmental bodies, such as the US Department of Transportation, the Bureau of Land Management and the Australian Department of Land Service, produce maps that are intended for purposes other than genealogy but that will also help you trace your roots. Several agencies, including the US

Geological Survey (erg.usgs.gov/isb/pubs/booklets/usgsmaps/usgsmaps.html) and the Ordnance Survey (www.ordsvy.gov.uk or www.ordnancesurvey.co.uk), also provide Internet access to their maps. Some such maps are available free of charge, others for a modest fee.

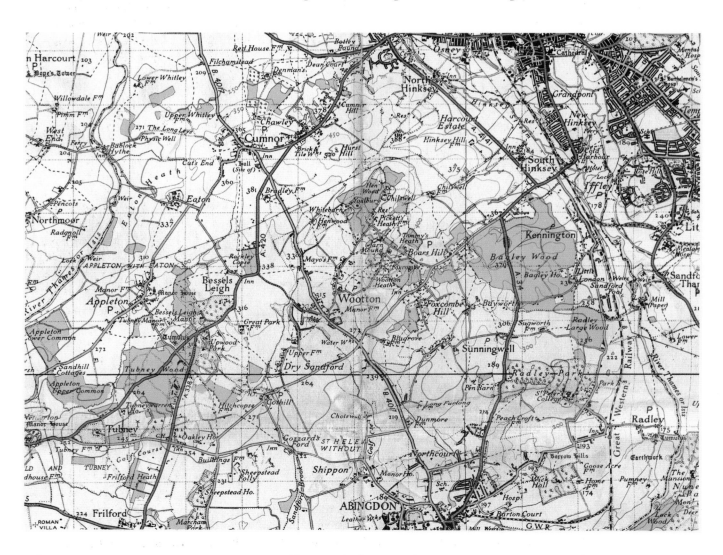

Ordnance Survey maps are among Britain's greatest gold mines of information, and can be used to pinpoint the location and plans of ancestral estates, buildings and residences.

Maps for UK research

UK maps are often so detailed that they can even provide you with a realistic impression of a site's appearance.

Ordnance Survey (OS) maps are superb resources. Initiated in 1791 by the Board of Ordnance as part of a defence project to survey the English countryside, OS maps not only display roads, lanes, topographical features and village names, they also identify houses, farms and other buildings, not just with a dot but with a name and a general outline of the structure.

Sadly, the Ordnance Survey has begun deleting some details from its new maps, removing information it believes is not necessary or of current public interest. Therefore, one of the best ways to locate your ancestral homestead, parish church or family cemetery is to examine maps from more than one period of time, starting with the most recent and comparing them with earlier maps of the same area. Fortunately, older OS maps are still quite available. Many can be purchased in second-hand bookstores and you can also find copies in the county record offices, public libraries (most of which have special local history sections) and other institutions, including the Royal Commissions on Ancient and Historic Monuments.

Almost all UK bookstores sell new OS maps, as do larger franchise bookstores in North America. You can also find them online. The Ordnance Survey itself provides a 'get-a-map' Internet service at www.ordnancesurvey.co.uk/getamap.

Manuscript estate maps show the physical layout of buildings and associated fields (with names and colour) on an estate. Use them to identify the structures and to pinpoint field boundaries, which often survive remarkably unaltered. Dating from at least as early as the 17th century, single maps document individual properties, whereas volumes of maps depict the entire estate. The maps provide detailed topographical pictures and display even minor features such as lanes, drovers ways, bridleways, tracks, fords, bridges and ferries.

Some estate maps are associated with reference books that name owners, tenants, fields, holdings, acreages and land usage. Repositories include county record offices, the British Library (www.bl.uk), the National Library of Wales, Oxford University's Bodleian Library (www.bodley.ox.ac.uk/guides/maps) and the National Library of Scotland (www.nls.uk).

Tithe maps, dating mainly from 1837 to 1850, feature detailed plans of parishes throughout the UK.

Beginning in the Middle Ages, tithes equivalent to one-tenth of a person's income were paid to the rector of the local parish church. In 1836 the British government decided to survey and map all titheable lands. It then imposed a monetary rent on landowners, most of whom had been paying their tithes in kind, usually with farm products.

A tithe award, the document that recorded the exact amount of rent, the owners' names and the names of the people who farmed the land and occupied its dwellings, normally accompanies a tithe map.

Repositories include county records offices, the National Archives at Kew and the National Library of Wales in Aberystwyth (www.llgc.org.uk/www_s001.htm).

Maps for US research

Although created for other purposes, specialized maps are a boon to family history research in the US.

Sanborn Fire Insurance Maps are very useful tools for family history research in the US. Intended to help fire-insurance agents determine the degree of fire hazard associated with a particular property, Sanborn maps provide a 'footprint' – or actual outline – of houses and other structures. Minute features like fire walls, locations of windows and doors, types of roofs, widths and names of streets, property boundaries, building usage and house and block numbers are identified on these maps.

Some 50,000 editions of Sanborn maps have been produced. In 1996 Environmental Data Resources, Inc. (EDR) purchased the Sanborn Map Company collection. EDR has digitized the maps and provides a searchable database (Sanborn Search Engine) on its website, www.edrnet.com/reports/historical.html.

The Library of Congress houses the maps in its special collections section. Sanborn maps can also be found in university libraries, fire departments, property assessor offices, real estate offices, title companies and city planning departments.

Plat maps, though technically classified as land records, are true maps that indicate land-ownership patterns established in counties throughout the US.

Initiated in 1785 by the Land Ordnance, the system (also known as the Public Land Survey System) documented property boundaries based on visual cues, such as landmarks like towers, on plat maps. Prepared from various sources, including census information, tax parcel maps, aerial photographs and property descriptions, plat maps provide land owners – and family historians – with a pictorial representation of an area of land. Drawn to scale, plat maps display the division of a parcel of land into lots and show topographical features, roads, waterways and railways, streets, alleys and rights-of-way.

Repositories for these maps include county courthouses, city halls, state archives, planning departments and real-estate agencies. The Family History Library, its Family History Centres and US public libraries also hold published plat books.

original records & transcriptions

Our human ability to create countless records in all sizes, shapes, materials and handwriting is partly what makes tracing one's roots such a challenge.

Long before word processors replaced the human hand as the writing instrument of the times, handwritten documents not only chronicled historic events but also recorded vital statistics, business and personal transactions, governmental and private agreements, and much more.

Primary versus secondary sources

Family history researchers should strive to locate original records, also known as 'primary sources', which were created on or about the time the event they document occurred. If you cannot review the originals themselves, try to obtain exact duplicates. In general, primary records are more reliable than documents produced even just a short while after an event.

However, never simply assume that primary sources are completely accurate accounts of your ancestor's life. Not only may they contain errors (spelling, dates, place names, other details) accidentally entered by the person gathering the information or deliberately proffered by the subject of the document, but archaic handwriting styles or the use of an unfamiliar or foreign language can also make them difficult to read.

Many researchers rely on second-hand transcriptions or translations rather than attempting to transcribe the information themselves. While 'secondary sources' – such as published family histories, indexes, transcriptions, Internet databases and personal websites, GEDcom files or a family member's inscribed pedigree chart – simplify the research process, using them as your main resources can cause giant problems. Quite often, the people you are relying upon for accurate transcriptions or error-free data make mistakes, misinterpret script or type an 'e' when they meant to type an 'r', for example.

The transcription challenge

When it comes to using primary sources, the further back in time you go, the more likely it becomes that you will encounter handwritten records. At some point you will want to transcribe an original document in its entirety, or, at the very least, add portions of the data on to your charts and into your notes. At first glance, you might think that merely copying words from a document is simple. Yet as you look closer, you'll become aware of strange letters, unfamiliar phrases and even misspellings that seem to fill the records. How do you cope?

Besides exercising extra caution when transcribing and interpreting data – even typewritten information – you will probably have to become something of a handwriting specialist – at least for the time frame, country and language in which your documents were created. For example, when is a 'y' not a 'y'? When it's a 'thorn' – which should be transcribed as 'th' rather than 'y'. That quaint English word 'ye' should actually be transcribed as 'the'.

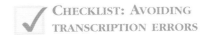

CHECKLIST: AVOIDING TRANSCRIPTION ERRORS

To help lessen the chances of you making your own transcription errors, try the following:

- Take a palaeography course and learn how to decipher old handwriting, the principles of letter creation and commonly used abbreviations. Developed in the early 13th century to distinguish between authentic documents and forgeries, palaeography is a very useful tool for modern genealogists.

- If spelling confuses you, compare the word or letters with others in the same document. Say the word out loud: when vocalizing a word or phrase in its context, you can often decipher it.

- When reviewing records someone else has transcribed, keep an eye out for mistakes made by misreading the handwriting. Identifying transcription errors can guide you past a sticking point in your research.

- Always record everything exactly as you see it. Even though a person's surname may be spelled several different ways in the same document, never correct the spellings.

Even in the 20th century, handwritten records, such as this divorce petition, were accepted as legal documents. When you come across such documents in the course of your research, you will need to pay extra attention to the unusual writing to ensure that you transcribe it accurately. Ask a friend or family member for a second opinion if the handwriting seems illegible to you.

the penitentiary of the said State
for a term of eight years, which
Judgment and sentence is in
full force and not reversed and
that said defendant is now confined as a prisoner in the penitentiary of the said State for said
Crime Wherefore the plaintiff
prays for a Judgment divorcing
said plaintiff from said defendant
and dissolving the said Marriage and that she be restored
to her maiden name of Barbara Stoner, And that the plaintiff be awarded the custody and
Control of said Child Nince
Seiser And for other and
proper relief

Barbara Seiser By A.
E. Walton her attorney

State of Ohio
Wyandot County Ss.

The Said plaintiff
Barbara Seiser being first
duly sworn says that the allegations
in this her petition are true

Barbara Seiser,

Subscribed in my presence
and sworn to before me this 26th
day of April A.D. 1848

surname variations

As you work your way through the records, you will reach dead ends, as trails lead nowhere, names disappear from histories and lineages seem to stop abruptly.

As always, when it comes to doing family history research, you must have an open mind, be imaginative and also be ready to move in new directions. The family tradition that claims your surname has always been spelled 'Taylor', for example, may have led you down the wrong road. Even if your relatives insist that the ancestral line has always called itself 'Taylor', consider other options: you might find out that you have blood-ties to people who spell their surnames 'Tailor', 'Talore' or 'Taylore'.

Patronymics

Even though the use of fixed surnames is commonplace today, the practice did not become standardized until the world's population expanded and people needed an improved, more concise way to distinguish individuals from each other. The 'patronymic' system of naming – where a child's surname is based on the father's forename – has been in place in many countries for several centuries. For example, the Scottish surname MacLeod indicates the bearer of the name was the 'son of' a man named 'Leod'. Consequently, each generation acquires a new surname and the cultures that use patronymics produce myriad names, which family historians must study with care in order to trace family roots accurately.

The Welsh have historically used patronymics to prove lengthy pedigrees. The name of one of Wales's great medieval princes of Gwynedd, Llywelyn ap Gruffydd ap Llywelyn ab Iorwerth, indicates that Llywelyn was the son of Gruffydd, who was the son of Llywelyn, who was the son of Iorwerth. In other words, Llywelyn's father was known as Gruffydd ap Llywelyn, his grandfather had the name Llywelyn ab Iorwerth, and so on.

Fixed surnames

By the 19th century, residents of most European nations, the US and Canada had adopted fixed surnames for self-identification. Ironically, however, the use of fixed surnames has also created confusion for family history researchers. Even though a surname has been transferred between generations within the same family, its spelling may have been changed over time, either accidentally or deliberately. So you should always consider alternate forms of a surname when you're searching official records or verifying data collected from several sources.

Reasons for surname changes

Surnames evolve for a variety of reasons. Some changes are deliberate: for example, a new bride often adopts her husband's surname. Some people use 'stage names' to pursue an acting or literary career or to create a more pleasing persona. Many continue to use their birth name when not in the public eye and sometimes their children acquire the new surname. Others change their names to escape the law enforcement system, slavery, an oppressive government or problematic family situations.

Immigrants often alter their surnames when settling in their new homeland as they seek not only to assimilate themselves more readily, but also to make their names easier to spell and pronounce. They may also do so to avoid retribution or discrimination based on name associations and nationality or even to sever themselves completely – emotionally as well as physically – from their past.

Immigrants may anglicize their surnames or change the spelling to conform with linguistic nuances. They may also translate their surnames into the language of the new country or modify the spelling for use with a different alphabet. A 'social climber' may deliberately change his or her surname to present a more upscale image of himself or herself, for example, changing a name like 'Black' to the more 'upwardly mobile' 'Blackwood'.

Inadvertent changes

Surnames also change inadvertently. Not only are transcription errors common (particularly on the Internet), but clerks, clergymen and other scribes who enter surnames into official documents mishear pronunciations and then misspell the names, either making creative changes owing to a lack of familiarity with the surname or just making careless mistakes. As many of our ancestors were probably illiterate, it is possible that they did not know how to spell their own names. They may have spelled them phonetically rather than literally or they may have allowed the transcriber to decide how to spell the surname. As a result, minute alterations occurred.

Owing to the similarities between certain letters or sounds, transcribers easily confuse 'b' and 'p', 'f' and 'v', 'dd' and 'th', 's' and 'z' and 'c' and 's'.

Finding a lost surname

Problem

My relatives insist that our surname has always been 'Stoner'. I have been able to trace my Stoner roots back to the 1890s, but then the surname seems to disappear from official records. What can I do to get past this dead-end?

Solution

- Devise a 'do-it-yourself' approach and develop a list of alternate spellings for the surname you are examining.

- If the time frame fits and your ancestor lived in the US, try using the Soundex system (see below) to identify alternate surnames to research.

- Say the surname aloud. Can you imagine other ways that the name may have been pronounced or spelled phonetically? How about 'Stowner' or 'Stonor' or 'Stawner'? Write them down.

- Ask several people to pronounce the name or listen to you say the name, so that you can identify alternative spellings or pronunciations and add them to your list.

- Rewrite the surname, adding or subtracting letters such as an 'e', 'y' or 's'. Could 'Stoner' be 'Stone', or 'Stoners' or 'Stones'?

- Interchange similar vowels, such as 'e' and 'i', or letters like 'j' and 'i', or 'v' and 'u' to create alternatives. 'Stonir'?

- List any variations that may once have started with an 'h' (often silent in English) but now begin with a vowel.

- Add or delete surname extensions, for example, changing Schwartzberg to Schwartz, or vice versa, or Johnston to Johnson, Johns to Jones?

- When possible, spell the surname as it might appear in a foreign language. For example, change 'Stoner' to 'Steiner'.

- Deliberately misspell the surname. How about 'Stover', 'Stainer' or 'Steener'?

- Join or contact a family or surname association, a one-name study group or an online bulletin board or newsgroup, whose members can offer guidance.

- Begin a new search, checking for the surname variants you have generated, keeping an open mind to the possibilities that Jane Stoner and Jane Steiner and Jayne Stone might very well be the same person.

The Soundex coding system

Developed by the US Works Projects Administration to sort out census data gathered from 1880 to 1930, the Soundex coding system indexes names by the way they sound rather than their spelling. Surnames that sound the same but are spelled differently have identical four-character codes, under which the data is filed. (NOTE: The Soundex system is only available for certain US census years and for certain states.)

One of the most confusing and complex concepts you will have to grapple with is how the Gregorian calendar affected the way dates were recorded.

From the Julian to the Gregorian calendar

Every serious genealogist needs a basic understanding of the 1752 calendar change in order to interpret official documents properly, particularly those written between 1582 and 1752.

In 1582 Pope Gregory XIII introduced a new calendar, created by his astronomer and mathematician, Aloysius Lilius, as a substitute for the increasingly inadequate Roman calendar that had been established by Julius Caesar. The two men determined that by the end of each year under the Julian system, the calendar had accumulated a surplus of five hours, 48 minutes and 45 seconds. So, by the 16th century, the human calendar was very much out of synch with nature's solar and lunar calendars.

Under the Gregorian system, also known as the New Style (NS) calendar, the first day of the new year shifted to 1 January from 25 March, which marked the beginning of the new year under the Old Style (OS), Julian calendar. To compensate for the errors, the Pope ordered the elimination of ten days from the month of October in 1582. Consequently, 15 October followed 4 October and the intervening days simply never occurred.

While most Roman Catholic nations around the world transitioned promptly to the NS calendar, many others did not. Protestant countries, including Great Britain, Ireland and the British colonies, waited until 1752 to adopt the Gregorian system formally in accordance with Lord Chesterfield's New Style Calendar Act of 1751 (Scotland adopted the NS calendar in 1600). Some countries, such as Russia, Greece and the Balkans, did not make the change until the 20th century. As in 1582, when the NS calendar was adopted in 1752, the year lost a number of days. This time, 11 days were dropped from September, so that 14 September 1752 immediately followed 2 September.

Double dating

When studying records created between 1582 and 1752, you will more than likely encounter the use of double dates for events occurring between 1 January and 24 March of those years. So you may find that two years are given for events recorded in town, court and church records, in wills and even on gravestones.

Using a slash mark (/) to distinguish between Julian and Gregorian dates, double dates often appear as '17 January 1687/1688' or '4 March 1724/5'. Be sure to record them exactly as they appear. If you have already done other research, you may wish to include your own interpretation of which is the correct year – but do so in brackets or with the notation that the interpretation is yours alone.

Regnal dates

To complicate matters still further, family history researchers using British records, especially those created in the Middle Ages and Renaissance, must know how to interpret regnal dates, which were based on their relationship to a particular monarch's reign rather than the Gregorian or Julian calendars. Appearing as early as the 8th century and used routinely after the coronation of Richard I in 1189, regnal dates were used with formal documents signed by or created for the monarchy. Regnal years started on specific dates, normally the monarch's accession date rather than 1 January or 25 March, and continued for an entire 12 months after that date. The next regnal year began on the calendar anniversary of the accession (not the coronation date, which usually occurred sometime later).

Interestingly, James VI of Scotland (crowned king in 1567), who became James I of England in 1603, used two sets of regnal years in his official documents. Even after the adoption of the Gregorian calendar in 1752, regnal dates continued to be used in official documents in Britain.

In 1936 three different kings ruled Britain consecutively; as a result, three different sets of regnal years exist: January to November marks the 26th regnal year of George V, November to December marks Edward VIII's first regnal year and, upon Edward's abdication in December 1936, his brother, George VI, began his first regnal year.

When researching early British records, be sure to account for date differences based on regnal years. Use a preprepared chart to identify the exact year.

Discrepancies with dates

Problem

Even though I understand that the Gregorian calendar replaced the Julian calendar, I am still having difficulty pinpointing the exact date that my ancestor died, as records seem to conflict on this issue. Have I missed something?

Solution

Like so many other aspects of family history research, there are always exceptions to the rule when it comes to determining dates for life-changing events. The following are just some examples:

- Even though 1752 marks the historic date when Britain and its colonies adopted the Gregorian calendar and the NS system was accepted worldwide, different populations have continued to use traditional systems of dating. For example, the Jewish calendar, a combined solar/lunar calendar, is used both for religious purposes and as Israel's official calendar. Many Islamic nations, including Saudi Arabia, follow a lunar calendar for both religious and administrative purposes, while others use the Gregorian calendar, but only for official purposes. Always consider the influence of a person's religion on the dates associated with key life events.

- After 1752 the Quakers and some other groups implemented a dating system whereby the months were identified by name rather than number. January became 'the first month', February was 'the second month' and September was 'the ninth month'. Before 1752 the 'first month' was March, 'the second month' was April, and so on. Be aware of these inconsistencies when reviewing Quaker and other religious records created before 1752.

pinpointing place names

If you think you've identified your ancestor's place of birth, burial or residence but can't find his or her name anywhere in local records, you may be looking at the wrong place!

Spelling inconsistencies

Before assuming that you have the wrong location, verify its spelling. Did you or someone else make an error transcribing the data? Did the writer of the original document misspell the name? Has the spelling of the place changed over time? Remember, official records contain typographical and transcription errors, so reconfirm the spelling of the place as it appears on whatever documents you have gathered before considering other possibilities.

Be aware, however, that different records may also refer to the same place but spell it differently. For example, the castle town of Criccieth in North Wales may appear as Crickaeth, Crikeith, Krickieth, Cricieth, etc. Look for spelling variants if you cannot pinpoint a place name.

The reliability of a place name

The place name you have listed for an ancestor may actually point to somewhere other than the town or village in which he lived or died. It may be the name of a larger jurisdiction, such as the parish, county, state or local unit that encompassed or governed the town. Or the place name may refer to a large city close to where your ancestor lived. Even today, it's not uncommon for someone born and raised in a suburb or hamlet several miles from a county town to say they are from the larger, better-known locality. If the records state that an ancestor came from a city, particularly a capital city or a county whose name is shared with a city, remember that she or he may have lived in a smaller community nearby. Expand your search accordingly.

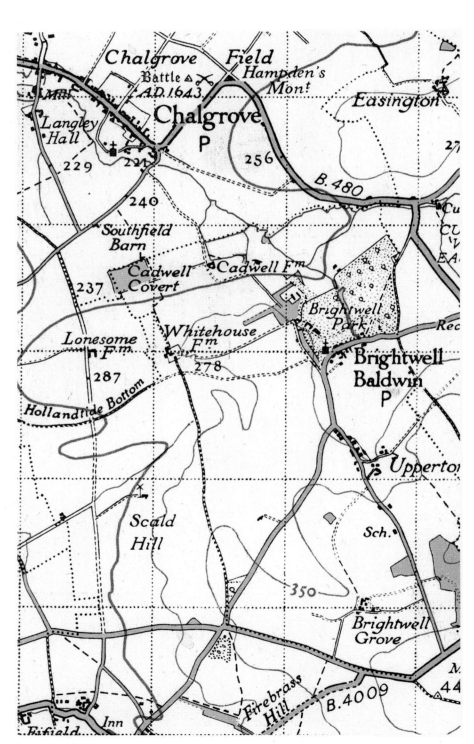

Multiple use of the same place name

Maybe you have confused the location of the place name, assuming that it is in one county or state when it's actually located in another. For example, Trefdraeth is the Welsh name for Newport in Pembrokeshire and also the name of a parish near Aberffraw on the Isle of Anglesey. And another Newport in Wales is located in what is now Monmouthshire.

Changing borders

Many places not only alter their names, they also change their locations – no, not physically, but legally and politically. If one country seizes another, the new government often renames the territory to reflect the change of power. When a country dissolves into several smaller countries or a colony wins its independence, the new nations often take on new names. City names may change as well.

Geopolitical units also shift as populations rise and fall and politicians realign boundaries to accommodate the variations: between 1974 and 1996, the Monmouthshire Newport mentioned above was officially part of the county of Gwent, while the Pembrokeshire Newport was part of Dyfed; before 1974 other county names applied for these places.

Place names often vary over time, and more than one region may contain the same place name. Maps make ideal finding aids for verifying that your ancestors lived in a specific place.

Determining exact locations

Problem

I am having trouble determining exactly where my ancestor lived before she emigrated to America. I am unfamiliar with the geography and political boundaries in what I believe to be my ancestor's homeland. How do I narrow down the possibilities?

Solution

Study historical maps, atlases, place name gazetteers and other references, which you will find in libraries, museums, bookstores and repositories such as the National Archives, the National Library of Wales and county record offices. Internet users will find the following websites of particular interest:

- geonames.usgs.gov – The Geographic Names Information System (GNIS) (for place names in the US and its territories).

- gnswww.nga.mil/geonames/GNS/index.jsp – GEOnet Names Server (GNS) (for international place names).

- www.ordnancesurvey.gov.uk – Ordnance Survey (Britain's national mapping agency).

- www.loc.gov/rr/geogmap/gmpage.html – Library of Congress Geography and Map Division.

- www.ga.gov.au/map/names – Geoscience Australia: Placenames Search.

- geonames.nrcan.gc.ca – Geographical Names of Canada.

- www.gazetteer.co.uk – Gazetteer of British Place Names.

- www.nla.gov.au/map/gazetteers.html – National Library of Australia: Gazetteers of Australia.

- www.old-maps.co.uk – Landmark Information Group's www.old-maps.co.uk.

This section takes a look at some of the special record types not covered in Part Three. These are prompted by certain social and historical circumstances. For example, illegitimacy and adoption often leave gaps in the official records. Unique record types have also been created through slavery and deportation.

Tracing one's male line can be a challenge, but it often takes even more diligence and creativity to find the branches on a female ancestor's family tree.

Tracing one's female ancestors, especially those who lived several generations ago, can be a daunting prospect. Not only has it been common practice for women around the world to adopt their husband's surname, either giving up their maiden name altogether or replacing their middle name with the maiden name, but also women's changing roles in society and the legal system have impacted on how their names have appeared in official documents over the course of time.

Women in society

You can make the task easier by taking the time to educate yourself about the social history of the era in which your ancestors lived. Learn about the rights women had when it came to signing and creating documents in their own name. In many cultures, women have not had the legal right to sign legal documents – this is their husband's right and duty. In some cultures, when women are able to sign documents, the law allows them to use only their maiden names.

In addition, in places where common law applies (or has applied during the course of history), a woman has no control over the property she brings into her marriage. Rather, the husband acquires full ownership and can dispose of it as he wishes. Even at her husband's death, the widow

receives only a percentage of the estate in common law countries. However, where civil law applies, spouses are considered equal owners of community property, which the husband manages, but the wife also has the legal right to possess and manage her own property separately from her husband.

When reviewing property and other records, remember to take into account the time period, whether the place followed common or civil law and what kind of constraints may have been placed on a woman that directly influenced the information you will find in official documents.

Early records of women are often difficult to locate, regardless of whether they were mothers and homemakers or nurses, teachers, military service members or worked in other trades.

Tracing a female ancestor's maiden name

Problem

Even though I have examined my family's archives and marriage records related to my great-grandmother, I am still having difficulty finding her maiden name. Where else should I look?

Solution

If the marriage records do not list the maiden name, try the following:

☐ Obtain a copy of any divorce, hospital, school or voting records, as applicable.

☐ Review migration records, particularly passenger lists, which can provide a wealth of individual detail, and naturalization papers.

☐ Locate your female ancestor's obituary for her maiden name or the names of her brothers.

☐ Locate birth and marriage announcements around the time you are searching.

☐ Find the applicable cemetery records, transcriptions or headstone inscription. A female ancestor may have her own grave marker or her name may be inscribed on a larger family stone that also lists the name and dates for her husband.

☐ Examine the husband's death certificate and any other documents that may contain a wife's full name, such as military and pension records, wills, deeds and land records. You may also find a man's in-laws (his wife's parents) listed on official records.

☐ Some census records provide clues, but you will need an investigative mind. Consider that neighbours or people living in the household may be relatives, the wife's siblings or her aged parent. Look at children's middle names for their mother's maiden name.

☐ Make a list of the husband's friends, business partners and associates in a fraternal society, religious group or even a sports team. They may be relatives of your female ancestor.

☐ Review published family and local histories and consult genealogical or historical societies in the region where your ancestor lived.

☐ Above all, widen your vision. Think in reverse – maybe a child was named after his or her grandparent (one of the mother's parents), whose records you can locate. Make educated inferences based on the names that do appear in your relatives' records.

☐ And don't give up!

Images of mother and daughter, such as this photo of Marie Clayton's grandmother, Ada Barker, and aunt, often identify maiden names. Check the back for handwritten details.

One of the few professions that Victorian society allotted to women was teaching. This photograph shows elementary schoolchildren in 1900 learning a lesson about shapes.

Finding a maiden name

When tracing female ancestors, begin by identifying the woman's maiden name, that is, the surname she was born with. Review everything you already know about this ancestor: her forenames, husband's surname, birth and death dates (if available) or the general time frame, etc.

Remember those family records and other treasures you gathered when you first started tracing your roots? Now's the time to take a fresh look at them for clues to your female ancestor's past. Look for maiden names in family bibles, old letters or diaries, on the backs of old photographs, on wedding invitations and on family heirlooms, such as embroidered samplers, which often display a family tree or the name of the creator somewhere on the piecework. Ask family members for their recollections, which may point you in the right direction.

Try to locate your ancestor's marriage record, which may document her maiden name. Check marriage registers and vital records, marriage applications and licences, marriage certificates, and marriage banns. Check church or parish registers: witnesses

To be used for a WOMAN only.

Form 10 Pen.

BOARD OF EDUCATION.

School Teachers (Superannuation) Act, 1918.

This Form should be filled up by any teacher desirous of having her service treated as Recognised Service or Qualifying Service under the above-named Act, and returned to the Board of Education, London, S.W.7.

NOTE.—I. Teaching or other service claimed as recognised or qualifying service, including War Service and Sick Leave, should be entered under the heading "Particulars of Service."

II. War Service should also be entered under the heading that follows. Unit, rank and number, if any, at the beginning and end of service should be stated.

III. Particulars of Sick Leave should also be given in the space provided for that purpose. Where during absence on Sick Leave payment has been made at varying rates, each rate and period should be stated separately. No period need be entered unless the teacher was on less than half-pay or unless it exceeded three months.

IV. Full-time service only should be entered. Where during any service a teacher's time has been divided between two or more Schools or Classes, the number of hours a week spent in each should be given.

V. No service before the age of 18 years should be entered.

VI. The Form must not be signed before 1st April, 1919.

	SURNAME.	CHRISTIAN NAME(S).
Name in full	Barker née Wicks	Ada

(If a married woman, state also Maiden Name.)

Number (if a Certificated Teacher) 6671

Date of birth 6. 6. 1856.

(A Registrar's Certificate of Birth must be furnished except in the case of Certificated Teachers recognised since 1.4.1899.)

PARTICULARS OF SERVICE.

Name of School.	County.	Status of School. (Elementary, Secondary, Day, Evening, &c.).	Date when service						Particulars required under Note IV.
			Commenced.			Ended.			
			Day.	Month.	Year.	Day.	Month.	Year.	
Seamore Girls	Stafford	"		Oct.	76	18	7.	78	
Melbourne Derby	Derby	Elementary	29	7	78	20	12	80	
Blakenall C.E	Stafford	"	10	1	81	8	8	90	
Bloxwich Inf.	"	"	22	9	90	14	5	91	
St. Andrews Wednesbury	"	"	14	9	91	31	8	93	
Blakenall Inf	"		3	9	93	still engaged here.✕			

Sep 1. June 6th 1921

(1008) W². 41290/475c. 135M. 2/19. P.P. Ltd.   [OVER.

This document reveals a lot about society and the place of women in in the early 20th century. These documents are worth tracking down if you know that one of your ancestors was a teacher.

who signed marriage records may have the same surname as your female ancestor. Also look at baptismal and christening records, which may indicate the maiden name of the child's mother. Many women revert to their maiden names upon divorce or use them while in the work force.

You may also be able to deduce maiden names from obituaries, where a brother's surname or that of another relative may be mentioned. Check all relevant records.

'To be used for a WOMAN only'

During the 19th century, the British Board of Education developed records that family historians can use to trace their female ancestors. The form, titled 'To be used for a WOMAN only' and was created in accordance with the School Teachers (Superannuation) Act, 1918, reveals much about a British teacher's service and also provides several key bits of personal information. The one shown here gives Ada Barker's maiden name (Wilks), and lists the names, dates and location of the schools where Ada taught. Each entry invites further research into Ada's tenure there.

Note: The spelling of Ada's maiden name is inconsistent with most other official documents, such as the certificate of her marriage to Joseph Barker, where her surname and that of her father are spelled 'Wilkes'. Ada's birth certificate, on the other hand, is consistent with the teaching record. More research should be carried out to confirm which spelling is correct.

illegitimacy and adoption

Gaps in your family tree may imply more than just missing information. They may indicate an ancestor's illegitimacy or that they were adopted.

While some problems can be traced to faulty transcription or misinterpreting the data, often researchers discover that something more intriguing or controversial occurred in their past. Events that may seem innocuous to you, the researcher, may have brought shame, embarrassment or legal problems to your ancestors. Your living relatives may consider them too intimate to discuss, let alone share with the rest of the world. So be sensitive and use tact when raising what may be an uncomfortable topic for your relatives.

Illegitimacy in social history

Historically, illegitimacy in the UK and US has long been a source of economic concern rather than merely something that brings shame upon an unwed woman and her family. The cost to a community of covering the welfare of an indigent woman and her children could be exorbitant if she had no viable means of support. As early as the 16th century, parents of an illegitimate child could be imprisoned, forced to provide a bond for the secure future of the child or made to move to another parish or community (perhaps where the father or mother was raised) that was legally responsible for the person.

During the 18th century, pregnant women were required to identify the father of an illegitimate child, who in turn was legally bound to provide either a lump sum of money to cover the child's welfare or to pay instalments over time. Commonly known as 'bastardy bonds', these payments released the parish or local authority from the legal responsibility and financial burden of caring for the child. During the 19th and 20th centuries, legislation changes increasingly placed the burden on the mother to sue the father if she wanted child support.

'Bastardy records'

Bastardy examinations, warrants, recognisance, summons, orders, certificates and bonds are excellent resources for researching illegitimate ancestors both in the UK and in certain parts of the US. They are normally stored in local records offices in both countries. Since bastardy cases were generally heard in Quarter Sessions and Petty Sessions courts, be sure to check court records as well. Parish Overseers' Accounts may also document the disposition of bastardy cases.

Adoptee ancestors

Parents place children into adoption for a variety of reasons, such as poverty or to avoid the stigma of illegitimacy. Many families legally adopt children, who take their surname. Having the same surname as the adoptive parents may disguise the fact of adoption and lead family history researchers to believe that an ancestor was the birth child of the adoptive parents.

Adoption often results in a name change for the child. Make sure that you locate the actual, original birth certificate to verify your adoptee ancestor's name. Sometimes adoptees change their name on their birth certificate to match the surname to that of their new parents.

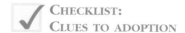

CHECKLIST: CLUES TO ADOPTION

If you believe an ancestor may have been adopted, consider the following:

- First, examine his or her birth certificate, which may reveal the names of birth parents (which will differ from the names you may already have on your pedigree chart).

- Look for an amended birth certificate, which often documents the birth parents' names.

- Review family records and memorabilia you have previously gathered for clues about the adoption.

- Check census or probate records, which may detail the relationships between individuals.

- Locate hospital records, guardianship records, court documents and child welfare and adoption agency records for information on your adoptee ancestor.

- You may also find details in state institution and workhouse records.

ADOPTION OF CHILDREN ACT, 1926.

A.C.A. 3.—*Form of Notice of Day appointed for Hearing of Petition.*

In the CROYDON **County Court.**

In the Matter of the Adoption of Children Act, 1926,

AND   E. 151.

In the Matter of the County Courts Act, 1934,

AND

In the Matter of ___David Roy Watson (to be known as David Roy Clark)___

of ___32, Nova Road, Croydon___ in the County of

___Surrey___ an Infant,

To ___Eric William Clark and Ruby Doris Clark___

of ___32, Nova Road, Croydon.___

Take Notice that a petition has been presented in the above matter praying that an order may be made for the adoption of the above-named

___David Roy Watson___

by ___Eric William Clark and Ruby Doris Clark, his wife___

of ___32, Nova Road, Croydon___

and that ___Croydon Corporation___

of ___Town Hall, Croydon___

has been appointed guardian *ad litem* to the said infant and that the said Petition will be heard at a Court to be held _____

at ___THE COUNTY COURT, SCARBROOK ROAD, CROYDON.___

on the ___28th___ day of ___February___ 19___49___

at ___10.15___o'clock in the ___fore___noon.

HOURS OF ATTENDANCE at the Court Office from 10 a.m. till 3.30 p.m., except on when the Office will be open from	Scarbrook Rd., Croydon, Saturdays Nine till Twelve o'clock.

BRUCE HUMFREY,

_____
Registrar.

(85210) 7/48

Gaps in a family tree are sometimes the result of childhood adoption. Adoption records can help adoptees identify parents and also provide leads for family history research into new lineages and changing surnames.

Recognizing illegitimacy

Problem

How do I recognize the illegitimacy of an ancestor in the documents I have already gathered?

Solution

Apply the investigative skills you have acquired during the course of your research and examine the records closely for the following clues:

- Compare birth and marriage dates for individuals and their parents. Did the marriage occur shortly after the birth of a child? Parents of an illegitimate child may take a few years to marry, if they did marry at all, so don't automatically rule out the husband of such marriages from being the child's father.

- Examine a child's full name. Illegitimate boys often acquired their father's surnames as their middle names. For example, James Williams Jones, son of Sarah Smith Jones, may have been the illegitimate son of Thomas Edward Williams.

- Check the records themselves. They may indicate, either directly or indirectly, that a child was illegitimate. Clues include descriptive phrases such as 'natural', 'base born', 'B', 'bastard', 'illegal', 'spurious', 'scapebegot', 'misbegotten', or the 'reputed' or 'imputed' child of X. Non-English language records often use similar terminology to indicate illegitimacy.

- Locate baptism or christening records for the names of both parents.

- Guardianship, wardship and apprenticeship records may also provide clues to the father's name, since illegitimate children often passed into their father's care in discreet ways.

- When you find conflicting information that seems to indicate an ancestor's illegitimacy, question relatives. Are there family stories about mysterious births and liaisons, or so-called 'black sheep'? They may be based in fact but distorted by time. Verifying the details can shed light on your past.

 DO

- consider the feelings and preferences of living relatives who may not wish to publicize a relationship they may consider embarrassing or 'no one else's business'.

- record and store all information – regardless of the status of your ancestor – to preserve it for future generations.

- document the fact of illegitimacy or adoption using a footnote or other method of notation.

- be respectful when documenting an ancestor's illegitimacy or adoptive status, particularly when preparing your family history for publication.

- use tact when questioning relatives about an ancestor's background, particularly if you believe that he or she was illegitimate or adopted.

 DON'T

- ignore the family history of the birth family, particularly if they are your blood relatives.

- include the adoptee's birth family on your pedigree chart, unless they have a definite blood connection to you.

- record or perpetuate misinformation just to assuage a

Adoption can be a time of joy and a time of sorrow. When researching adoptee and illegitimate ancestors, always consider the feelings of your relatives and consult their wishes before making your findings public.

CONNAUGHT
HOUSE
NATIONAL
ADOPTION
SOCIETY'S
BABIES'
HOSTEL

You may already know that you have Native American ancestry, but such family heritage may never have been examined in detail.

Tracing one's native heritage generally follows the same pathway discussed throughout this book. Begin at the beginning by recording all information you know about yourself, and then proceed backwards in time to parents, grandparents, etc. Write each ancestor's names and other details on a pedigree chart and/or family group sheet. Gather evidence at home first. Talk to relatives. Contact local, state and national repositories. Document your findings cautiously and methodically.

The unsettled and often tragic history of the world's native peoples has created its own archival information. Once you identify a gap in your research, you may find yourself stuck on where to turn next. Unfortunately, even the Internet is relatively lacking in guidance on tracing indigenous ancestors.

Native American ancestry

Information on Native American tribal groups other than those forcibly removed to reservations in the American South and Midwest can be much more difficult to find than records dealing with the Trail of Tears. Despite widespread family traditions that claim links to the Cherokee, there were well over 500 tribes in the US before settlement by European migrants. So

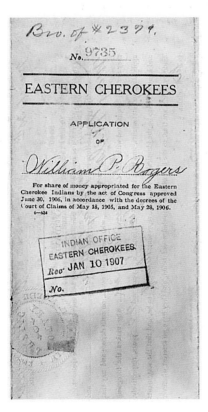

Eastern Cherokee applications, such as this one for William P. Rogers (famously known as Will Rogers), were filed to obtain compensation from a decree passed by the US Court of Claims in 1906. These applications are filled with useful genealogical information.

Finding Native American ancestors

Problem

My uncle has always claimed that we have Native American ties. What steps should I take to determine if his stories are true?

Solution

First of all, you'll need to establish your ancestor's tribal affiliation. If you cannot determine the tribe with a reasonable degree of certainty, identify the most likely possibilities based on geographical and historical information and other details you have gathered. Next, you should do the following:

- Educate yourself about the tribe's history.

- When searching official documents, always look for spelling variations and surname variants rooted in tribal naming customs (which may require extra research).

- Make a list of each ancestor's full name (including their Native American name), name of tribe, birth dates and relationships between you and the individuals you wish to research.

- Head to libraries, historical society centres and even the nearest Family History Centre. Do research in state archives, state historical societies and state universities.

- Email, write to or telephone the applicable indigenous museums or tribal headquarters. Most Native American tribes maintain a cultural or research centre staffed by individuals who should be able to point you in the right direction. See the Resources Directory for more information.

- Educate yourself about what you may find in records relating to Native Americans.

- Search the official records created by the Bureau of Indian Affairs and the agency assigned to the tribes you are studying. Many are available on microfilm at the US National Archives or one of the regional branches. You may also find information on the Familysearch.org website.

- Check federal census records, tribal census rolls, the Final Rolls, the Congressional Serial set: 1817–89, Indian school and hospital records, military records, tax and voting registers and land allotment rolls.

The second page of Will Rogers' application documents information you might not find anywhere else, such as the Indian names of family members, their birthplaces, and that they were listed on Emigrant pay rolls and the Cherokee Authenticated roll of 1880. Try to locate documents like these to learn more about these family members.

tip Aboriginal peoples in Canada

The Library and Archives Canada holds records for the Department of Indian Affairs and Northern development, which are inventoried by band, agency and district. Researchers with Canadian aboriginal ancestry should check Indian registers, membership records and lists and census, land and school records stored at the Library and Archives Canada. Start your research at the website for the Canadian Genealogy Centre: http://www.collectionscanada.ca/index-e.html.

the chances are higher than average that, if you do have Native American ancestors, they belonged to one of the other tribal nations.

If you hope to prove Native American ancestry, first check out your family traditions. Identify where they originated. Did your ancestors live in Oklahoma or Idaho, Arkansas or Arizona? If you narrow down the location, you improve your chances of discovering with which tribe he or she was actually affiliated.

Dawes Rolls

Among the most helpful resources for researching Native American ancestors are the so-called 'Dawes Rolls', named after Senator Henry Dawes, the author of the General Allotment Act of 1887. The legislation divided reservation lands into parcels, which were granted to eligible Native Americans and others who were living in Indian Territory.

Produced between 1898 and 1914, the rolls were created to identify those members of the 'five civilized tribes' who qualified for land allotments based on their enrolment category. These included people with Native American blood and their newborn and minor children, individuals married to Native Americans and freedmen (former slaves who had been adopted into a tribe) and their newborn and minor children.

Also known as the Final Rolls, these documents list names and other details for members of the Cherokee, Chickasaw, Choctaw, Creek and Seminole tribes whose enrolment applications were approved by the Secretary of the Interior and who actually received land. Enrollees received an enrolment (or census) card, which confirmed their affiliation with one of the five tribes. Descendants of Native Americans listed on the Final Rolls are eligible for membership in the same tribe as their ancestors – but only with proof of their ties to the enrollee.

The National Archives maintains microfilm copies of the Dawes Rolls. For copies of census cards, contact the National Archives – Southwest Region, PO Box 6216, Fort Worth, Texas 76115-0216. Internet users can find more information on the Southwest Region's website at www.archives.gov/facilities/tx/fort_worth.html and also on the NARA's main website at: www.archives.gov/research_room/arc/arc_info/native_americans_final_rolls_index.html.

Indigenous ancestors in Australia

As the governmental organization of Australia evolved over time, different state agencies were assigned responsibility for managing and administering the lives of Aboriginal and Torres Strait Islanders. Each agency created its own records. Family historians who wish to trace their Aboriginal roots should first educate themselves about this history before delving into the documents.

You may find records created by the following:

- Colonial Secretary's Office

- Aborigines Protection Board

- Aborigines Department

- Department of Aborigines and Fisheries

- Department of Native Welfare

- Department of Indigenous Affairs

- Health Department

- agencies relating to law enforcement and the court system

Fortunately, all offices of Australia's National Archives hold at least some of the above materials. If you are uncertain about the particular area where your ancestors lived, you may want to begin at the archives in Canberra, Melbourne or Darwin, which hold the most extensive collections. Alternatively, contact the applicable State Records Office, such as the State Records Office of Western Australia, the Public Record Office of Victoria or the State Records Office of South Australia, or visit the Indigenous Resource Unit at the John Oxley Library of Queensland in South Brisbane (www.slq.qld.gov.au/jol), which has a noteworthy collection related to Australia's indigenous peoples. Public access is restricted to certain records and you may need to obtain permission to view them; to avoid disappointment and wasted effort, be sure to check regulations before heading to the repository.

New Zealand's indigenous records

Like the other native populations mentioned above, the Maori of New Zealand have experienced significant sociocultural changes since the arrival of European migrants in their homeland. A number of agencies were established to govern the indigenous peoples, including the Native and Maori Affairs Department and the Maori Land Courts.

Not surprisingly, a variety of official documents exist that family history researchers may find of use, many of them stored at Archives New Zealand. These include Maori vital records, government and tribal census records, adoption records, tribal registers, probate and trial records, divorce records, coroners' reports, election records and native schools records.

Many of these records are specific to the Maori; others, however, are archived according to their more general classification, e.g., divorce records. Access to some of these records is restricted, so be sure to contact staff before visiting the repository. The head office is located in Wellington and Archives New Zealand has branches in Auckland, Christchurch and Dunedin.

Archives New Zealand holds many types of Maori records, including vital and census documents, native school records and more.

Millions of people with African ancestors live far from their ancestral homeland, where abundant records of more than three centuries of slavery survive.

The slave trade

As early as 1501, Spain granted permission to colonists to transport slaves forcibly from Africa to work their holdings in the Caribbean. By the 16th century, the British, Dutch, French and Portuguese had also entered the slave trade and had shipped thousands of West Africans to the Americas to work on their plantations. Scholars estimate that well over 10 million Africans journeyed to the Americas to labour as slaves. Most were plucked from their homelands in Senegal, Gambia, Sierra Leone and the Gold Coast. Others were shipped from Mozambique, Madagascar, the Cameroons and Nigeria. These men and women became the personal property of their white landowners. Just as any other property, they could be sold, inherited, given as gifts or donated to other owners. Not surprisingly, the majority of African-ancestored people in the US, the Caribbean nations, Canada, Latin America and the UK are descended from slaves.

Tracing African ancestors

Even though not all African-ancestored individuals are descended from slaves, family history researchers whose African relatives lived in the 'New World' before the turn of the 20th century should seek out special slavery and free black records for the genealogical information they contain.

However, before leaping into the records, use the guidelines detailed in Parts One and Two of this book to establish a well-organized, written research plan. Only once you reach back to 1870, when the federal census first lists all African-Americans (and Native Americans) by name, and after you have thoroughly examined all the record types you would normally research for any genealogy project – vital records, obituaries, census records, military records, court records, etc. – should you begin to examine slave records. However, never assume that you will find information on African ancestors in the same records as whites. Even in the late 20th century, certain record types were still segregated by race.

You should also be aware that at least 400,000 African-ancestored people in the US had become free years before the end of the Civil War. So you need to determine whether or not your ancestor was enslaved until 1863, when Lincoln signed the Emancipation Proclamation (officially ratified as the 13th amendment to the US Constitution in 1865). Also be aware that many Africans willingly emigrated to the Americas as early as the 17th century to serve as indentured servants, who were legally free. Others were freed from illegal slave ships upon reaching the Caribbean islands or settled in the Americas after being discharged from military service (as after the Revolutionary War, when the British army acquired slaves). So, your first step should be to determine whether your African ancestor was a slave or free black before 1870.

Before delving too much into the records, educate yourself about the African slave system, the history of emancipation and the legal status of African slaves. Study the histories of the nations, states, regions and localities where Africans were enslaved during the time period you are researching. Identify any religious groups or special organizations that may have played a role in the history of African-ancestored peoples and read about the Underground Railway that carried runaway slaves to freedom. Each topic will help you gain insight into the realities of the slave trade and its lingering impact on African-ancestored people around the world.

A portrait of Harriet Tubman (c. 1820–1913). Tubman, herself an escaped slave, helped hundreds of slaves escape the South by means of the Underground Railroad and nursed Union troops during the Civil War.

Date of each Manumission	Names of Persons Manumitted	Sex	Age	Price in currency paid for Slaves Redemption	At whose expence Effected	Amount of Tax or Fine	Fees paid at the Register Office
1823							
March 10	Alexandrine	Female			George Burton		1..16..
" 22	John	Male			Celestin Moiese		1..16..
" "	John Anislas & Joseph	Males			Alice Newcomb		1..16..
" "	Jeanne	Female	45 Years		Ismael Noirlin		1..16..
" "	Elizé	Male			Peter Larocque		1..16..
" "	Justine	Female	18 Years		Bartholomew Gray		1..16..
April 1	Rachael Williams Paine	Female			Meade Stone Daniel & Wife		3..12..
" 16	John Creantive	Male		166	Elizabeth M.S. Wykes		2..14..
" 19	Sarah Ann	Female			Sarah M Blair		1..16..
" "	Henry	Male			Ditto		1..16..
" "	Catherine	Female			Sarah Gamble Cumming		1..16..
" 28	Anthony Henry Bellot	Male			Frederic Bellot		1..16..
" "	Arsene	Female	18 Years		Gabriel St Rose		1..16..
" "	François	Male	25 Years		Ditto		1..16..
" "	Louis Marie	Male	22 Years		Ditto		1..16..
" "	Jeanne	Female	55 Years		Ditto		1..16..
" "	Marie Louise	Female	30 Years		Mondesir Lili		1..16..
" "	Marie	Female	23 Years				
" "	Marie François	Female	6 Years		Ditto		1..16..
" "	Zephorine	Male	8 Months				
" "	Felix	Male	17 Years		Ditto		1..16..
" "	Elizabeth	Female			Ditto		1..16..
" "	Ubrie	Male	25 Years		Ditto		1..16..
" "	St Rose (alias Hypolite)	Male			François Tavernivo		1..16..
" "	Coco	Male	35 Years		Noël Eloi		1..16..
" "	Alexandrine	Female			Grs of Valérine B. Tavernivo		1..16..
" "	Jervais	Male			Joseph Kavarier		1..16..

Records like this list of slaves showing date of manumission, names, sex and ages of slaves could prove invaluable in the search for one of your ancestors.

Record types associated specifically with African-ancestored peoples

Slave records

- Slave sales and importation declarations.

- Slave shipping lists and US Customs Service records.

- Records of the ports involved in the slave trade, particularly those from which the ships sailed.

- Slave registries and the records of the Slave Compensation Commission (for British West Indian slaves); located in island archives or register offices and UK National Archives.

- Slave census schedules and census records for free African-Americans.

- Census mortality schedules.

- Plantation records, including punishment books, inventories, accounts, and other documents.

- Apprenticeship bonds for freedmen.

- Declarations of freedom and manumission records.

- Free Black registers.

- Records gathered for UNESCO's Slave Trade Archives Project.

Other records

- Segregated records, including marriage records and vital statistics, tax records, deed and property records, and school records.

- African-American military records (for example, the United States Colored Troops regimental records or the records of the Tuskegee airmen) – for all US wars, and including service and pension records, discharge records and draft registration cards. The US National Archives acts as a repository for these documents.

- The records of the Bureau of Refugees, Freedmen and Abandoned Lands (commonly known as the Freedman's Bureau) and the records for the Freedmen's Savings and Trust Company, which the US National Archives has made available on microfilm.

- African-American church records and cemetery records.

WHEN RESEARCHING AFRICAN ANCESTORS...

✓ DO

- learn about African naming traditions, particularly those in use during the slavery years. Some slaves only took on new forenames when arriving in their new country; others switched surnames when sold to new owners. Members of the same family often had different surnames.
- examine military records, school records, vital records, cemetery records and church records for information on slave ancestors.
- explore Native American connections.

✗ DON'T

- limit your research to slave and free black records
- assume that freed slaves adopted the surname of their former owners. Many took the surname 'Freeman' or 'Freedman' to reflect their new status, but others took the surnames of people they admired, like George Washington, or a close friend or benefactor.
- assume a person listed as 'white' in census or other early records was actually Caucasian. Often, African and Native Americans and people with mixed ancestry identified themselves as white to avoid racial prejudice and social stigmatization. Clerks sometimes misassigned people to certain racial groups simply because of skin colour.

Tracing slave ancestors

Problem

I have worked my way back through my family history to 1870 and am ready to move further back in time, but I am aware that earlier records are less likely to list individual slaves. How can I find details about my specific ancestors?

Solution

Records dealing with individual slaves are exceedingly rare. So you have a better chance of finding relevant documents if you can identify the name of your slave ancestor's final owner.

- **Most often, individual slaves are listed on deeds and other property records or on other documents, such as plantation records, wills and probate records, inventories, appraisements and estate financial records, and bills of sale (some are stored with the Library of Congress or local repositories).**
- **Then, look for any documents or personal records created by the slave holder, such as correspondence, family bibles and diaries, for clues to slave names.**
- **Check local histories, state records, the records of the Freedman's Bureau and Freedman's Savings and Trust Company (located in the National Archives and regional centres), and Civil War records.**
- **Review church records, which may name owners who gave permission for slaves to marry or to baptize their children and also identify the slaves involved in the ceremonies.**
- **Check newspapers for slave sales, obituaries and other events.**
- **Visit the cemetery where a slave owner and his family are buried. Often, associated graves, marked or unmarked, may belong to slaves.**
- **Try to obtain burial records from the sexton's office. The same cemetery may have a separate section for African-Americans.**
- **To trace African ancestors in the Caribbean, look through the slave registers (established in 1814), which list details of owners and slaves, including name, age, colour, country of birth and the slave's occupation, manumission and the transfer of ownership.**

Research in Africa

Once you have checked all records that might pertain to your African ancestors that are stored in local, regional or national repositories, consider extending your efforts to Africa. First, look for information that relates to African origins, including their tribal association. Try to verify any connections mentioned by family members.

The next step is to examine maritime, port and slave shipping records and determine which ship transported your ancestor. Consult scholars who specialize in African history and the history of the slave trade. Become familiar with UNESCO'S Slave Trade Archives Project, launched in 1999 with the aim of improving access to and safeguarding original documents related to the transatlantic slave trade and slavery throughout the world (www.unesco.org/webworld/slavetradearchives). People with African ancestry linked to the Caribbean and Latin America will find this website of special interest.

UK Slave Registries

Mandated in response to the Slave Registration Act of 1819, a central registry of slaves was established in London. In 1821 the British government began enforcing the Act and required island governors to submit slave registries. Every three years from 1822 to 1834, when the Act was abolished, returns like those shown here for Mary Rosannah Rigby and Aaron Sims ('a free man of colour') were completed for each slave owned by a particular person. These documents record the owner's name and each slave's name, gender, age, colour, place of employment and – sometimes – the country of birth.

Bahama Islands 341

Return of Two Slaves the property of Mary Rosannah Rigby of the Island of New Providence the First day of January 1822

Number	Name	Sex	Age	Colour	Place of Employment at the time of the return	Whether African or Creole
1	Hannah	Female	Years 25	Black	Grand Bahama	Creole
2	Joe	Male	18 Months	Black	Grand Bahama	Creole

Bahama Islands W.W. Rigby

William Wade Rigby of the Island of New Providence Esquire, the Husband of the above named Mary Rosannah Rigby being duly sworn saith, that the above is a full perfect and faithful return to the best of the deponents knowledge and belief of all the Slaves the property of the said Mary Rosannah Rigby, within or appertaining to these Islands, on the First day of January instant.

Sworn to at Nassau New Providence this Thirty first day of January 1822 W.W. Rigby

Before me

James Armbrister

Registrar

Bahama Islands 342

Return of Nine Slaves the property of Aaron Sims of the Island of New Providence free Man of Colour, Mariner, the First day of January 1822.

Number	Name	Sex	Age	Colour	Place of Employment at the time of the return	Whether African or Creole
1	Rose	Female	Years 36	Black	New Providence	Creole
2	Harry	Male	2	Black	New Providence	Creole
3	Sarah	Female	3	Black	New Providence	Creole
4	Maria	Female	40	Black	New Providence	Creole
5	Chatham	Male	1	Black	New Providence	Creole
6	Charles	Male	18 Months	Black	New Providence	Creole
7	Jane	Female	Years 3	Black	New Providence	Creole
8	Jack	Male	4	Black	New Providence	Creole
9	Hannah	Female	6	Black	New Providence	Creole

Bahama Islands Aaron Sims

Aaron Sims of the Island of New Providence free Man of Colour, Mariner being duly sworn saith, that the above is a full perfect and faithful return to the best of the deponents knowledge and belief

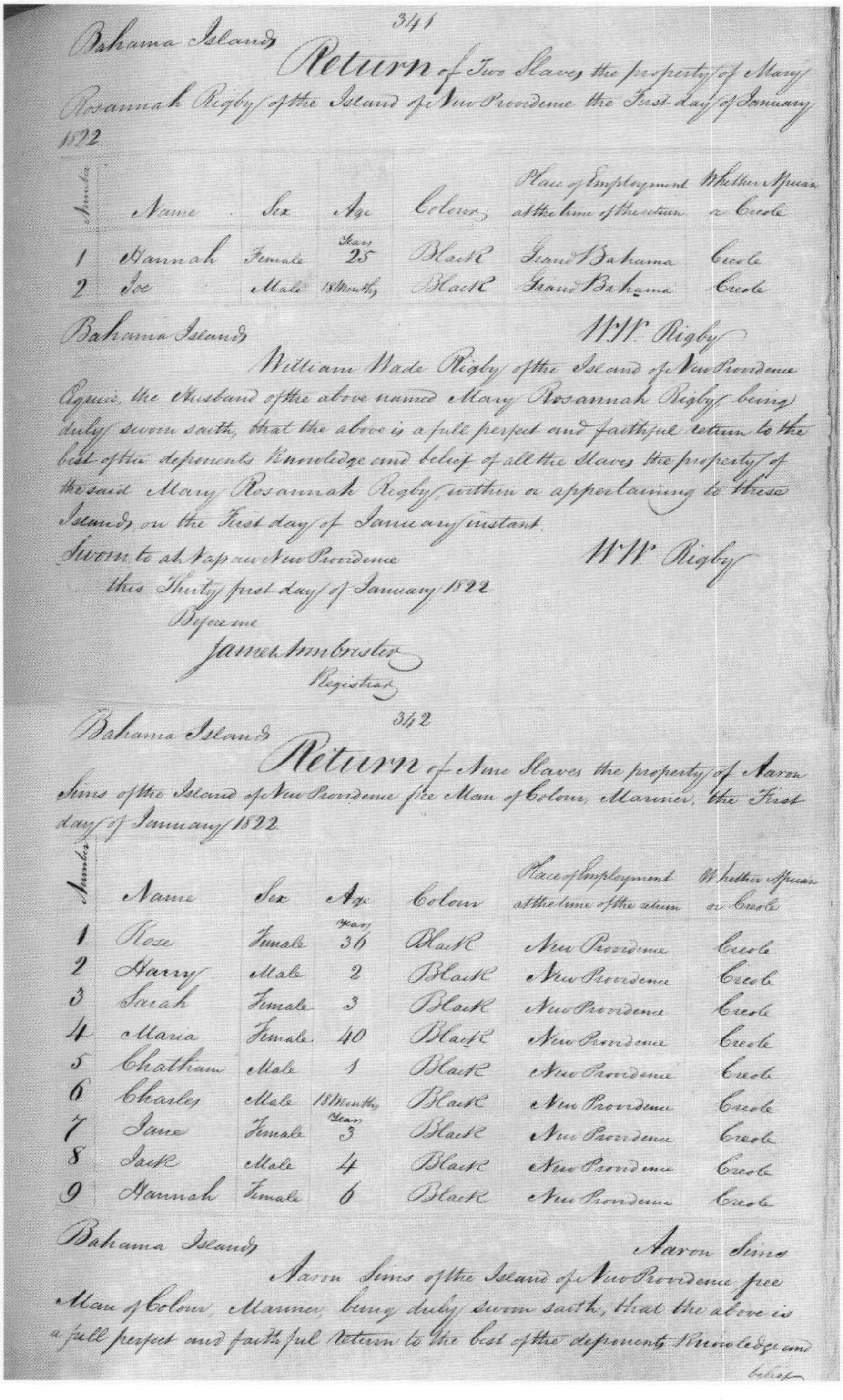

In the slave returns shown here, the registrants were identified either as 'African' (born in an undocumented African nation) or 'Creole' (born in the Bahamas). Additional research may reveal that several of Aaron Sims' slaves were actually related.

tip **Extend your research to the Caribbean**

African-Americans should also extend their research to Canada and the Caribbean, where their ancestors may have lived before migrating to the US.

tracing transported convicts

Britain's history of transporting convicted criminals to their overseas colonies began in the 17th century and continued well into the mid-19th century.

Seen as more humane, 'transportation' became the alternative to corporal punishment for many offences, with the exception of murder. Typical sentences were 14 years for major felonies and seven years for lesser crimes. Jailed criminals were known as 'prisoners', while transportees and those sentenced to hard labour were classified as 'convicts'.

Before the 1770s, the destination for many transportees – most of whom were petty thieves, burglars, pickpockets and shoplifters – was America or the West Indies.

Later, Britain established a series of 'floating prisons' – convict ships known as 'hulks' – which docked in the River Thames and in Portsmouth and Plymouth harbours. However, the ships rapidly became overcrowded and disease spread.

In consequence, in 1787, a new penal colony was founded to handle the increasing convict population. Between 1787 and 1868, when the practice of transportation was abolished, more than 160,000 male and female convicts were transported from Britain to Australia.

Convict records

To manage the convict population, documentation of all types was created both in Britain – where the crime and trial occurred – and at the convicts' final destination.

Family historians will find these convict records of considerable value to their research. Not only do these records document the convict's name and other vital information, they often also provide details such as the person's physical appearance, health, assignment in the penal colony and family background.

Finding out about the crime committed by a convict

Problem

My great-great grandfather was transported to Australia on a convict ship. I know his name, the date he arrived in Australia and when he finished his sentence. Where can I find information about the crime he committed?

Solution

- Try to obtain copies of the relevant trial records, petitions for clemency, and judges reports, many of which are located at the National Archives in Kew.

- If you do not know the date or place of trial, you will have to do more research. Check prison registers or convict transportation registers, which documented that data.

- If the trial took place at Quarter Sessions, contact the local records office where the trial occurred.

- If the trial occurred at the Assizes, check the National Archives in London.

- If the trial occurred at the Old Bailey, check the Corporation of London Records Office (in the Guildhall) for trials in London before 1834, the Greater London Record Office for those held in Middlesex before 1834 or the Central Criminal Court records held at the National Archives for Old Bailey trials after 1834.

Types of convict records

Held in Britain
(with copies in Australia):

- Admiralty medical journals
- Convict transportation registers
- Hulk registers
- Judges' reports
- Petitions for clemency
- Trial records
- Warrants for pardons
- Wives' petitions

Held in Australia:

- Assignment records
- Census records (especially 1828)
- Certificates of freedom
- Convicts' bank accounts
- Convicts' permissions to marry
- Indents
- Musters
- Pardons
- Tickets of exemption
- Tickets of leave

Locating the records

In order to begin your research, you need some basic information, including your ancestor's full name and the date (at least approximately) when he or she was convicted of the crime and/or sailed to Australia, or to whichever colony he or she was sent.

Check published censuses or musters and convict registers (arranged by county) held by the National Archives at Kew or by one of the county record offices, including Devon, Kent, Lancashire, Lincolnshire, Nottinghamshire and Yorkshire, for additional information. Unfortunately, no exclusive index exists that covers the more than 160,000 people who

Captain W. L. Phillip, who founded Sydney in 1788, inspects a group of convict settlers arriving in Australia. If one of your ancestors was a convict, illustrations like this can give background detail to their lives.

were sent to Australia between 1781 and 1868, when the last ship sailed.

Relevant records originating in Britain are stored mainly at the National Archives in Kew. The Australian Joint Copying Project, initially undertaken by the National Library of Australia (NLA) and the State Library of New South Wales (NSW), has created microfilm copies of these records for use by researchers in Australia. The State Records New South Wales

(www.records.nsw.gov.au) acts as the main repository for Australian convict records, which provide an astounding array of details about the convict, the crime and other data. The Society of Australian Genealogists (SAG) offers a CD-ROM version of The Australian Biographical & Genealogical Record for purchase on its website: www.sag. org.au. Microfilm copies are also available at the National Library of Australia and state libraries.

Using the Internet

Indexes to all sorts of convict records are available online, easing the initial research effort. For example, the website of the State Archives of New South Wales features indexes to certificates of freedom, convict bank accounts, pardons, tickets of leave and exemption from government labour and other documents. The National Archives at Kew also provides links to indexes of convict records. Internet sites specifically devoted to convict history and records, such as 'Convicts to Australia' (www.convictcentral.com), also feature searchable databases.

Trial records

Trial records document the initial phases of a person's history as a convict and include case papers, indictments, depositions, agenda and minute books, petitions for clemency and judges' reports.

Depending on the type of case and where it was tried, when seeking English or Welsh trial records you may need to check Quarter Sessions records, normally held at the pertinent local archives office; Assize court records, located at the National Archives at Kew or the National Library of Wales; or records of Old Bailey trials, which are held in several repositories in the UK. Check the National Archives of Scotland for Scottish trial records and

Examining a ticket of leave

Problem

I have obtained a 'ticket of leave' for my ancestor, who was transported to Australia in the 19th century. What is a 'ticket of leave'? What kind of information should I take from the document? And what further research leads can it provide?

Solution

Besides obtaining conditional and absolute pardons or fleeing into the back country, convicts often earned a ticket of leave (TOL), which granted them limited freedom to work and live within a specific police district before the end of their sentence. Even with a TOL, the convict had to report regularly to the local TOL Muster, attend church services and renew the TOL annually. Revocation of the TOL could occur if the convict left the district without permission, was found to be drunk or disorderly in public or committed another criminal offence.

James Broderick's TOL, shown here, provides great insight into the convict's life and criminal past. It includes:

- the name of the ship that carried him to Australia

- the place and year of the trial

- the crime with which he was charged

- the sentence

- his former occupation

- his year of birth

- his 'native place'

- a fairly detailed physical description

A close look at this document will provide a number of leads for further research. For example:

- Broderick worked as a 'servant' – for whom?

- Why did he steal the cows from his employer – for food or to sell?

- How did he receive the cuts on his face and thumb – during military service, fighting, while working?

- Was Galway City his birth place, residence or the nearest large city to where he was raised or worked before transportation?

- What did he do after obtaining the TOL?

- Did he remain in Sydney for the remainder of his life?

TICKET OF LEAVE.

No. 31/785   29 September 1831.

Prisoner's No. ——

Name, ———— James Broderick

Ship, ———— Mariner (3)

Master, ———— Norsworthy

Year, ———— 1827

Native Place, ———— Galway City

Trade or Calling, ———— Servant

Offence, ———— Stealing cows

Place of Trial, ———— Galway

Date of Trial, ———— 29 July 1826 per MM

Sentence, ———— Seven years

Year of Birth, ———— 1787

Height, ———— 5 feet 4½ inches

Complexion, ———— Sallow

Hair, ———— Black & little bald

Eyes, ———— Dark brown & weak

General Remarks, ———— Small mole on left side of nose, mark of a cut on corner of left eye. Cut on first joint of thumb, left hand.

Allowed to remain in the District of Sydney

On recommendation of ———— Bench,

Dated 20 July 1831

One of the best resources for family historians tracing transportee roots is the Ticket of Leave. These documents often include the convict's name, vital statistics, crime, and his or her physical appearance and special identifying features.

tip   **Join the convicts mailing list**
When visiting the 'Convicts to Australia' website, consider joining the Convicts Mailing List, where you can ask specific questions about convict ancestors and research or network about your findings.

the State Paper Office in Dublin for Irish trial records. Several Australian state archives and genealogical societies also provide microfilm copies of these records. You will need the date of the trial in order to locate these records.

Indents

Rich in genealogical detail, indents should be the first type of convict record you attempt to find. These papers document the formal transfer of each convict from the custody of the transport ship's master to that of the governor of the colony taking control of them.

In them you will find convict names, date and place of trial, the crime, sentence, prior convictions, marital status and number of children, religion and a physical description (identifying marks, height, and colour of hair, eyes and skin). Indents may also include tickets of leave, pardons or certificates of freedom and information on crimes committed in the penal colony.

When starting this research, refer to indexes to convict indents, some of which are accessible on the Internet.

Tickets of exemption from government labour

Issued when convicts were assigned to work for and live with relatives, these documents, like indents, provide a wealth of information. Along with a description of the convict's physical appearance, details of his or her employment and name and relationship of the relative, these tickets of exemption provide information about convicts such as the name of the ship that transported them to the penal colony, crimes they committed in the colony and how they acquired their freedom.

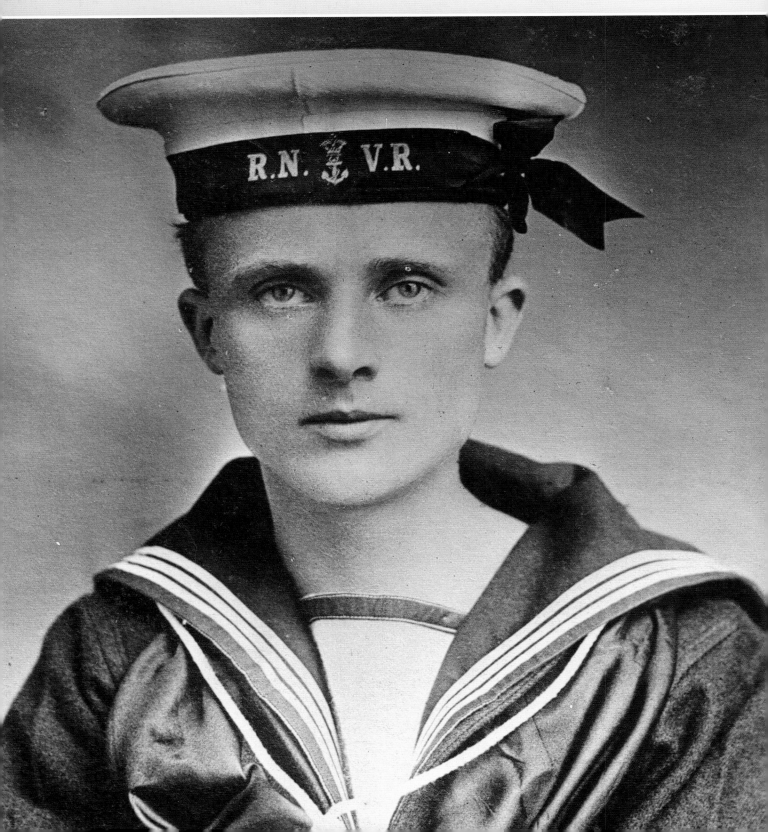

After thoroughly researching genealogical records, family historians often find themselves 'hitting the brick wall'. Don't admit defeat! Write up the biographical notes you have compiled and note any conflicting information or gaps in the records. Then ask yourself whether the time is right to travel to your ancestral homeland.

doing overseas research

Hitting a brick wall in your family history research can provide the perfect opportunity for you to broaden your search overseas.

By now, if you have followed the suggestions in Parts Two and Three of this book, you have probably already initiated contact with record repositories located at quite some distance from where you live, perhaps in another state or overseas.

Although the Internet can ease the research process, the results, as we have seen, can pose new questions, particularly when the information you find has been inadequately researched or incorrectly transcribed. Travelling to your ancestral homeland will enable you not only to do your research in person but also to meet local residents and experience for yourself the culture, landscape and history of the region where your forebears lived.

The benefits of going global

Actually seeing and touching your family's historical records can be exhilarating. You may uncover pieces of your past about which you had never known to ask. Rather than having to rely on a stranger to go through the documents and decide what might be of interest to you, when you go global you control the process

and make the decisions. You are in charge of how much time you wish to concentrate on doing the research rather than having to do it bit by bit, haphazardly, or not at all, because of your distance from the facility. And you can save money by first viewing the documents in person and then deciding for yourself whether or not you want copies.

Following up local leads

If you are in the repository or the land where the records were actually created, you can immediately follow up the new leads by heading to the local library, governmental office, museum or historic site for answers. You may even be able to find local residents who have specific knowledge of your ancestors or living relatives. They may know details of the history of the area that can reveal more about your past. Members of the local historical or genealogical society may also be willing to meet you. They may know the background behind family traditions or turning points, or at least be able to direct you to someone who has the information you require.

 WHEN PLANNING AN OVERSEAS RESEARCH TRIP...

✓ DO

■ as much research as possible, using the Internet and other locally accessible resources.

■ clarify what you wish to accomplish before you travel.

■ develop a reasonable plan for completing your research within the time constraints.

■ take time to enjoy being in a new place and explore the locality with a sense of wonder.

■ interact with local residents, not only to learn what they may know about your ancestors, but also to gain an appreciation for their culture.

✗ DON'T

■ wait until you arrive at the records repository to contact staff to ensure that they can accommodate your needs.

■ underestimate the time it may take you to locate, examine and copy relevant records.

■ expect staff to be able to attend to all your records requests at once – they may be busy with other researchers.

■ be judgemental about unfamiliar cultures, lifestyles and traditions; after all, they may be part of your heritage.

 tip **What to bring**
When packing for your trip, don't forget to include a copy of your pedigree chart or family group sheets, and a list of questions or topics you plan to research. Determine before you depart if you will have access to a computer. If so, consider carrying copies of your files on CD-ROM and/or floppy disks. You will lighten your load and save room in your suitcase for photocopies, books and any hand-written notes you may take during your stay.

Finding out more about an ancestor's property

Problem

My great-grandparents, both now dead, were relocated by the military during World War II so that the army could use the land for a training facility, which it remains to this day. How can I find out more about my ancestors' property?

Solution

Even though the area is an active training facility, you have several ways to do research and can even access the site with the proper authorization.

- Visit the nearest county records office and research not only your ancestor's name and the place name of the property, but also the locality and the training facility.

- Visit the local public library and ask the reference librarian for assistance with researching the above subjects.

- Take complete notes and make photocopies, as applicable.

- Purchase and/or review any local histories of the region. Find author contact details and arrange for an interview or telephone meeting.

- Identify any surviving local residents who were alive during the time when the relocation occurred. They may not only know what happened to your family but also be able to describe the historical events in detail.

- Ask if they would agree to an interview or to recording their memories.

- Prepare interview questions before a meeting. Be polite and considerate – memories may be faulty!

- Record the conversation, ask follow-up questions and clarify any confusion before you end the interview.

- Write to the commander of the army's training facility for permission to gain access. Be sure to explain exactly why you wish to visit and what you want to see.

- Explore the training facility as extensively as possible, taking photographs and notes and asking lots of questions.

- Follow up new leads as time permits.

During WWII, residents of Imber, England, hurriedly left their homes and farmsteads to make way for the army. Buildings like this that remain standing can provide a physical connection to the genealogical past.

retracing ancestral footsteps

Tracing your family roots can spark a yearning to visit your ancestral homeland and physically connect with your past.

You have reviewed scores of genealogical records, documented names, birth, marriage and death dates and identified the places where your ancestors lived. You may know where they are buried, or at least where their graves might be located. You have created a family tree. You know from the records that they are your ancestors, that you have their DNA in you. You may have ageing photographs that offer visual proof that they once lived. Yet, despite all the evidence, you may still feel disconnected from your past, as if these distant ancestors never truly existed, because all you have is paper and words. But, the paperwork has aroused your curiosity. It may now be time to see for yourself how and where they lived, and to honour them in a more personal way by visiting the places where they lived and died.

Cemetery research

Cemeteries are not just repositories of the dead, they are the final resting places of the actual people who lived and contributed to the person you are today. They are places filled with history – your history! Wandering the stone rows can be fascinating, all the more so when you finally stumble upon the spot where an ancestor is buried. Like heirlooms and photographs, burial sites provide physical proof that your ancestors did in fact live.

If you do not know the exact name or location of the cemetery, begin your search with what you do know, e.g., the last place your ancestors lived in, where they died, where they owned land. Identify cemeteries and churches in that area or property formerly held by ancestors that may hold a private burial ground. These are all leads for you to follow.

Finding the gravesite

Once you locate the cemetery, be methodical as you search the grounds. If you have difficulty finding a particular grave, do not give up! It may be disguised by bracken or so worn that inscriptions are unreadable. If your ancestor's grave was unmarked, you may pass it by. Do not assume that the gravesite is where cemetery records indicate, either: records may be

Gravestones document your ancestor's past as much as their vital records. Examine inscriptions closely. Clues about the deceased are revealed in epitaphs and also in symbolic carvings.

Locating the cemetery

Problem

I know what region my family came from and want to visit their gravesites, but I haven't managed to locate the cemetery where they should be buried. What should I do?

Solution

As with all genealogical research, when you search for your ancestor's gravesite you should begin with what you already know. Take the following steps:

- Identify the last house, village – or at least the general location – where your ancestors lived.

- Find out where they died.

- Research churches in the village or surrounding area that have associated cemeteries.

- Identify community cemeteries using topographic and Ordnance Survey maps or land, tax and census records.

- Determine if your ancestor owned land: property formerly held by ancestors may contain a private burial ground.

- Contact the local genealogy or historical society, who often compile and preserve cemetery records and may know the location of cemeteries off the beaten path.

- Check the library for local history books identifying cemeteries or noting where specific individuals are buried.

- Contact funeral directors, who should know the locations of area cemeteries and may hold cemetery records.

- Travel to the village, area, landholding or church, locate the cemetery and examine the headstones. Even on a casual visit, you may find just what you are seeking.

- Determine, if possible, where that ancestor's relatives – parents, spouse, children or siblings – may be buried. Visit those cemeteries and check the headstones to see if the ancestor you are researching is buried there, too.

inaccurate. Over time, the cemetery may have been cleared or built on or grassed over and the headstone may have broken or moved. So look around. You may find headstones lined up along the perimeter fence of the grounds or in a storage shed.

Gravestones

Gravestones are amazing records. They may identify maiden names, birth places and dates, ages at death and spouse and children's names and may provide evidence of military service or membership in a fraternal organization or religious group. Even if you already have a transcription of the inscription, remember to record everything on the headstone exactly as you see it. Even if the language is foreign to you, transcribe what you see as it appears. If you have doubts, ask a companion to double-check your writing. Transcriptions are often inaccurate, so it is imperative that you document what you see with extreme care. Follow the same process for each relative's headstone.

Be sure to record or sketch the location of each ancestor's grave, not only relative to each other but within the entire cemetery as well. Take photographs of each stone from many different angles, including the back, and sketch any emblems, symbols or carvings.

After recording your ancestor's details completely, look carefully at nearby stones. You may spot the graves of other relatives and burials of stillborn or very young children, which were often omitted from historical records. If the grave is located adjacent to a church, look inside for family effigies, tombs or memorials. Note when a grave is well tended or adorned with fresh flowers, which may have been placed by living relatives whom you can track down.

Family burial grounds may be on land still owned by relatives, who may live in houses actually built by your ancestors. Connecting with them can open new doors into your past.

While published family histories may provide artistic renditions of an ancestral home, such as this picture of Sissinghurst Castle (which still survives in Kent, England), researchers will find great satisfaction in visiting the site itself.

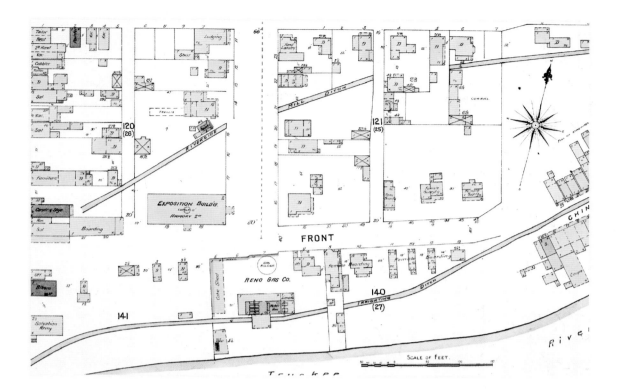

Sanborn Fire Insurance Maps such as this one from Reno, Nevada, dating from 1899 provide 'footprints' of houses and other buildings, and can help you identify where your ancestor lived.

Locating ancestral homes

During your records research, you may find house names, addresses, locations or other identifying information. You may decide to do a thorough house history, tracing title deeds, building permits, census and tax records, to identify previous owners, house contents and their dispersal over time. Or you may decide to visit the house in person to walk the same dirt or cobbled tracks or to gaze down the hallways that your ancestors knew.

If your ancestors occupied stately homes, houses or farmsteads now preserved as sites of architectural or historical importance, you may have little trouble finding them. However, it is more likely that the home of your ancestor will have been torn down, reoccupied by strangers, remodelled or engulfed by later development. In some cases, homes long proclaimed as part of a family's heritage – such as the log cabin in which Abraham Lincoln was reputedly born in Springfield, Illinois –

are determined by scientific methods to be not old enough to have witnessed such historic events! Finding the structure may challenge your research skills, but, as long as it still stands, you should be able to locate the building.

Using maps

Maps are marvellous research tools for locating ancestral homes. Even if the area has physically changed (and it probably has!), you can identify the house with the aid of a good map. For houses in North America, obtain the Sanborn Fire Insurance Map for the town or city you are researching. Dating from 1867, these large-scale maps show in great detail the business, industrial and residential areas of 12,000 cities and towns in the US, Canada and Mexico.

Ordnance Survey (OS) maps pinpoint houses and farms in the UK, not just with a dot but with a name and a general outline of the structure. If possible, purchase a map from your

nearest large bookstore before your visit or stop at a tourist information centre, local bookstore or newsagent in the community where you believe your ancestors originated. The staff at tourist information offices and local bookstores will not only have local maps for sale, they may also be knowledgeable enough about local history to offer assistance. Be sure to tell them why you are there and ask if they have any information that might help your search.

Some maps, like early atlases and town plans, manorial or tithe maps, which are often hand-drawn, show the physical appearance of a community, an individual house or the surrounding lands (identified with field names) as they looked centuries ago. In the UK these fascinating historical relics are stored in local records offices, the National Archives and libraries, such as the National Library of Wales in Aberystwyth, from where you can obtain photocopies.

Do

■ ask local residents you may
come across for assistance in
finding the house or discovering
its history.

■ ask locals if any family members
still live in the area who either
resided in the house or might
have knowledge of its fate.

■ seek out the local historical
society or civic trust, which may
hold archives or photographs
pertaining to your ancestral
home or have members who can
point you in the right direction.

■ arrive at the house, if you find it,
prepared with copies of personal
records, your genealogy and any
other documents that might
persuade current owners to let
you explore the house.

 Don't

■ expect the current house owners
to allow you to roam freely
through their home or across
their property.

■ be surprised that, if you do find
the building, you become so
inspired that you decide to
document its history.

■ forget your camera: you will
want to have a lasting image of
the site for future reference and
to share with your relatives.

■ overlook the possibility that a
family cemetery may also survive
on the same property as your
ancestral home.

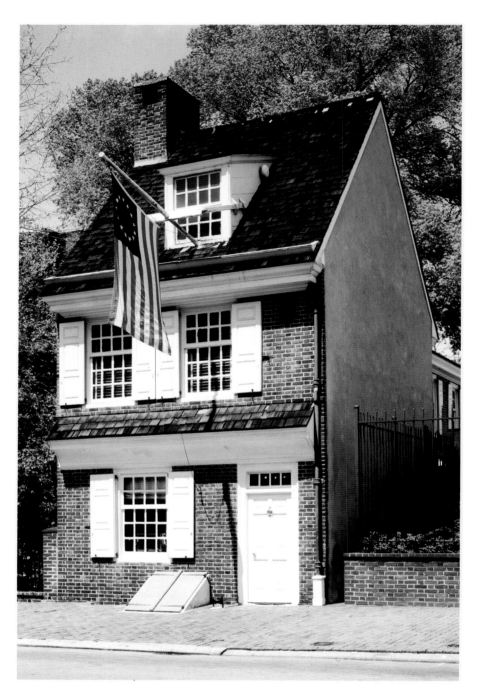

You may be fortunate to have had a famous ancestor whose historical house has been preserved, as has the Betsy Ross House in Philadelphia, Pennsylvania, which contains memorabilia related to life of the woman who reputedly helped design and sew the first American flag.

Local histories

Like genealogy, researching a locality's history has become increasingly popular over the past several decades. Indeed, the two topics go hand-in-hand, one documenting personalities, the other providing the socio-historical and topographical context. Family historians and local historians will frequently use the same primary sources and the same records repositories to uncover details relevant to their respective research topics. Like family historians, local history

Using local histories

Problem

I have a copy of a local history, but it seems to contain mainly obituaries and peculiar news items. How can such a book help me retrace my ancestors' footsteps?

Solution

Local histories will often contain countless clues to your past. As well as giving vital details and names of relatives, they may help you in the following ways:

- Obituaries may point you to community cemeteries, many of which are now way off the beaten track, where your ancestors may be buried.

- News items may record an ancestor's job – perhaps he was a miner, steamship engineer, teacher or farmer – and may point you to maritime, military, religious or museum archives.

- News items often relate details of awards, organizations or memberships or accomplishments or discuss key events in an ancestor's life.

- Use the information you have gleaned as leads for researching business, organization, court and other records.

- Head to the applicable records repositories or museums that may house the documents.

- Trace the reality behind the folklore. Does the book mention a place name or describe a location – for example a cross-shaped stone embedded in the hedgerow? Visit the spot and see what you can uncover. Often, fact-based, strange and epic tales can guide you along new pathways to discovery.

researchers find relevant details about a town's or county's past on maps and in manorial, estate and personal documents, land and tax records, probate records and wills, business and court records, census and vital records and other papers. Like family historians, local history researchers gather and assimilate their data in files.

Since many local historians publish their findings in readable form in books, journals and magazines, shrewd genealogists will read published histories for the region, town or community in which their ancestors lived. Not only will you discover what life may have been like during your ancestor's lifetime, you may also find references to specific ancestors, their jobs, families, homes, occupations or military service.

Some local histories trace the entire history of a region, while others focus on specific time periods or communities, large and obscure. They frequently mention individuals who played critical roles in the community's development, individuals who may actually be your relatives. Some, such as Nigel Nicolson's history of Sissinghurst Castle, contain copies of old maps, town plans, photographs and documents that may pertain to your heritage. Many are invaluable records of the past, of buildings and establishments long since demolished or replaced and the people who were involved with them.

Professional and amateur historians, local history societies and hobbyists often publish local histories. Some donate their findings to regional

libraries, which compile and publish the details in very readable, inexpensive formats.

Locating local histories

When visiting the community or region where your ancestors lived, check the local history section at the public library, the records office, the bookshop or the local museum or family history centre. Even check the Internet, including ebay.com, where some very obscure but valuable histories are often advertised.

Try communicating with the local historian directly. Sometimes books contain the author's contact details. Or the publishers may provide that information. You may also be able to find an author's email or postal addresses on the Internet.

locating living relatives

Unlike any other time in human history, we can now quickly, simply and efficiently connect with family members living around the globe.

High-speed air, rail and automobile transportation eases movement between nations and across the oceans. Fibre-optic cables and satellite technology allow us to communicate almost instantly, whether we are in the next house or on another continent. Where the research process was once often gruellingly slow, family historians can now not only learn about their heritage by reading books and visiting local records repositories, they can also use the Internet to discover, talk to and arrange to meet with living relatives.

Genetic genealogy

For years, DNA analysis has been vital in forensic studies, verifying a child's paternity and indicating the likelihood of inheriting life-threatening or disabling diseases. Now, DNA profiles can also help family historians connect with their ancestors.

Dr Bryan Sykes, a geneticist at Oxford University in England, pioneered the field of genetic genealogy. His company, Oxford Ancestors, Ltd, puts researchers from the US, Canada, Australia and the UK in touch not only with their ancestors but also with living relatives around the globe.

Known for his innovative research conducted in the early 1990s on the remains of Czar Nicholas II of Russia and his family, Sykes has also associated the DNA of two ancient humans, the so-called 'Ice Man' and the 'Cheddar Man', to living relatives. In 2001 he published The Seven Daughters of Eve: The Science That Reveals Our Genetic Ancestry. After

examining the DNA of several thousand participants, Sykes concluded that everyone in Europe is descended from one of seven women. Today, Oxford Ancestors is just one of an increasing number of companies that help family history researchers make connections with their past, and their present. Many participants go on to meet living blood relatives.

Top five genetic genealogy-testing websites

- Oxford Ancestors: www.oxfordancestors.com
- Family Tree DNA: www.familytree dna.com/default.asp
- Relative Genetics: www.relativegenetics.com
- GeneTree DNA Testing Center: www.genetree.com
- AncestryByDNA: www.ancestrybydna.com

Surname associations and DNA studies

Many surname or one-name associations have begun to participate in DNA studies. Before deciding to spend the money to have yourself tested and placed in a database for comparative purposes, make sure that you find out which surnames have already been studied. You may find leads on the Internet; however, the results themselves are generally confidential. If you decide to contact these associations, make your initial enquiry brief and to the point, and don't expect an immediate reply.

WHEN SEEKING LIVING RELATIVES ...

 DO

- ask known relatives for contact details about distant family members.
- obtain relevant city directories to identify relatives' addresses and telephone numbers.
- use Internet search engines and forums to try to contact relatives.
- share your records and your discoveries about your past both on the Internet and by written correspondence.
- join a surname association.

 DON'T

- hesitate to contact potential relatives if you have sufficient evidence based on your research that indicates these people may be part of your family tree.
- assume that the name and contact details you find on the Internet pertain to your living relatives.
- communicate by telephone first; always make initial contact by written correspondence.
- harass a potential relative, especially if they do not respond to your initial enquiries or if they say they are not the person you are hoping to find.

Case Study: The Clough DNA/Surname Analysis

For several years, Connecticut resident Sheila Andersen has been investigating her Clough family connections. Along with other members of the John Clough Genealogical Society, Anderson used the services of Oxford Ancestors, Ltd to identify genetic links to a 16th-century Welsh merchant, Richard Clough yr Hen (the elder). The American Cloughs had tracked their roots to a John Clough, who had emigrated from England to Salisbury, Massachusetts, in 1635. Then they hit the ever-threatening brick wall because John Clough had apparently left no record of himself in his homeland, and they could not trace their roots any further back in time.

In 2001 Andersen was busily organizing the first Clough Family trip to Britain to visit Clough-related sites and meet Cloughs living in Wales and England. When another member learnt about the work of Oxford Ancestors, the society promptly decided to do a genetic study of the male line. Five men, including an Englishman known to descend from Sir Richard Clough (Richard yr Hen's son) through his illegitimate son by a Dutch mistress, sent cells from their cheeks to Oxford for DNA analysis.

When Brian Sykes revealed that the Y-chromosome signature of a donor from the New England branch of the Clough Society (a direct descendant of John Clough) and that of the English descendant of Richard Clough yr Hen were identical, the group realized that they had discovered a living blood link to their British ancestry and were elated to have the chance to meet him.

Dean Hart's ancestors migrated from Lithuania to Johannesburg, South Africa. This photograph, taken in 1931, indicates that his genetically bonded relatives may live not only in England, but in distant lands as well.

Using a genetic genealogy testing firm

Problem

I am interested in using the services of a genetic genealogy testing firm. How do I determine which one is best for me?

Solution

As with choosing a professional genealogist, thoroughly review your options before investing your time and money in a specific testing firm.

- First of all, you need to identify your goals: you may decide that hiring a professional genealogist is more appropriate at this stage of your research.

- Evaluate each company, not only to identify their fees and what services they provide but also to understand how they process the data, your role in the procedure and who will have access to the data.

- If applicable, ask if they do special studies for certain ethnic or racial groups.

- Review client testimonials, which are often posted online.

- Obtain a list of references and contact them to find out whether or not they had positive experiences.

- Contact surname associations that have used each company.

- Determine if you can participate in an ongoing study related to your surname or ancestry and, if so, what kinds of information you might obtain.

- If you decide to proceed, choose the firm that best meets your requirements and whose fees are within your budget.

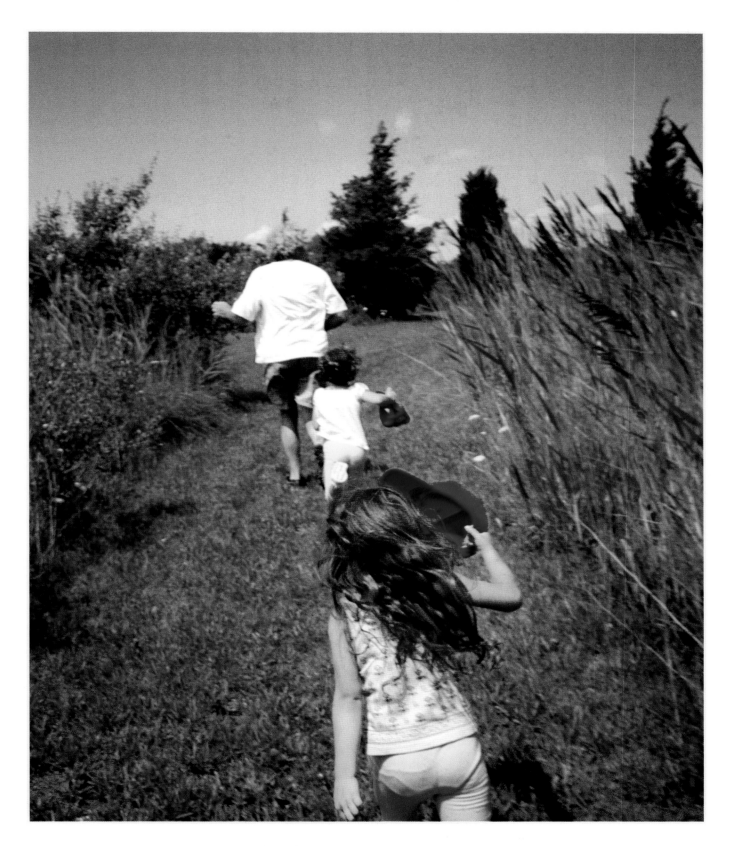

Bonding with newly discovered relatives can be one of the most rewarding experiences that can result from submitting your DNA for genetic testing. Getting to know family members can also help you fill in the blanks on your family tree.

Once you have accumulated a reasonable amount of paperwork, it's essential that you begin to preserve the data, the records and your family heirlooms.

Hopefully by this point in your research, you have made ample use of the tips suggested throughout this book. You have organized your data using standard charts, logs and other forms. You have established a logical and reliable filing system for easy retrieval of information. And you have kept meticulous records of your findings. By now, you have probably created plenty of notes, made mountains of photocopies and obtained copies of primary sources.

Whether you have access to a computer or store everything in a filing cabinet, preserving your findings will not only ensure that all your hard work is retained for future generations and other genealogists, but will also help prevent unexpected loss – from natural disasters or the wearing effects of ageing – so that you can refer to your own research whenever you wish.

Software programs

Technological advances have made it possible for family historians to store their data on software programs that have been specifically designed with the genealogist in mind. As a result, computers and the Internet have become essential tools for professional researcher and hobbyist alike.

Many genealogists use GEDCOM files to store and share their findings via email or to upload them into Internet databases that other researchers can access, such as Ancestry.com, HeritageQuest.com and RootsWeb. The LDS website also encourages researchers to upload family records to the Pedigree Resource File, which requires users to register

(for free) before participation (www.familysearch.org/Eng/Share/Preserve/frameset_preserve.asp). See the Resources Directory at the end of this book for more information on genealogy software.

While some programs allow the user to manipulate the data, input information onto pedigree charts and other forms and to share the details with other computer and Internet users, they do have their flaws.

Backing-up your files

Because standardized software is frequently updated, upgraded and modified, new versions often cannot properly manage data stored on older versions. Software programs become obsolete relatively quickly, so your files may become inaccessible and other users may not be able to access the data. Even though the thought of permanently copying data on to a computer disk or burning it on to a CD-ROM may seem the ideal (and permanent) solution to your storage needs, no system is completely foolproof. Disks degrade, information is lost or garbled, and no one can guarantee that the digital backups will survive indefinitely.

Despite these potential problems, however, inputting data on to computer files and saving the files to disk or CD-ROM is wise, at least for the short term. But make sure that you always keep paper copies as well.

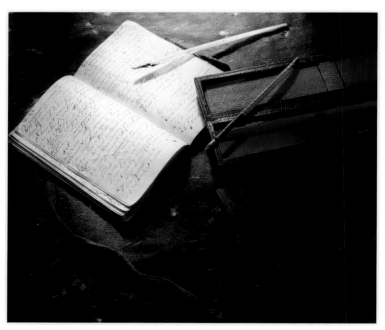

Family treasures such as this old diary need special care and handling to ensure proper preservation.

State-of-the-art family-tree software and other software programs now allow you to preserve your family photographs. To ensure your photographs remain in excellent condition, use archival supplies to store the originals safely as well.

 Do

■ make multiple copies of your files, original and photocopied records and all other materials.

■ use professional archive storage materials, such as acid-free paper, sheet protectors, boxes and folders, to prevent deterioration and fading.

■ use archival materials for storing photographs in albums. Make black-and-white copies of colour prints and negatives, as they last longer.

■ give copies to family members for safekeeping.

■ donate copies to local libraries or genealogical societies, the Family History Library or your nearest Family History Centre.

■ ask another family member to take over responsibility for your family history records if you become incapacitated.

 Don't

■ store your copies in only one place.

■ attach paperclips and other metallic items to documents: they will rust, stain and rip paperwork and photographs.

■ fold paperwork before storage in acid-free folders.

■ expose your family history documents to excessive lighting, temperatures or humidity.

■ store items near a heater, oven, fireplace, dishwasher or clothes washing machine – nor in the bathroom.

sharing what you have learnt

Family history research isn't just about keeping the information you find to yourself. Others are tracing the same family roots, so share your discoveries.

You have spent hours and hours researching your family tree, collecting information and copying records. You have found answers about your heritage, confirmed family traditions and discovered that your roots began far away from where you were born and raised. Perhaps you have become so engrossed in the search that genealogy has become your passion! Now is the time to share your discoveries with the world. Don't wait until some nebulous day in the distant future. Take the next step and let others know what you have learnt.

Writing your family history

Writing a family history book takes time and effort, but the end product will keep your heritage alive, can be used by other researchers and is an outstanding way to preserve the data you have uncovered.

As with any book writing project, be professional about how you present the information: review the National Genealogical Society's 'Standards for Sharing Information with Others' (see page 206) to ensure your work meets ethical and legal guidelines.

Shop around for publishers to get the best deal and to find a company who will produce a quality product. Once your family history is published, present copies to family and friends. Donate copies to the Family History Library, your nearest Family History Centre and similar organizations.

Bringing your past to life

The process of writing any book requires careful organization and the same degre of planning you used to carry out your research. Define your goals and understand why you wish to write a family history. Think about how you can make the facts, dates and records come alive. Before you sit down to write up your personal past, ask yourself the following questions:

- What audience do you want to reach – family, friends, other genealogists or the world at large?

- Which surnames do you wish to include? Do you want to trace a single line or multiple lineages?

- Is there a particular ancestor you want to concentrate on or a particular story you want to relate?

- Do you know enough social history to enliven your writing?

- What kind of book do you want to write – narrative, memoir, biography, cookbook or pictorial?

- Do you know how to tell a story? (If not, consider taking a creative writing course.)

- Will you illustrate the book? If so, with family photos, letters, birth and marriage certificates?

- Will you embarrass any living relatives by telling their stories?

CHECKLIST: HOW TO SHARE YOUR FINDINGS

- Duplicate your files, and then give copies to your children, siblings or parents.

- Write your family history – and then publish it.

- Create a personal or family history website on the Internet. (Review the National Genealogical Society's 'Guidelines for publishing web pages on the Internet', see page 207, for tips on setting up a user-friendly site.)

- Form a genealogical association devoted to your surname or join one already accepting members.

- Publish a newsletter devoted to your family's history or any aspect of genealogy that intrigues you.

- Become active in a local, regional or national genealogical and/or historical society.

- Become an amateur family history researcher or pursue professional certification.

Sharing your family history can be an emotionally rewarding experience. Grandparents can bond with grandchildren over a photo album displaying old or deceased relatives and use the opportunity to pass on information about the past.

THE NATIONAL GENEALOGICAL SOCIETY'S
RECOMMENDED PUBLISHING STANDARDS
STANDARDS FOR SHARING INFORMATION WITH OTHERS

(Recommended by the National Genealogical Society)

Conscious of the fact that sharing information or data with others, whether through speech, documents or electronic media, is essential to family history research and that it needs continuing support and encouragement, responsible family historians consistently:

■ respect the restrictions on sharing information that arise from the rights of another as an author, originator or compiler; as a living private person; or as a party to a mutual agreement.

■ observe meticulously the legal rights of copyright owners, copying or distributing any part of their works only with their permission, or to the limited extent specifically allowed under the law's 'fair use' exceptions.

■ identify the sources for all ideas, information and data from others, and the form in which they were received, recognizing that the unattributed use of another's intellectual work is plagiarism.

■ respect the authorship rights of senders of letters, electronic mail and data files, forwarding or disseminating them further only with the sender's permission.

■ inform people who provide information about their families as to the ways it may be used, observing any conditions they impose and respecting any reservations they may express regarding the use of particular items.

■ require some evidence of consent before assuming that living people are agreeable to further sharing of information about themselves.

■ convey personal identifying information about living people – like age, home address, occupation or activities – only in ways that those concerned have expressly agreed to.

■ recognize that legal rights of privacy may limit the extent to which information from publicly available sources may be further used, disseminated or published.

■ communicate no information to others that is known to be false, or without making reasonable efforts to determine its truth, particularly information that may be derogatory.

■ are sensitive to the hurt that revelations of criminal, immoral, bizarre or irresponsible behaviour may bring to family members.

The National Genealogical Society's
Recommended Publishing Standards
Guidelines for Publishing Web Pages on the Internet

(Recommended by the National Genealogical Society, May 2000)

Appreciating that publishing information through Internet Web sites and Web pages shares many similarities with print publishing, considerate family historians:

- apply a title identifying both the entire Web site and the particular group of related pages, similar to a book-and-chapter designation, placing it both at the top of each Web browser window using the <TITLE> HTML tag, and in the body of the document, on the opening home or title page and on any index pages.

- explain the purposes and objectives of their Web sites, placing the explanation near the top of the title page or including a link from that page to a special page about the reason for the site.

- display a footer at the bottom of each Web page which contains the Web site title, page title, author's name, author's contact information, date of last revision and a copyright statement.

- provide complete contact information, including at a minimum a name and e-mail address, and preferably some means for long-term contact, like a postal address.

- assist visitors by providing on each page navigational links that lead visitors to other important pages on the Web site, or return them to the home page.

- adhere to the NGS 'Standards for Sharing Information with Others' regarding copyright, attribution, privacy and the sharing of sensitive information.

- include unambiguous source citations for the research data provided on the site, and if not complete descriptions, offering full citations upon request.

- label photographic and scanned images within the graphic itself, with fuller explanation if required in text adjacent to the graphic.

- identify transcribed, extracted or abstracted data as such, and provide appropriate source citations.

- include identifying dates and locations when providing information about specific surnames or individuals.

- respect the rights of others who do not wish information about themselves to be published, referenced or linked on a Web site.

- provide Web site access to all potential visitors by avoiding enhanced technical capabilities that may not be available to all users, remembering that not all computers are created equal.

- avoid using features that distract from the productive use of the Web site, like ones that reduce legibility, strain the eyes, dazzle the vision or otherwise detract from the visitor's ability to easily read, study, comprehend or print the online publication.

- maintain their online publications at frequent intervals, changing the content to keep the information current, the links valid and the Web site in good working order.

- preserve and archive for future researchers their online publications and communications that have lasting value, using both electronic and paper duplication.

NATIONAL ARCHIVES & OTHER REPOSITORIES

UNITED STATES & CANADA

Allen County Public Library, Historical Genealogy Department
200 East Berry Street
Fort Wayne, IN 46802
tel: 1-219-421-1200
URL: www.acpl.lib.in.us/
genealogy/index.html

Daughters of the American Revolution Library
1776 D Street NW
Washington, DC 20006-5303
tel: 1-202-879-3229
URL: www.dar.org/library/
default.cfm

Denver Public Library, Western History and Genealogy
10 W. 14th Avenue Parkway
Denver, CO 80204
tel: 1-720-865-1111
URL: www.denver.lib.co.us/whg/
index.html

Family History Library
35 North West Temple Street
Salt Lake City, UT 84150-3400
tel: 1-801-240-2584 or
1-800-346-6044 (x21054)
URL: www.familysearch.org

Library and Archives Canada
395 Wellington Street
Ottawa, ON K1A 0N4
Canada
tel: 1-613-996-5115 or
1-866-578-7777 (toll free in
Canada & the US)
URL: www.collectionscanada.ca/
index-e.html

The Library of Congress
101 Independence Avenue SE
Washington, DC 20540
tel: 1-202-707-5000
URL: www.loc.gov

National Archives and Records Administration
700 Pennsylvania Avenue NW
Washington, DC 20408
tel: 1-866-325-7208
URL: www.archives.gov

New York Public Library, The Irma and Paul Milstein Division of United States History, Local History and Genealogy
Room 121
Fifth Avenue and 42nd Street
New York, NY 10018-2788
tel: 1-212-930-0828
URL: www.nypl.org/research/
chss/lhg/genea.html

The Newberry Library
60 W. Walton Street
Chicago, IL 60610-7324
tel: 1-312–943–9090
URL: www.newberry.org/
genealogy/genealogyhome. html

UNITED KINGDOM & IRELAND

Family Records Centre
1 Myddelton Street
London EC1R 1UW
tel: 020-8392-5300
URL: www.familyrecords.gov.uk

General Register Office for England and Wales,
see **Family Records Centre**

General Register Office for Northern Ireland
Oxford House
49/55 Chichester Street
Belfast BT1 4HL
tel: 028-90-252000
URL: www.groni.gov.uk/index.htm

General Register Office for Scotland
New Register House
3 West Register Street
Edinburgh EH1 3YT
tel: 0131-314-4433
URL: www.gro-scotland.gov.uk

The National Archives
Kew, Richmond
Surrey TW9 4DU
tel: 020-8876-3444
URL: www.nationalarchives.gov.uk

National Archives of Ireland
Bishop Street
Dublin 8, Ireland
tel: 353 1-407-2300
URL: www.nationalarchives.ie

National Archives of Scotland
Historical Search Room
HM General Register House
2 Princes Street
Edinburgh EH1 3YY
tel: 0131-535-1334
URL: www.nas.gov.uk

National Library of Wales
Penglais Hill, Aberystwyth
Ceredigion, Wales SY23 3BU
tel: 01970-632-800
URL: www.llgc.org.uk

**Public Record Office of
Northern Ireland**
66 Balmoral Avenue
Belfast BT9 6NY
tel: 028-9025-5905
URL: www.proni.gov.uk

CONTINENTAL EUROPE

**Archivo de la Corona de
Aragon**
Calle Condes de Barcelona 2
Barcelona, Spain
tel: 934-854-318

Archivo General de Indias
Avenida de La Constitucion
Sevilla, Spain
tel: 954-500-530

Archivo Historico Nacional
Calle Serrano 115
28006 Madrid, Spain
tel: 917-688-500

Czech Republic State Archives
Archivni Sprava
Ministerstva vnitra CR
Milady Horakove 133
166 21 Praha 6
Czech Republic
tel: 420-2-321173

**Federal Archives
(Bundesarchiv) of Germany**
Abteilung B
(Federal Republic of Germany)
56064 Koblenz; Potsdamer Str. 1
56075 Koblenz, Germany
tel: 0261-5050
URL: www.bundesarchiv.de

National Archives of Hungary
1014 Budapest Bécsi kapu tér 2-4
Budapest, Hungary
tel: 36-1-225-2800
URL: www.natarch.hu/mol_e.htm

**The National Archives
(Riksarkivet) of Norway**
Folke Bernadottes vei 21
Postboks 4013
Ullevål stadion
N-0806 Oslo, Norway
tel: 47-22-02-26-00
URL: www.riksarkivet.no/english

**The National Archives
(Riksarkivet) of Sweden**
Fyrverkarbacken 13-17
SE-102 29 Stockholm, Sweden
tel: 46-8-737-63-50
URL: www.ra.se/en

State Archives in Poland
Archiwum Glowne Akt
Dawnych, 00-263 Warszawa ul.
Dluga 7, Poland
tel: +48-22-831-54-91
URL: www.archiwa.gov.pl/
?CIDA=43

AFRICA

**Gambia National Records
Service**
The Archives Directorate
The Quadrangle
Banjul, The Gambia
tel: 00220-226700
URL: www.nrs.gm

**National Archives and Records
Service (NARS) of South Africa
(Head Office)**
The National Archivist
24 Hamilton Street
Arcadia, Pretoria 0001
tel: 012-323-5300
URL: www.national.archives.gov.
za

LATIN AMERICA

Archivo General de Nacion
Avenida Leandro N. Alem 246
C1003AAP Buenos Aires
Argentina
tel: 54-11-4331-5531/33
URL: www.mininterior.gov.ar/agn

Archivo General de la Nacion
Eduardo Molina y Albañiles s/n
Col. Penitenciaría Ampliación
Deleg. Venustiano Carranza
15350 México, DF
tel: 5133-9900
URL: www.agn.gob.mx

Archivo Nacional de la Republica de Cuba
Calle Compostela No. 906
Esq. San Isidro
Habana Vieja, CP. 10100
Cuidad de la Habana, Cuba
tel: 53-7-862-9470
URL: www.awrnac.cu

ASIA/PACIFIC

Archives New Zealand (Head Office)
10 Mulgrave Street, Thorndon
Wellington, New Zealand
tel: 64-4-499-5595
URL: www.archives.govt.nz

National Archives of Australia (Canberra BC)
Queen Victoria Terrace
Parkes, ACT
2600 Australia
tel: 02- 6212-3900
URL: www.naa.gov.au

National Archives of Japan
3-2 Kitanomaru Koen
Chiyoda-ku, Tokyo, Japan
URL: www.archives.go.jp/
index_e.html

National Archives & Records Service
(302-701) 920 Dunsan-Dong
Seo-Gu, Daejeon
The Republic of Korea
tel: 82-42-481-6271
URL: www.archives.go.kr/gars/
english/overview.asp

National Archives of India
Director General of Archives
Janpath, New Delhi
110001 India
tel: 3073462
URL: www.nationalarchives.nic.
in/landing.html

Note: The vast number of records repositories around the world preclude a complete listing. The following websites provide contact details for various regional and local archives, and is not intended as all inclusive.

A2A (Access to Archives)
URL:www.a2a.org.uk

Archives Canada
URL: www.archivescanada.ca/
english/networks. html

ARCHON online directory of archives repositories in the UK & Ireland
URL: www.archon.
nationalarchives. gov.uk/archon/
default.htm

Directory of Archives in Australia
URL: www.archivists.org.au/
directory/asa_dir.htm

Research in Courthouses by State
URL: www.cyndislist.com/
courthouses.htm#States

US State Level Repositories
URL: www.cyndislist.com/
lib-state.htm#States

GENEALOGICAL SOCIETIES & OTHER ORGANIZATIONS

Note: The following selection represents the broad variety of organizations that exists for family historians. It is not intended as all inclusive.

UNITED STATES: NATIONAL & REGIONAL SOCIETIES

California Genealogical Society
1611 Telegraph Avenue
Suite 100
Oakland, CA 94612-2154
tel: 1-510-663-1358
URL: www.calgensoc.org

Genealogical Forum of Oregon
1505 SE Gideon
PO Box 42567
Portland, OR 97242-0567
tel: 1-503-963-1932
URL: www.gfo.org

Genealogical Society of Pennsylvania
215 S. Broad St, 7th Floor
Philadelphia, PA 19107-5325
tel: 1-215-545-0391
URL: www.libertynet.org/~gspa

Midwest Historical and Genealogical Society
PO Box 1121
Wichita, KS 67201-1121
tel: 1-316-264-3611
URL: skyways.lib.ks.us/genweb/
mhgs/index.html

Minnesota Genealogical Society
5768 Olson Memorial Highway
Golden Valley, MN 55422
tel: 1-763-595-9347
URL: mngs.org

New England Historic Genealogical Society
101 Newbury Street
Boston, Massachusetts 02116
tel: 1-617-536-5740
URL: www.newenglandancestors.org

National Genealogical Society
4527 17th Street North
Arlington, VA 22207-2399
tel: 1-703-525-0050 or
1-800-473-0060
URL: www.ngsgenealogy.org/index.htm

New York Genealogical and Biographical Society
122 East 58th Street
New York, NY 10022-1939
tel: 1-212-755-8532
URL: www.newyorkfamilyhistory.org

UNITED STATES: ETHNIC GENEALOGICAL SOCIETIES

African American Genealogy Group
PO Box 27356
Philadelphia, PA 19118
tel: 1-215- 572-6063
URL: www.aagg.org

Czechoslovak Genealogical Society International, Inc.
PO Box 16225
St. Paul, MN 55116-0225
tel: 1-763-595-7799
URL: www.cgsi.org

Hispanic Genealogical Society of New York
309 West 105th Street
New York, NY 10025
URL: www.hispanicgenealogy.com

The Irish Ancestral Research Association
Dept. W, PO Box 619
Sudbury, MA 01776
URL: www.tiara.ie

Polish Genealogical Society of Connecticut and the Northeast
8 Lyle Road
New Britain, CT 06053-2104
URL: www.pgsctne.org

Welsh-American Genealogical Society
60 Norton Avenue
Poultney, VT 05764-1029
URL: www.rootsweb.com/~vtwags

UNITED KINGDOM: NATIONAL, REGIONAL & ETHNIC SOCIETIES

Dyfed Family History Society
Mrs E Williams, Chairman
8 Penllwyn Park
Carmarthen, Carmarthenshire
SA31 3BU
URL: www.dyfedfhs.org.uk

Federation of Family History Societies
PO Box 2425
Coventry, CV5 6YX
URL: www.ffhs.org.uk

Gloucestershire Family History Society
c/o Alex Wood
37 Barrington Drive
Hucclecote, Gloucestershire
GL3 3BT
URL: www.gfhs.org.uk

Guild of One-Name Studies
Box G
14 Charterhouse Buildings
Goswell Road
London EC1M 7BA
URL: www.one-name.org

Gwynedd Family History Society
c/o Yvonne Edwards
36 Y Wern
Y Felinheli, Gwynedd LL56 4TX
URL: www.gwynedd.fsbusiness.co.uk

Institute of Heraldic and Genealogical Studies
79-82 Northgate
Canterbury, Kent CT1 1BA
tel: (0)1227 768664
URL: www.ihgs.ac.uk

Kent Family History Society
c/o Mrs. Kristin Slater
Bullockstone Farm
Bullockstone Road
Herne, Nr. Herne Bay
Kent CT6 7NL
URL: www.kfhs.org.uk

Lincolnshire Family History Society
Research Centre, Unit 6
33 Monks Way
Monks Road, Lincoln LN2 5LN
tel: (0)1522 528088
URL: www.lincolnshirefhs.org.uk

London and North Middlesex Family History Societ
c/o William and Joan Pyemont
57 Belvedere Way
Kenton, Harrow, Middlesex
HA3 9XQ
URL: www.lnmfhs.dircon.co.uk

Norfolk Family History Society
Kirby Hall Library
70 St. Giles Street
Norwich NR2 1LS
tel: (0)1603-763718
URL: www.norfolkfhs.org.uk

North of Ireland Family History Society
c/o Graduate School of Education
The Queen's University of Belfast
69 University Street
Belfast BT7 1HL
URL: www.nifhs.org

Quaker Family History Society
c/o Liz Butler
1 Ormond Crescent
Hampton, London TW12 2TJ
URL: www.rootsweb.com/
~engqfhs

The Scottish Genealogy Society
15 Victoria Terrace
Edinburgh, EH1 2JL Scotland
tel: (0)131 220 3677
URL: www.scotsgenealogy.com

Society of Genealogists
14 Charterhouse Buildings
Goswell Road
London EC1M 7BA
tel: (020) 7251 8799
URL: www.sog.org.uk

Wiltshire Family History Society
10 Castle Lane
Devizes, Wilts SN10 1HJ
URL: www.wiltshirefhs.co.uk/
home.htm

Yorkshire Archaeological Society
Family History Section
c/o Claremont
23 Clarendon Road
Leeds, West Yorkshire LS2 9NZ
URL: www.yorkshireroots.org.uk/
core.htm

AUSTRALASIA

Australasian Federation of Family History Organisations Inc.
PO Box 3012
Weston Creek, ACT
2611 Australia
tel: 04 0090 3866
URL: www.affho.org/index.php

Australian Institute of Genealogical Studies, Inc.
PO Box 339
Blackburn, Victoria
3130 Australia
URL: www.aigs.org.au

New Zealand Society of Genealogists, Inc.
PO Box 8795
Symonds Street, Auckland
1035 New Zealand
URL: www.genealogy.org.nz

Queensland Family History Society
PO Box 171
Indooroopilly
Brisbane, Queensland
4068 Australia
URL: www.qfhs.org.au

Society of Australian Genealogists
Richmond Villa
120 Kent Street
Observatory Hill
Sydney, New South Wales
2000 Australia
URL: www.sag.org.au

Tasmanian Family History Society, Inc.
PO Box 191
Launceston, Tasmania
7250 Australia
URL: www.tasfhs.org

Western Australian Genealogical Society, Inc.
6/48 May Street,
Bayswater, Western Australia
6053 Australia
URL: www.wags.org.au

CANADA

Alberta Family Histories Society
712 16th Avenue NW
Calgary, Alberta T2M 0J8
tel: 403-214-1447
URL: www.afhs.ab.ca

East European Genealogical Society
PO Box 2536
Winnipeg, Manitoba R3C 4A7
URL: www.eegsociety.org/
Index.html

Genealogical Institute of the Jewish Heritage Centre of Western Canada
C116–123 Doncaster Street
Winnipeg, Manitoba R3N 2B2
tel: 204-477-7460
URL: www.jhcwc.org/geninst.htm

Genealogical Institute of the Maritimes
PO Box 36022
Canada Post Postal Office
5675 Spring Garden Road
Halifax, Nova Scotia B3J 1G0
URL: nsgna.ednet.ns.ca/gim

New Brunswick Genealogical Society, Inc.
PO Box 3235, Station B
Fredericton, New Brunswick
E3A 5G
URL: www.bitheads.com/nbgs

Ontario Genealogical Society
40 Orchard View Boulevard
Suite 102
Toronto, Ontario MR4 1B9
URL: www.ogs.on.ca/ogs/
first.html

Saskatchewan Genealogical Society
2nd Floor, 1870 Lorne Street
PO Box 1894
Regina, Saskatchewan S4P 3E1
tel: 306-780-9207
URL: www.saskgenealogy.com

FRATERNAL & BENEVOLENT ORGANIZATIONS

Independent Order of Odd Fellows
The Sovereign Grand Lodge
Headquarters
422 Trade Street
Winston-Salem, NC 27101, USA
tel: 1-800-235-8358 or
1-336-725-5955
URL: www.ioof.org

Moose International, Inc.
155 South International Drive
Mooseheart, IL 60539, USA
URL: www.mooseintl.org/public/
default.aspx

The National Grange of the Patrons of Husbandry
1616 H Street NW
Washington, DC 20006, USA
tel: 1-202-628-3507
URL: www.nationalgrange.org

The Order of Knights of Pythias
Supreme Lodge Knights of
Pythias
59 Coddington Street, Suite 202
Quincy, MA 02169-4150, USA
tel: 1-617-472-8800
URL: www.pythias.org

The Shrine of North America, Shriners International Headquarters
2900 Rocky Point Dr.
Tampa, FL 33607-1460, USA
tel: 1-813-281-0300
URL: www.shrinershq.org/shrine/
index.html

The United Grand Lodge of England (Freemasons)
Freemasons' Hall
60 Great Queen Street
London WC2B 5AZ, UK
tel: 020 7831 9811
URL: www.ugle.org.uk

Woodmen of the World/ Omaha Woodmen Life Insurance Society
Woodmen Tower
1700 Farnam Street
Omaha, NE 68102, USA
tel: 1-800-225-3108
URL: www.woodmen.com

HISTORICAL SOCIETIES

Convict Trail Project
URL: www.convicttrail.org

The Foxearth and District Local History Society
c/o Alan Fitch
Orchard House
Foxearth, Essex CO10 7JG, UK
tel: (0)1787 311913
URL: www.foxearth.org.uk

Guelph Historical Society
100 Crimea St, Unit B-9
Guelph, ON N1H 2Y6, Canada
URL: www.guelphhistoricalsociety.
ca

The Hawaiian Historical Society
560 Kawaiaha'o Street
Honolulu, HI 96813, USA
tel: 1-808-537-6271
URL: www.hawaiianhistory.org

Manitoba Historical Society
304–250 McDermot Avenue
Winnipeg, MB R3B 0S5, Canada
tel: 204-947-0559
URL: www.mhs.mb.ca

Ohio Historical Society
Ohio Historical Center,
1982 Velma Avenue,
Columbus, OH 43211, USA,
tel: 1-614-297-2300, URL:
www.ohiohistory.org/index.html

Oregon Historical Society
1200 SW Park Avenue,
Portland, OR 97205, USA
tel: 1-503-222-1741,
URL: www.ohs.org

South Carolina Historical Society
The Fireproof Building,
100 Meeting Street
Charleston, SC 29401, USA
tel: 1-843-723-3225
URL www.schistory.org

GENEALOGY SOFTWARE

Note: This section surveys the software programs available to family history researchers. Always shop around for software to fit your particular needs, interests and finances before making a purchase.

Ancestral Quest

Incline Software, LC
PO Box 95543
South Jordan, UT 84095, USA
tel: 800-825-8864
URL: www.ancquest.com

Clooz: the electronic filing cabinet for genealogical records

Ancestor Detectives
PO Box 6386
Plymouth, MI 48170-8486, USA
tel: 734-354-6449
URL: www.clooz.com

Family Historian: Genealogy Software

Calico Pie Limited
Effingham Road
London SE12 8NZ, UK
tel: 01284-828271
URL: www.family-historian.co.uk

Family Tree Legends, Pearl Street Software

1630A 30th Street, #106
Boulder, CO 80301, USA
tel: 800-326-5816
URL: www.familytreelegends.com

Family Tree Maker

Genealogy.com
tel: 800-548-1806 (North America) or 801-705-7696 (outside North America)
URL: familytreemaker.genealogy.com

Genmap UK and LDS Companion

Archer Software
c/o Steve Archer
90 St. Albans Road
Dartford, Kent DA1 1TY, UK
tel: 01322-291509
URL: www.archersoftware.co.uk/genmap01.htm

GenSmarts

Underwood Innovations, LLC
4436 Heathmoor Court
Long Grove, IL 60048, USA
tel: 847-910-3761
URL: www.gensmarts.com/index.asp

Legacy Family Tree

Millennia Corporation
PO Box 66
El Mirage, AZ 85335, USA
tel: 800-753-3453
URL: www.legacyfamilytree.com

The Master Genealogist

Wholly Genes Software
5144 Flowertuft Court,
Columbia, MD 21044, USA
tel: 877-864-3264 (in the US) or 410-631-4735 (outside the US)
URL: www.whollygenes.com

Personal Ancestral File

The Church of Jesus Christ of Latter-day Saints
free download available on FamilySearch website
URL: www.familysearch.org/eng/paf

Reunion, Leister Productions, Inc.

PO Box 289
Mechanicsburg, PA 17055, USA
tel: 1-717-697-1378,
URL: www.leisterpro.com/

RootsMagic Genealogy Software, RootsMagic, Inc.,

PO Box 495,
Springville, UT 84663, USA,
tel: 877-766-8762,
URL: www.rootsmagic.com

The Times Family Tree,

GSP: Global Software Publishing,
GSP Ltd.,
Meadow Lane
St. Ives, Cambridgeshire
PE27 4LG, UK
URL: www.gsp.cc

GENEALOGY & ARCHIVAL SUPPLIES

Ancestry.com
(downloadable ancestral charts),
URL: ww.ancestry.com/save/
charts/ancchart.htm

Conservation By Design Limited
Timecare Works
5 Singer Way, Woburn Road
Industrial Estate, Kempston
Bedford MK42 7AW, UK
tel: (0)1234 853555
URL: www.conservation-by-design.co.uk

The Family History Store
Kindred Trails Worldwide
Genealogy Resources' online
store, www.thefamilyhistorystore.com

Family Tree Magazine
(free downloadable forms)
URL: www.familytreemagazine.com/ forms/download.html

Genealogical Storage Products
9401 Northeast Drive
Fredericksburg, VA
22408 USA
tel: 1-800-634-0491
URL: www.genealogicalstorage
products.com

Genealogy Printers
Mr. Ronald ONeill
Genealogy House
15 Linley Drive, Bushbury
Wolverhampton WV10 8JJ, UK
tel: (0)1902 836284
URL: www.genealogyprinters.com/
catalog/default.php

My History
Tony Beardshaw
8 Gough Close
Rotherham, South Yorkshire
S65 3BS UK
tel: (0)1709 830782
URL: www.my-history.co.uk

Origins
1521 E. Racine Street
Janesville, WI 53545, USA
tel: 1-608-757-2777
URL: origins.safeshopper.com

Preservation Equipment Ltd.
Vinces Road
Diss, Norfolk IP22 4HQ, UK
tel: (0)1379 647400
URL: www.preservation
equipment. com

Preservation Technologies, L.P.
111 Thomson Park Drive
Cranberry Township
PA 16066 USA
tel: 1-800-416-2665 or
1-724-779-2111
URL: www.ptlp.com

Preservation Technologies
B.V, Pluim-es 18
2925 CM Krimpen a/d IJessl
The Netherlands
tel: 31-0-180-521188
URL: www.ptlp.com

S&N Genealogy Supplies
West Wing, Manor Farm
Chilmark, Salisbury SP3 5AF, UK
tel: (0)1722 716121
URL: www.genealogysupplies.com

University Products,
the Archival Company
Archivalsuppliers.com
University Products Inc.
P.O. Box 101
517 Main Street
Holyoke, MA 01041, USA
tel: 1-800-336-4847
URL: www.archivalsuppliers.com
OR www.universityproducts.com

Your Family Legacy
87 Edmonton Road
Bellville, OH 44813, USA
tel: 1-877-493-2935
URL: www.webyfl.com

further reading

BOOKS

Carmack, Sharon DeBartolo (1998).
A Genealogist's Guide to Discovering Your Female Ancestors: special strategies for uncovering hard-to-find information about your female lineage.
Cincinnati, Ohio: Betterway Books.

Chamber, Margaret (1998).
Finding Families: The Guide to the National Archives of Australia for Genealogists.
Alexandria, New South Wales: Hale & Iremonger.

Christian, Peter (2003).
The Genealogist's Internet.
London: The National Archives.

Crowe, Elizabeth P. (1998).
Genealogy Online: researching your roots.
New York: McGraw-Hill.

Dollarhide, William (1999).
Managing a Genealogical Project.
Baltimore, Maryland: Genealogical Publishing Company, Inc.

Eichholz, Alice, ed. (2004).
Ancestry's Red Book: American State, County & Town Sources.
Provo, Utah: MyFamily.com, Inc.

Everton George B. (2002).
The Handybook for Genealogists: United States of America.
Draper, Utah: Everton Publishers.

Filby, P. William (2002).
Passenger and Immigration Lists Index: A Guide to Published Records More Than 4,181,000 Immigrants Who Came to the New World Between the Sixteenth and the Mid-Twentieth Centuries.
Detroit: Gale Group.

Fitzhugh, Terrick VH and Susan Lumas (1998).
The Dictionary of Genealogy.
London: A&C Black.

Fleming, Ann C. (2004)
The Organized Family Historian: How to File, Manage, and Protect Your Genealogical Research and Heirlooms (National Genealogical Society Guides).
Nashville, Tennessee: Rutledge Hill Press.

Grannum, Guy (2002).
Tracing Your West Indian Ancestors.
London: Public Records Office.

Hendrickson, Nancy (2003).
Finding Your Roots Online.
Cincinnati, Ohio: Betterway Books.

Hey, David (2004).
Journeys in Family History.
London: The National Archives.

Hoskins, W.G. (1993).
Local History in England.
London: Longman.

Howells, Cyndi (2004).
Planting Your Family Tree Online: How to Create Your Own Family History Web Site (National Genealogical Society Guides).
Nashville, Tennessee: Rutledge Hill Press.

Jones, Steve and Chris Pomeroy (2004).
DNA and Family History: How Genetic Testing Can Advance Your Genealogical Research.
London: The National Archives.

Kemp, Thomas Jay (1994).
International Vital Records Handbook.
Baltimore, Maryland: Genealogical Publishing Company, Inc.

Kershaw, Robert (2002).
Emigrants and Expats.
London: Public Records Office.

Lennon, Rachel M. (2002).
Tracing Ancestors among the Five Civilized Tribes: Southeastern Indians prior to Removal.
Baltimore, Maryland: Genealogical Publishing Company, Inc.

Melnyk, Marcia Yannizze (2000).
The Weekend Genealogist: Timesaving Techniques for Effective Research.
Cincinnati, Ohio: Betterway Books.

Mokotoff, Gary (1955).
How to Document Victims and Locate Survivors of the Holocaust.
Teaneck, NJ: Avotaynu, Inc.

Nevius, Erin, et al. (2003).
The Family Tree Guide Book to Europe: your passport to tracing your genealogy across Europe.
Cincinnati, Ohio: Betterway Books.

Public Records Office (2004).
Using Birth, Marriage and Death Records (Pocket Guides to Family History).
London: The National Archives.

Reakes, Janet (1999).
How to Trace Your Convict Ancestors: Their Lives, Times, and Records.
Alexandria, New South Wales: Hale & Iremonger.

Riden, Philip (1998).
Local History: a handbook for beginners.
Cardiff: Merton Priory Press, Ltd.

Rowland, John and Sheila, eds.
Welsh Family History: a guide to research.
Birmingham: The Federation of Family History Societies (Publications) Ltd.

Smith, FC and Emily Croom (2003).
A Genealogist's Guide to Discovering Your African-American Ancestors.
Cincinnati, Ohio: Betterway Books.

Stewart, Alan (2004).
Gathering the Clans: Tracing Scottish Ancestry on the Internet.
Phillimore, 2004

MAGAZINES

Ancestry Magazine,
360 West 4800 North,
Provo, Utah 84604, USA,
URL: www.ancestry.com

Australian Family Tree Connections,
AFTC Publishing Pty Limited,
ACN 094 561 332,
PO Box 322,
Gosford, New South Wales 2250,
Australia, URL: www.aftc.com.au

Everton's Genealogical Helper,
PO Box 187,
Morgan, Utah 84050, USA,
URL: www.myancestorsfound.com

Family Chronicle,
US: 2045 Niagara Falls Blvd., Unit 7,
Niagara Falls, New York 14304-1675;
Canada: 505 Consumers Road,
#500, Toronto, Ontario M2J 4V8,
URL: www.familychronicle.com

Family Tree Magazine,
4700 E. Galbraith Road,
Cincinnati, Ohio 45236, USA,
URL: www.familytreemagazine.com

Family Tree Magazine,
ABM Publishing Ltd.,
61 Great Whyte, Ramsey,
Huntingdon, Cambridgeshire PE26
1HJ, United Kingdom, URL:
www.family-tree.co.uk

Practical Family History,
ABM Publishing Ltd.,
61 Great Whyte, Ramsey,
Huntingdon, Cambridgeshire PE26
1HJ, United Kingdom, URL:
www.family-tree.co.uk

index

Picture credits

Chrysalis Books Group Plc is committed to respecting the intellectual property rights of others. We have therefore taken all reasonable efforts to ensure that the reproduction of all content on these pages is done with the full consent of copyright owners. If you are aware of any unintentional omissions please contact the company directly so that any necessary corrections may be made for future editions.

Author's acknowledgements

The challenges of preparing such a comprehensive book as *Tracing Your Family Roots* were eased by the contributions of staff members at Chrysalis Books, who enthusiastically shared their family histories, records and insight, especially Alex Myers, who answered multiple questions about her fascinating links to Sissinghurst Castle, Major William Bridges Webb and the Baker family.

To my parents, Nina and Harold Ewald, for sharing their interest in our family tree and their documents with me.

To Marvin Hull, my husband, whose feet have grown by leaps and bounds from the tiny baby's footies shown on his birth certificate to a man's size 13. Who'd have imagined?!

My thanks to Everton's Publishers for recommending me for this project.

My special thanks to Anne McDowall, who was there at the beginning and has been my rock as we completed this massive project.

And, to Robert S. Miller, III, my attorney and friend, for his pearls of legal wisdom and perspective. Who knows, with Lamonts in both of our family trees, maybe we are related!

Lastly, my steadfast gratitude to the US Navy, who sent me to Britain in the first place.